Studies on the Chinese Mark

Rapid Economic Development in China and Controlling Inflation

Chief editors:
Gao Shangquan *and* Chi Fulin
Written by:
Zhu Huayou

FOREIGN LANGUAGES PRESS BEIJING

First Edition 1997

The project is aided by
(Hainan) China Foundation for Reform and Development Research.

ISBN 7-119-00025-x

Published by Foreign Languages Press
24 Baiwanzhuang Road, Beijing 100037, China

Distributed by China International Book Trading Corporation
35 Chegongzhuang Xilu, Beijing 100044, China
P.O. Box 399, Beijing, China

Printed in the People's Republic of China

Foreword

What do we make of and how do we deal with the relationship between inflation and economic growth? This is probably a major practical question which every nation in the world must face. In the past decade and more, a relatively high level of inflation has repeatedly sprung up in the course of China's rapid economic growth. And in the past two years, the inflation problem has become a prominent contradiction closely linked with the quick development of China's marketization. How to effectively control inflation and to properly handle the relationship between reform, development and stability without impeding rapid economic growth is the problem which we must conscientiously study during the period of economic transformation.

In November 1994 in Haikou, the China (Hainan) Reform and Development Research Institute, China Restructuring Economy Research Society, UN Development Program and the German Technology Cooperation Company jointly held the International Seminar on the Asia-Pacific Regional Rapid Economic Growth and Stable Development. Specialists from the UN Development and Planning Office, Asia Development Bank, Ford Foundation, the United States, Germany, Canada, Japan, the Republic of Korea, Singapore, Vietnam, the Philippines and high ranking leaders and well-known economists of China held extensive discussions on international comparisons of experiences in controlling inflation, of problems involving economic reform, of the relationship between opening up and inflation, of controlling inflation while maintaining rapid economic growth and other problems, and many important theoretical viewpoints and thoughts on policy options were put forward during discussions. Based on the research into inflation problems made by the China (Hainan) Reform and Development Research Institute and relevant materials discussed at the seminar and speeches by experts there we wrote and edited this book; we have also referred to the research results of experts on questions of inflation from recent years. We aim to provide a relatively comprehensive and objective analyses of the problem of inflation and measures to be taken to keep inflation under control during rapid economic growth.

Gao Shangquan and Chi Fulin are chief editors of the book, Chi Fulin edited the draft and Zhu Huayou did the actual writing.

Financial assistance for its publishing was provided by the (China) Hainan Foundation for Reform and Development Research for which we express our sincere gratitude!

The Editors
March 1995

Contents

Chapter 1
Inflation in the Changing of Economic Structure

I. The Reasons for Inflation in China

(I) In the last decade, China's inflation has always been connected with its cyclical economic fluctuations

In the last decade or so, large scale inflations appeared repeatedly in China. Each time the economy moved into a period of growth, a relatively high level of inflation occurred. In the past decade, China's economy fluctuated on three occasions and inflation has also exhibited three peaks.

1. The Inflation of 1985

By 1985 the traditional planned economic system had already been weakened gradually; urban and rural production of non-state-owned economy already constituted approximately half of the GNP; the autonomy of state-owned enterprises extended step by step. By freeing up prices on small commody products and part of farm produce and sideline products, and the implementation of the double-track price system for the products produced by the state-owned industrial enterprises (for products covered by the state plan controlled pricing was maintained; for products outside the state plan market prices were adopted), thus the prices of two thirds of the products were adjusted by the market.

In the first quarter of 1985, economic growth reached a peak, and the economic growth rate compared with the average of the previous four years was faster by 12 to 14 percentage points, showing an overheated state. Beginning from the second quarter, prices rapidly went up. For the period from September to December the price increasing rate was more than 10 percent higher than that of the same period in 1984. In 1985 the GDP increased by 12.8 percent; at the same time the resident cost-of-living index went up 9.3 percent from the previous year and the retail price index of commodities rose by 8.8 percent over the year before.

To counter this, in July 1985, the government began to carry out mainly administrative means, measures including re-examining the investment projects of state-owned enterprises; strictly controlling the scale of fixed assets investment; reducing the scale of credit. Besides, the savings-deposit interest rate and that for fixed assets loan were raised twice first in April and then in September of the same year.

By early 1986, prices had dropped noticeably; however, the speed of economic growth dropped rather quickly, in February 1986, industrial production experienced no increase. Due to political considerations and pressure from local governments and state-owned enterprises, the Central Government began to relax control over credit in the second quarter of 1986, causing currency issuing for the following three quarters to experience a consistently high speed of increase. By the end of 1986 the amount of broad currency (M2) was 32.3 percent higher than that at the end of 1985.

2. The Inflation of 1988

In 1988 several new reform measures were introduced: overall implementation of the enterprise contract responsibility system, further expanded autonomy for enterprises; the Central Government implemented different types of all-round contract systems for local financial budgeting; in the area of price system reform the policy of combining readjusting with freeing up while stressing the latter was adopted so as to gradually increase the proportion of market-set prices and, at the same time, raised the purchase price of grain and edible oil as well as coal and shipping prices.

In March 1986 after relaxing control over banks, the increasing rate of broad currency (M2) went up step by step, so that during the first three quarters of 1987 it maintaining an increase above 30 percent. As a result, there was a recovery of rapid economic growth. Despite the adoption in October and November

1987 of the "tightening policy" in finance and banking to control the overheating economy, however, after December 1987, a policy of pouring in large amounts of capital to spur on the industrial growth was again put into effect. In the second and third quarters of 1988 economic growth reached a new peak. Because of this there was a concurrent swift, violent increase in prices. By the third quarter of 1988, people began to pull out their savings and a purchasing rush occurred.

From the third quarter of 1988, in order to bring a halt to the emerging vicious inflation, the government adopted strict controlling measures to stablise the economy. The major ones included: strengthening administration of prices by taking over operation of major agricultural means of production such as chemical fertiliser and setting ceiling prices for major means of production; strictly controlling the amount of loans and the scale of currency issuing, once even halting loans to rural and township enterprises; firmly reducing the scale of fixed assets investment, halting loans to projects outside the state plan; checking companies and straightening their affairs, especially trust investment companies; controlling the purchasing power of social groups; and increasing twice the interest rate for savings deposit.

In 1989 the rising trend of prices went down swiftly. At the end of the third quarter, the inflationary rate (compared to the retail price index of commodities of the previous month) fell to zero, and the price index of urban residents' average costs for daily necessities in 1990 went up by only 3.1 percent. At the same time, the selling on market was sluggish, the speed of industrial production growth fell steeply; enterprises operated under capacity or halted production; pressure on the job market increased; and the general financial situation was worsening. Beginning in the fourth quarter of 1989 the government adopted a policy of credit expansion in order to restart an economy that had fallen into dire straits.

3. The Inflation of 1993

From 1992 to 1993 price reform took a relatively big steps forward; commodity prices for the vast majority of items, including grain and edible oil, were relaxed, and only a minority of commodity prices, constituting between 10 to 20 percent of gross sales, remained under administrative control. Concurrent with this, non-state-owned enterprises developed rapidly, the proportion of these enterprises among the gross industrial output value went from 22 percent in 1978 up to 52 percent in 1992.

After relaxing the hold on banks from the fourth quarter of 1989, the banking system by means of granting loans poured large amounts of currency into national economy. However, from 1989 to 1991 the influx of large amount of currency did not bring about any obvious increase in inflationary pressure. The reason for this lies perhaps in the fact that during this period finance underwent a rapid and deepgoing development, new financial messures emerged continually, large plots of land which were originally allocated free were being sold in the form of bulk rentals; all of this led to the large-scale emergence of new financial capital and real estate, enabling the rapidly expanding credit and capital to be absorbed and saved up instead of bringing any immediate inflation.

But, after 1991, the continued large-scale influx of currency caused the situation afterwards to undergo a great change. In the middle of 1991, the increase in broad currency reached 30 percent, and this level remained all the way through the middle of 1993. The inflationary pressure following this increased steadily; by the second half of 1992 the price index began to climb step by step. However, the Central Bank did not take any effective regulatory measures for a long time. On top of this, some people took advantage of the chaos in the financial system to speculate for profit, thus intensifying the inflation.

In May and June 1993 the Central Government began to strengthen its macro-regulatory efforts; the major measures issued include: halting loan issuing power of the branches of the Central Bank; requiring specialised banks to take managerial responsibility over the entire bank's risk. It demanded that all banks recovered capital lost to breaching of regulations for loaning; put the amount of bank loans under control; strengthened the examination and approval of new investment projects; tightened financial outlays and strengthened tax collection and management; raised the interest rate of savings deposit and loans twice in a row, and for resident deposit accounts of three years or longer implemented inflation proof savings deposits.

Following the promotion of the stabilising program in early July 1993, during the third quarter of that year, currency growth and production development both slowed down noticeably. By October, the growth rate of the currency supply (M1) went down from 34 percent in June to 15.6 percent: the growth rate of industrial output value also fell from 30.2 percent in June to 16.4 percent; the growth rate of investment by state-owned industrial sectors went down from 74 percent to 58 percent; the increase rate of the price for production means fell from 52.95 percent to 31.35 percent (All of these are figures compared with those of the same month in the previous year).

However, the pulling back in credits influenced the operational activities of state-owned enterprises. As a result, enterprises particularly state-run enterprises were short of funds, which caused industrial growth to slow down, and local governments raised the need to ease controls on credit. Under such circumstances, between September and October 1993, the Central Bank poured huge amounts of money for short-term loans into state-owned banks (totalling 170 billion RMB yuan). Although strict loan quotas of an executive nature limited bank's function of creating currency, in November and December 1993 the growth rate of broad currency (M2) rose again. At the same time, the price increasing trend eased by the retraction in currency growth in the period from August to October 1993 sprang up again and went up sharply from November 1993. In the four months from November 1993 to February 1994 the retail price index rose 3.4 percent on average over each preceding month. In 1994 more important reform measures continued to be introduced with the establishment of a socialist market economic system as their objective, and all in all things progressed relatively smoothly. Viewed from the relationship of gross supply and gross demand, a fundamental balance was maintained; for more than 90 percent of consumer products supply remained higher than or was equal to demand, and nothing like the purchasing rush of 1988 occurred. Therefore, inflation in 1994 was quite different from the previous ones. Many major economic indicators make clear, in comparing the economic situation of 1994 with that of the first half of 1993, there was a marked improvement. The basic economic objective of "soft landing" was reached.

(II) An expanded demand for investment is the direct incentive for inflation

China's economy has all along had an incredibly deep-set internal drive seeking to expand and broaden the scale of investment. This drive originated in the merging of the state political authority with economic authority under the past system of planned economy. It is precisely this merger that put the policy decision on investment and the allocation of capital investment under the government control; and the financial restrictions were ineffective to enterprises, and they did not need to pay anything when they used or held investment capital. Even though the state changed from allocating investment capital to providing loans, a weak effect brought about by the interest rate on loans, could not change the situation fundamentally. Following the Central Government's granting more power to localities, local authorities had greater power to decide on investment strategy and with this, the drive to expand the economy also got stronger. Since the 1980s almost all of the inflations were induced by excessively expanding investment. The major factor inciting the 1993-1994 inflation in China was also the swell in investment that had occurred since 1992.

Due to the factors known to everyone, an expanding investment mechanism has existed in China for a long time; every area, every work unit strives for investment project, causing, first of all, the basic construction plan to grow ever larger. Moreover, many construction projects adopt the method of under-reporting their construction budget to gain approval. As a result, these projects often remain unfinished before the fund allocated for the projects have long been used up. This forces department of higher authority to have no choice but to allocate additional investment. Under such a mechanism the actual level of investment will by necessity exceed the project quota that had been worked out according to the amount of materials that could be provided. The public finance sector has to make an overdraft on the Central Bank to make narrow currency (Mo) increase. This is one of the holes through which currency expands. Corresponding to this is the fact that the government cannot but approve the People's Bank's expansion of credit quota, thus creating the second loophole by which currency expands (broad currency also increases). Inflation, thus follows inevitably.

Table: The Increase Rates of Investment and Inflation (%):

	1984	1985	1986	1987	1988	1989	1990	1991	1992	1993	1994
Society-wide fixed assets investment	28	38	18.7	20.6	23.5	-8	7.5	23.8	42.6	50.59	28.50
Fixed assets investment of units owned by the whole people	24	41.8	17.7	16	20	-8	15	24.3	45.4	51	
Imported foreign investment	35	70	59	16	21	-1	3	11	65		35
Rate of inflation	2.8	8.8	6	7.3	18.5	17.8	2.1	2.9	5.4	13.2	21.7

Source: China Statistics Yearbook.

It is apparent from the table that during and before the year inflation occurred, society-wide fixed assets investment, including the fixed assets investment of the units owned by the whole people, unexceptionally experienced large scale increase. For the corresponding periods, the growth rate of imported foreign capital were also at a high level. If we consider the process from the input of investment to the point of the actual rise in prices, one can see clearly from the chart that the increase of investment is the direct inducement of each instance of inflation in China.

In 1993, when China's economy continued to take big steps forward, a new set of contradictions and problems appeared. Especially serious were indiscriminately raising funds, unjustifiably providing short-term loans and arbitrarily establishing financial institutions (known as three disorders), all of which contributed to the breakdown of the normal financial order, and moreover forced currency issuance to shoot-up, wreaking havoc on the macro-economic environment. The "three disorders," brought about by the customers' searching for loans, gave financial support to the "real estate boom" and the "development zones boom." The "three disorders" and the "two booms" fueled to the flames, creating a vigorous demand for investment and leading directly to price increases for steel and other construction materials for domestic construction projects. The large-scale imports of steel caused the exchange rate to climb higher. Though the Central Government promptly adopted stronger macro-regulating measures, curbed further soaring of steel prices, and even stabilised the exchange rate between the US dollars and RMB yuan at about 1:8.7, the sharp rise in steel prices, however, gave way to a general rise in prices of industrial products.

The symptoms of investment starvation and thirst resulted from the traditional investment system serve as the crux of the swelling of fixed assets investment. Let us analyse the increase in commodity prices caused by the swell in the total scale of fixed assets investment: First, in the past the great majority of China's fixed assets investment was formed by allocated funds from the budget, but following the replacement of allocated funds by loans and the emergence of multiplying investment bodies, now a large amount of them come from bank loans. In the past, the expansion of fixed assets investment increased the budget deficit, now it increases the credit deficit. Regardless of whether it is a budget deficit or a credit deficit, in order to remedy them, both require issuing more currency. Second, fixed assets investment is such a type of economic activity that within one year or more than a year, no means of production or means of livelihood, or any useful result will be provided, but it will take labour, means of production and means of livelihood from the whole year's total production. That is to say, to put same amount of money for other economic activities, although it is also necessary to increase society's overall demand (taking away labour, means of production and means of livelihood from the year's gross production), it quickly brings with it an increase in society's overall supply (goods or services). However, for fixed assets investment, before projects have actually been completed and put into production, not only requires an increase in society's total demand but will "take away" the total supply of the society. This doubly widens the margin between society's total supply and its total demand. Third, the bottleneck effect. The swelling of fixed assets investment certainly leads to the shortage of energy and raw material supply and the pressure on transport, thus forming a bottleneck restricting the national economy as a whole, and furthermore, causing the prices of products in short supply and services to skyrocket. Within several months from the winter of 1992, the price of wire rods used in construction was more than doubled, a prominent example of this phenomenon. Fourth, when fixed assets investment is really hot, there are always enterprises and work units which shift circulating capital to basic construction projects, and the result was to force the bank to provide more circulating capital or delayed the repayment of the loans, leading to the occurrence of triangle debts among enterprises. No matter which situation arises, it will increase the amount of currency to be issued.

The root cause of problems resulting from frequent swelling of fixed assets investment is the traditional investment system. Before a capitalist makes an investment, he will repeatedly carry out research on the feasibility of the project. But, according to China's traditional investment system, the decision-makers of the investment do not have to bear any responsibility for the final outcome of the investment; those who make decisions on providing loans do not actually bear any responsibility either as to whether or not the loans can be recovered as scheduled. This type of investment system is the root cause leading to China's inflation.

At present, China's inflation problem results directly from an economic strategy of seeking high-speed development by relying on high investment. In 1992 the GDP growth rate reached a 13.2 percent. However, this type of high growth counts on the support of great capital input. According to estimates, about 60 percent of the annual economic growth was brought about by the increased capital investment, and in 1993, demand on investment continued to going up. For the first half of the year, the total fixed assets investment of the whole society was 354.2 billion yuan, of which 219 billion yuan was from state-owned work units, 70.2 percent higher than that of the same period in the previous year; the increase in investment pushed up the issuing of currency. Another 52.8 billion yuan was issued in the first half of the year, and by the end of June the value of narrow currency (M1) had increased 34.2 percent over the same period of the previous year. This caused prices to skyrocket. After a year of continued effort in macro-control, the inflation rate still would not come down. This was again related to the high capital input. In 1994 fixed assets investment rates dropped a little, but remained at a relatively high level. The fixed assets investment of state-owned work units for the second half of 1993 totalled 613.1 billion yuan, an increase of 53.3 percent over the same period of the previous year; in the first half of 1994, the amount totalled 308.1 billion yuan, an increase of 37.5 percent and the figure of July showed 72.9 percent increase compared with the same period of the previous year. Obviously the high inflation rate in China, to a large extent, can be attributed to the continuous large scale of fixed assets investment. An excessively large scale of construction projects put pressure not only on the currency market, but also on the commodity market, especially on the means of production market; all of this pushed up prices.

The investment demands which caused inflation not only blew up the sum total of investment but, more seriously, destroyed the structure of investment demands. In periods of economic growth, exuberant investment demands were focused on processing industries. Rapid growth usually begins from the processing industries. After a period of speedy development in the processing industries, energy, raw materials and other basic industries and transportation cannot bear the pressure, thus pushing up prices in all areas.

Inflation is a typical feature of an economy which is unstable and fluctuating. Economic growth pushes up inflation rates, which in turn serve as the typical sign of economic growth.

However, it also anticipates that the whole economy will decline and retract, because it is at this point that the government will inevitably adopt measures necessary to adjust and control the situation. Therefore, inflation becomes the ending point of the period of economic growth and the beginning of the period of economic decline. With the declining economy, the rate of inflation falls accordingly.

Confronted with the sustained high inflation rate, the policy objectives are to continue controlling the scale of fixed assets investment and adjusting the structure of investment demands.

(III) Market monetization acts as a long-term driving power of production cost and results in structural price increases

In recent years, China's high inflation has been mainly structural:

1. Before reforms, the price structure of products and production essentials was irrational.

a. Low prices for primary products (grain, basic raw and processed materials), basic services (public service charges and house rent). For instance, during the early 1980s, compared with the prices on the international market, China's grain price was 2-4 times lower, crude oil price, 5 times, and rents, 10 or more times lower.

b. High prices for industrial products (primarily machinery, household electrical products). This shows the wide gap that existed between the capital and profit margins of different businesses. In 1979, an early year of reform, the average profit margin of state-owned industrial enterprises was 12.3 percent, among which the profit margin of processing industry reached 33.1-61.1 percent and that of basic industry was only 1.4-4.4 percent.

c. Low remuneration for production essentials. Wages, land-use costs, interest rates and exchange rates were all relatively low.

2. The process of turning toward a market economy is also the process of rationalizing prices. However, as the adjustment of income distribution (taxes, wages, etc.) involved a relatively high

degree of difficult, price reform could neither bring about significant price reduction for industrial products nor raise the prices of primary goods. The result was that the overall price level remained unchanged or without any fundamental change. What could be done was to keep the price of industrial products unchanged or increasing as little as possible while raising the prices of primary goods so as to gradually ease the disparity in the relative prices. The depreciation of the Chinese currency against foreign currencies enabled domestic prices to match international market prices.

In this way, if not considering the costs of information, the rationalized prices following the success of reform will serve as a long-term impetus to production costs, this will inevitably cause the level of prices to go up.

By 1992, compared with the prices of 1978, the year before reform began, the purchasing price for agricultural products had risen accumulatively 176.5 percent, prices of rural industrial goods, 83.2 percent, prices for industrial excavation products, 165.7 percent, and prices for raw materials, 150.2 percent; the latter two had increased respectively 50.9 percent and 35.4 percent more than the prices of their processed products.

3. According to statistics, the rise in structural prices brought about by long-term production cost incentives will result in an increase of overall price level by approximately 1-1.5 times. Supposing it takes 20 years to complete the system transformation, then long term production cost incentives could bring about a price increase of approximately 3-5 percent a year. This is the risk which is necessarily taken in the process of transition into a market economy.

However, to speed up the process of marketization is in a sense, the price must be paid in reform.

The year of 1993 is a year of significance, in which the most price reform measures were put forward by the Central Government. In 1994 a series of macro reform measures were put into effect and this was the major reason leading to an excessively fast rise in prices.

In the area of wage reform, government organs and institutions implemented new wage systems to solve the problem of low wages for government staff and intellectuals. This required a large amount of currency. Moreover, a number of enterprises having the proper conditions also copied these institutions and government organs and raised wages accordingly. In 1994, the national wage in budget plan was 18.4 percent higher than that of the previous year, but the actual increase in wages was much higher than 30 percent.

Opening up to the outside world brought about changes in the overall level of prices. Especially when doing away with the state-fixed rate for foreign currency exchange, the exchange rate quickly adjusted to previous levels of the foreign exchange market and the exchange rate for Chinese currency fell by a large margin. The most direct effect from this change was a large-scale increase in the costs of imported materials. In addition, entering the international market had different effects on China's industries and their products. Due to the fact that China, on the whole, still has low wages, low consumption and low prices, so to gear to the global market will naturally force the overall price to go up. At the same time, merging with the global market will also cause fluctuations on the international market, which will in turn have an even more direct impact on the domestic market. As a result strong fluctuation in prices may occur on the domestic market.

When the state-set exchange rate was replaced by the market exchange rate, prices were pushed up. The exchange rate for the Chinese currency (RMB yuan) against the American dollar dropped from 5.8:1 to 8.7:1, with RMB depreciating 40 percent. The most direct impact of this depreciation was the rise of the domestic purchasing price for exported goods and the prices for imported goods, semi-processed goods and industrial raw materials; this resulted in inflation pressure. First, due to the adoption of the market exchange rate and the large scale reduction in financial subsidies for imported goods, primarily means of production and the collection of customs tariffs on the basis of market prices, prices for imported items and the cost of domestic products using imported goods as raw materials were inevitably driven up. Second, 80 percent of China's exported items were primary products, of which the majority were in short supply on the domestic market; therefore an increase in exports also meant an increase in the prices of exported items. Third, with the state-set exchange rate being replaced by the market exchange rate, the expense on important imported products such as products used for national defence, even after it was minimized to US$ 5 billion, would require an annual increase of 15 billion yuan of the country's total expenditure. And other imported items of national importance such as large set of equipment for state key projects, medical equipment and educational instruments would require outlays of 10 billion yuan or more. Fourth, the burden created by payments of the principal and interest on foreign debt increased. At present, China's foreign debts have already reached US$ 80 billion, and the majority of which were borrowed during the period of the Seventh Five-Year Plan. They have consecutively entered the peak period for repayment, meaning that each year US$ 5-6 billion of dept is due for repayment. Fifth, the imported foreign investment requires a big increase for RMB as supporting fund. By the end of May 1994 China had already approved the establishment of 194,000 joint ventures and enterprises with sole foreign investment, which had actually used a total of US$ 72.6 billion. In the first half of 1994 alone, the government had approved 30,000 such enterprises, using actually US$ 20 billion. After the market exchange rate was adopted the domestic supporting fund, calculated on the basis of a 1:1 ratio, had increased by 40 percent over the figure before the state-set exchange rate was replaced by the market exchange rate. Beside, the amounts of imported foreign capital, including both foreign loans and foreign investments, have greatly increased. Apart from a portion of the equipment and raw materials which had been imported from abroad, the vast majority of the foreign capital needed to find a corresponding amount of material guarantee from the domestic market. This was especially true as a large amount of foreign investment went into processing industries and tertiary industries, thereby exacerbating the bottleneck restrictions on energy, raw materials, transportation, communications and information exchange.

(IV) An excessively fast increase in the currency supply creates inflation

1. Inflation is essentially a phenomenon involving currency. The currency supply is the whole society's savings; it is the overall amount of currency which the whole society at a certain point of time uses as its means of circulation and payment, including primarily the cash possessed by institutions, enterprises, rural and urban residents as well as the savings and other kinds of capital held by financial organizations. Granting that the holders are willing, the cash and savings can be used to purchase goods and pay for labor and services; therefore, the currency supply reflects the overall currency demand of the society.

According to the liquidity of currency, the overall supply currency can be broken up into different levels. Referring to generally recognised international principles, and based on China's current situation, the People's Bank of China has divided the supply of Chinese currency into the following four levels: M0: circulating cash; M1: M0 + enterprises' current savings + savings of government organs, organisations and army units + savings of rural areas + savings of individual credit cards holders; M2:M1 + savings deposits of rural and urban residents + fixed deposits of enterprises + foreign savings + deposits of trust funds; M3: M2 + finance bonds + business bills + large sum negotiable instruments. M1 is generally known as narrow-sense currency supply, its liquidity is fairly high. M2 refers to broad-sense currency supply. The margin between M2 and M1 is quasi-money and its liquidity is low. M3 is a concept which was created by taking into account the new circumstances brought about by finance; at present, the figure cannot be estimated. The currency supply, created and provided by the banking system, is an integrated reflection of wealth, taxes, finance, investment, consumption and international revenue and expenditure.

Inflation is always connected with the increase of the amount of currency in circulation during a set period; under many circumstances it is brought about by an increase in currency supply.

Presently, the most prominent problem in China's economy is the excessive increase in currency supply and the serious inflation. By the end of October 1994, enterprises' savings of banking institutions of the country had increased 315 billion yuan over the beginning of the year, 3.6 times that of the same period in 1993. Of this figure, fixed savings of enterprises had increased 53.6 billion yuan compared with the figure at the beginning of 1994. The shortage of capital still exists in some areas, some trades and business sectors as well as in many state-run enterprises, however, if we take overall situation of the country as a whole the present currency supply still tends to be too great. At the end of the third quarter of 1994, 614.3 billion yuan (MO) was in circulation in China, an increase of 26.4 percent, or an increase of 7.5 percentage points over the second quarter of the year. And narrow-sense currency (M1) totalled 1900.9 billion yuan for the third quarter of 1994, an increase of 32.5 percent or 11.7 percentage points over that of the second quarter of 1994. The excessive increase in currency supply, particularly in the supply of M1 (narrow-sense currency), inevitably intensified the pressure on current inflation. The national retail price index increased by 20.9 percent from January to September 1994, and in October retail prices increased by 25.2 percent. The overall level of consumer prices increased by 27.7 percent and the inflationary situation was quite grave.

2. The major reasons for the increase of currency supply were: a raise in the prices of primary products such as grain and cotton; the excessive growth in fixed assets and funds for consumption; a relatively large increase in the amount of bank loans and financial expenses; and a large-scale increase in the amount of foreign exchange reserve.

The raise in the prices of grain, cotton, oil, coal and other primary products and the corresponding increase in the currency supply led to a rise in the structural prices. In order to establish a socialist market economy, the prices of primary products must be raised and an equal value exchange system must be implemented between various kinds of goods. This reform will be fundamentally completed in twenty years from 1979, and it will make prices move up 3-5 percentage points a year. Since the state raised purchasing prices of grain and cotton and other farm produce in 1994, from January to October the banks increased the amount of cash for purchasing agricultural and sideline products by 43 percent over 1993, and thereby increased the initiative of peasants to produce and sell agricultural products, thus setting up conditions to lower prices in 1995. However, due to random price rises brought about by the disorder in circulation, and, added to this, the crippling of the function of state-owned commercial enterprises in regulating supply and demand in the marketplace, the actual price burden on the consumers far exceeded the scale of price rise set by the state.

Excessively fast growth of fixed assets investment and consumer funds remains a major reason for the excessive increase in the amount of currency supply and the sustained high inflation rate. From January to October of 1994, the national fixed assets investment made by the state-owned work units was 40.4 percent more than in the same period of 1993; although there was a drop in the increase rate compared with that of 1993, this still represented an upsurge on the basis of rapid increase in 1993. The national investment rate in fixed assets (the ratio between the total amount of the fixed assets investment of the whole society and gross domestic product) was 38 percent from January to October, add to this, the annual amount of over 100 billion yuan of industrial and commercial circulating capital which were used as fixed assets investment instead, and a number of other fixed assets investments which were not included in national statistics, the actual fixed assets investment rate exceeded 40 percent. From January to October national bank payment for wages and personal withdrawal exceeded that of the same period in 1993 by 41.34 percent; and the cash paid out for the cost of administration and management of enterprises increased by 37 percent over the figure of the same period in 1993.

There were relatively large increases in the amounts of bank loans and financial payments and a corresponding increase in the savings of enterprises and institutions, both leading to an increased currency supply. For January to October of 1994, national bank loans increased 107.2 billion yuan over that of the same period in 1993, of which loans for purchasing agricultural and sideline products went up by 76 billion yuan, industrial loans, agricultural loans and fixed assets loans went up by 21, 13 and 14 billion yuan respectively, a breakdown of this sort is reasonable and the scale of credit and loans for the entire year was kept basically under the control of the plan. However, investigations into credit and loans have not been strict and the quality of loans tended to be low; up to now, there have been no real lines drawn between banking industries and credit and securities businesses, and for this reason part of capital for loans has inappropriately gone into the stock market and real estate market, adding yet more pressure to credit and loans. The percentage of the state revenue in the gross national product is too low, and the percentage of the Central Government revenues in the total state revenues is too low, so the Ministry of Finance is powerless to help out state-owned enterprises with additional capital. There are a number of enterprises whose wages and expenses have gone beyond the control of management. From January to September 1994 financial expenditure increased at a faster rate than last year. These are all major reasons for the increase in the currency supply and inflationary pressure.

A new factor for the large-scale increase in the currency supply during 1994 was the huge increase in the national foreign exchange reserve. By the end of October 1994 the foreign exchange reserve was 2.1 times over the figure at the beginning of the year, and the amount of RMB it tied up was 2.7 times compared with early 1994. The increase in the foreign exchange reserve represents the growing strength of China's ability to make payments internationally and, so it is a good thing. However, this, on the one hand, created an export surplus of goods and services and a domestic supply deficit; on the other, as foreign exchange equivalent RMB entered the market, increasing the currency supply. As a result, the growing demand domestically created more pressure on inflation.

(V) During the transformation of economic systems there exists a great risk of inflation

The influence on inflation during system switch presents itself in two ways. First, during the period of the system change, due to friction and contradictions that exist between the new and old systems, there are still many things out of order and without standards or even illegal phenomena. For instance, the major distinguishing characteristic of a growing economy is increased investment; and this makes it easy to lead to increases in loans and currency, and thus to inflation. In addition, a "frothing economy," "companies in name only," and a chaotic financial system all serve to add more pressure on inflation. Second, the system transformation itself, in the process of replacing the old system with a new one, will also bring with it inflation.

The most notable characteristic of China's original planned economy lies in the fact that all major economic factors were at the disposal of the government while enterprises had little or no power of self-determination. Related to this is the fact that the prices of goods and major factors were all controlled by the government. Therefore, although the publicly recognised level of inflation was not high, a hidden inflation still existed. For example, many loss-making enterprises relied on government aid for survival, and the government issued many kinds of coupons which actually carried value to subsidize residents' consumer items and social service payments. Even more serious is that under such a system the entire pricing system was distorted for the prices of ordinary goods as well as the pricing of key factors.

Obviously, the low price level under a planned economy system was base on low individual consumption, an unbalanced structure and low efficiency; moreover, the mechanisms used to stabilise such a low level of prices were rather fragile and difficult to maintain for a long time.

This is to say, reform itself is not the cause leading to inflation; the goal of reform is to straighten out the system and maintain a stable level of prices. The crux of high inflation lies in the old economic system, manifested primarily as hidden inflations mentioned above. The influence created by the transformation of the system is manifested prominently as following:

1. The influence from the change of the price mechanism on prices.

The irrationality of the pricing system is expressed in three major areas: prices of commodities, prices for services and prices for essential factors. First, let's look at prices of commodities. Irrational pricing of commodities is prominently reflected in the double scissors difference: First, for the price ratio between agricultural and industrial products, the former tends to be too low, the latter, too high. Second, for the price ratio between basic industrial products and processing industrial products, the former tends to be too low, and the latter, too high. It is worth pointing out that the generally low prices of agricultural products and primary industrial products were not the result of a high labor productivity or a lack of market demand, but were related to the strict state price policy under a planned economy. The state price reform in regard to commodities has taken this as its focus. Within a certain period of time, the state adopted a policy combining adjusting prices with freeing up prices, with emphasis on adjusting. Due to the fact that price adjustment cannot fundamentally solve the unreasonable discrepancy in price ratio, therefore, in the late 1980s the state gradually shifted toward mainly to free up prices. No matter how great the scale of the adjusting or the freeingup, both imply that the prices of products from basic industries will rise, and more products are involved in adjustment or freeing up in pricing, faster the prices will rise. Furthermore, if prices for most commodities are freed up or for all commodities, the price increase will be even faster.

The warping of prices for services is reflected either in too low prices or a large portion of services are unpaid because no price has ever been set for these services. To change the situation, it calls for an overall raise of the prices in the services industries and this will result in price increases in non-service industries, including industry and agriculture due to the increases in production costs to produce products related to service industries. In contrast to the reform for prices of commodities, reforms for service prices came about much more slowly. The first real step in reform was taken at the end of the 1980s while an overall reform in this area began in the 1990s. It could be said that this was a major reason for the high inflation of the late 1980s and the vicious price growth during the first half of 1994.

Prices for essential factors, including interest rates, the exchange rate, wages, land usage rents and others, are also in a seriously warped situation. And the fundamental reason is that these prices were always under the government control and were kept at a very low level. As a result, they have lost their sensitive reaction to the market which they should have. Even more serious is that, to enterprises, the prices for essential factors constitute part of overall costs, and any change in the prices of these essential factors will affect the enterprises' costs and their production costs. Therefore, in the course of the transformation of the economic system, all the government can do is to relax its control over the prices of essential factors or make an adjustment on essential factor prices, and these moves often end up in raises of essential factor prices, which will lead to an overall rise of all prices.

2. The influence from the structural transformation on prices.

The content of the structural transformation varies, including the coordination between basic industries and processing industries, the upgrading of industrial technology, the expansion of the structural scale of industrial organisations, etc. However, closely related to the rise in prices is the shift in the agricultural labor force during the transformation from a dual structure to a single structure economy. After the reform in rural areas began in 1978, farmers had more freedom in making job choice and the agricultural productivity was improved. Therefore, large numbers of farmers began shifting from the limited farmland to non-agricultural industries. From 1978 to the present, this shift has gone through four phases. (1) The period from 1978 to 1983 was the primary phase, and in the five years 10.391 million people shifted. (2) The period from 1984 to 1986 witnessed a rapid shift. During this period 25.249 million people shifted between 1984 and 1985, constituting 43.9 percent of the total number between 1978 and 1991. (3) The years from 1987 to 1990 was a period of gradual shift, and compared with the previous period, the speed of the shift receded greatly. This was especially true after the economic readjustment and consolidation in 1989, during this period a trend for farmers to return to their villages appeared in some areas. (4) In the period from 1991 to the present the shift of agricultural work force has picked up again. These four periods correspond in time with the system transformation and the cyclic fluctuations in prices. It is clear that, on the one hand, the economic system transformation is a direct motive factor inciting the agricultural labor force shift; on the other, the shift in the agricultural labor force is one of the factors promoting the rise in prices. The reason is quite obvious: before the farmers shifted, they were primarily self-sufficient or partially self-sufficient for basic necessities; however, after shifting to non-agricultural industries, this group of people became commodity consumers. Moreover, along with their increased income, their consumption level continued to increase too. This inevitably pushed up the market demand and lead to rises in prices.

3. The influence from the transformation in enterprise mechanisms on prices.

For a long time, prices were determined by the state and enterprises were not allowed to change prices as they wished to. However, the power of self-determining prices was a very important factor for enterprise activities. Under the condition that enterprises were powerless in determining prices themselves and the government kept the prices at a very low level, it was impossible for enterprises to maintain a relatively high productivity. Because of this, in the early 1980s, the government began implementing reforms which granted enterprises more rights and profits and this continued all the way through to the end of the 1980s. When we look back and find that these reform measures did not solve the problem in enterprises' operational mechanism, but enterprises has gradually expanded their power of self-determination for businesses, particularly the power to set prices. According to statistics, in the past, 97 percent of the total retail prices of commodities in society were set by the government, whereas, now 95 percent of them have already been freed up. In the past, 100 percent of the prices of the total sales of the means of production were determined by the government; now, 85 percent have already been freed up. After enterprises were given greater self-determination power for business, profit-making has become their major goal, and prices have naturally gone up.

In order to get out of this predicament, the most important thing is to chang people's viewpoint through media, letting the whole nation realise that the system transformation will to a certain extent lead to inflation, and, they should strengthen their inflation endurance. In the past, our news media placed more emphasis on disseminating the necessity of reform, the guiding principles and direction of the reform, the reform program and measures, and the positive effects, and benfits and improvement, after the reform measures and programs were put into effect. However, there has not been enough exposition on the difficult nature of achieving reform or on the risks and price that come in the course of reform. This has strengthened an attitude among people that reform only has a positive effect and no negative effect. Obviously, this attitude is extremely harmful for pushing reform forward. A major reason why a number of reform measures have been difficult to develop or have suffered immediate failures soon after they were put into practice is the people's lack of endurance of risks involved in reform.

At the same time, another fundamental job that needs to be done at present is to find out the people's actual inflation endurance, so as to decide the corresponding speed of the system change. China is a large country with a huge population; the average income and the general cultural quality of its population are still low. Therefore, the social stabilisation mechanism is fairly weal. If rampant inflation were to occur in China, the result will be too ghastly to contemplate. It would not only forfeit the results already brought about by reforms, but would also block further economic development. Looking at things from this perspective, China's reform must be pushed forward step by step and any idea that a small amount of work will yield large results is not feasible.

In the course of changing tracks, more reasonable prices imply a change in the way in which the entire economy moves: from a planned allocation of resources to market controlled allocation of resources; however, this transformation cannot be implemented in a smooth manner. When the Central Government is not powerful enough in macro control and adjustment inflation will also occur.

During the transition process into a market economy the competition mechanism was introduced and the prices became rationalized, causing profits in industrial enterprises to drop and an increase in revenues in the essential factors of production. Because of this, tax sources must switch from a small number of processed industrial products to all products and essential factors. To guarantee financial revenues tax structure and the tax collection system must also undergo through changes.

Due to the re-allocation of resources, in the process of price reform, production subsidies should be given to product at relatively low prices. In addition, the weak adaptability of enterprises to competition, the difficulties in reassigning surplus employees in organisations, and other factors will cause an increase in temporary financial subsidies, settlement costs and other expenses. Therefore, financial expenses must be maintained at a certain level.

At the same time, only after general laws and regulations which accord with a market economy as well as China's special characteristics are set up, will it be possible to maintain a stable financial policy. However, in regard to these two aspects, China's reality for carrying out such a policy is not so optimistic. For example, the financial all-round contract system has been put into practice but there is no mechanism to guarantee an increase of tax revenues. Therefore, the transition process into market economy causes inevitably an annual decrease of the proportion of tax revenues in the GNP, thus bringing about financial deficit. In reality, the years from 1979 to 1993, excluding 1985 for special reasons, all have financial deficit.

In the area of currency policy, pricing reform was implemented in stages; for sectors whose prices were relatively low, the banks adopted low interest rate policy. Where financial functions were lacking, the finance bureau overdrew money from the Central Bank to offset the deficit. The Central Bank also provided loans directly, thus creating deficit in public departments. Ever since the division of one unified bank into the Central Bank and commercial banks, both the Central Bank and commercial banks have to adapt themselves in regard to the technology, quality of staff and the distribution of interests; at the same time they have to face immense pressure from governments and departments at various levels. Due to this, the possibility for a relaxed currency policy is quite high. This inevitably causes the currency supply to rise rapidly: from 1985 to 1993 the M2 currency supply increased 25.2 percent on average, much faster than the average increase speed of 9 percent in the GDP.

Financial deficits and a relaxed currency policy can create an increase in overall demand, thus resulting in inflation. We must work hard to reduce most possibly the risk of this type of inflation.

Therefore, it is reasonable to think that it should be up to the Central Bank to input currency to alleviate the inflation brought about by deficits in the public sector.

Naturally, during the transition period there are also beneficial factors to reduce inflation. When an economy is in the process of monetization, it attracts a larger amount of currency and expands its capacity to absorb currency and the speed of currency circulation slows down. From 1985 to 1993, the circulation speed of M2 revenue decreased on average by 5.7 percentage points annually. Due to opening up and the transition into a market economy, the efficiency of the overall economy of the transitional period has risen gradually.

Experts hold that the reasons that cause inflation in China's economic transition period are quite complex. A certain level of rise in structural prices is an unavoidable cost that reform must pay. At the same time, during this period, technology transfer and the redistribution of interests must all pay a necessary cost; even though we should do our best to minimize this cost, we must nevertheless pay the cost in the form of additional inflation. Although there exist the fact that inflation is somehow subdued by the increase of the overall efficiency, generally speaking, during a transitional period, an average annual price rise of 6-8 percent may occur. Moreover, if due caution is not maintained it is quite possible that two-digit inflation might appear. As the system transforms, efficiently controlling overall demand and decreasing the deficits of smaller public sectors are absolutely necessary for controlling inflation.

(VI) Inflation is due to competition under soft restriction within the state-owned economy after devolving rights and profits

The devolving rights and granting profits, particularly in a sense of opening up, has played an important, positive role in the reform of the Chinese economic system. In more than a decade of reform, many things were created and accomplished by enterprises and individuals at the grass-roots after they had been granted certain autonomy while the Central Government merely plays a role of confirmation. Finally, the market economy established on the basis of volunteer trades of countless people will be improved by the countless participants into such a market economic mechanism that can deal with countless specific situations. If, in order to pursue some short-term goals, we withdraw the profits and rights that have already been granted, the market reforms will not be able to go any further and nor will it be possible to establish a new market economy system. It does not mean that a market economy needs no macro control by the government, but it definitely does not want everything to be decided by the Central Government. The essence of the market mechanism is one of separating powers; any violation of this principle in carrying out reform can only lead one away from a real market economy.

However, the division of powers without the precondition of reforming the state property rights relationship has its limitations. The significance of effective property rights on the economic behavior of an enterprise or any actual economic entity lies, first of all, in the restrictions they set for the capital user or operator (no matter how residual claim power is allocated). Owing to the lack of effective property rights (the power could be clearly delimited to someone, but in reality it might have no effective restrictions on capital operators), the so-called soft-budget restrictions always exist in the state-owned economy. However, under the traditional planned system, since the basic level unit had no autonomy and profit incentives, the soft-budget restrictions had played a very limited role in the actual economic activities. This is because the amount of income that a basic unit was able to control was limited and all investment and pay-outs are controlled by the central planners. Granting rights and profits and the reform of the management system (including the financial and taxation system, the banking system and the enterprise management system), to a certain extent, have solved the problem of the economic operators lacking initiative and autonomy. Therefore, it has instilled vitality into the economy, it has not solved the problem of lacking effective restrictions. This manifested in the fact that enterprises did not have to go bankrupt even if they had suffered big losses for they could continue borrowing money from the bank, and the government still had the right to interfere in the banks' loaning activities, etc. As a result, the effort to divide powers in the reform created a special economic system: the basic units of the state-run economy (local governments, state-owned enterprises, state-run enterprises and state banks) had all obtained "autonomy," but the "restrictions" on them were still too "soft."

When all grassroots units have both ample profit incentives and the autonomy to pursue its own interests, they naturally are in a relationship of competition with each other. Competing for one's own interest is in itself a good thing, it is the motivating force for an economy to develop. The problem lies in that this competitive environment began under conditions where the soft-budget restrictions had not yet been hardened. Therefore, the competition between state-run economic units appeared to go through the market, however, it actually was not the same as market competition but can only be called competition under soft restrictions. Its basic difference from market competition is this: under a market economy, production costs, prices, interest rates (the cost of the use of capital) and investment risks all function as major factors restricting decision-makers while under soft-restriction competition, they play only a minimal function.

The soft-restriction competitions, under the condition of dividing economic powers between different localities and enterprises, have resulted in the present inflation and the increase in overall demand. In a traditional planned economy, the final policy decisions on economic activity were all made by the central planners, therefore the effort of grassroots units to compete with each other and to obtain more resources was primarily reflected in their struggle for projects with larger investments and more material allocations. And under a divided-power system, when localities or enterprises can "approve" projects by themselves and all materials can be bought on the market, the effort of grassroots units to obtain more resources is mainly seen as competition for funds. And under the condition of soft-budget restrictions, he who obtains more funds will also have more income and enjoy an unfair advantage. And those whose economic development is faster will also enjoy a faster increase in their income and, therefore, will be less fearful of inflation. And those who have less funds for fewer projects will use less capital, have lower employment rate and slow increase of income, and suffer greater losses during inflation. Therefore, the practice of soft restrictions often calls for endless demands for funds. Regarding the soft-restriction competition in terms of fighting for more funds, it is by no means milder than market competition, and in fact it is even fiercer and the competitors are ready to resort to any means; this easily leads to greater inflation.

1. The expansion of autonomy of local governments and enterprises in investment.

From 1980 the financial contract system was implemented. The initial purpose of the Central Government was to shift the financial burden. While lightening the responsibilities of the Central Government this also helped strengthen local economic development and increase the income of localities. Following the implementation of this system, local governments' power to allocate financial resources continued to increase, the amount of income which localities were able to allocate grew in proportion in the gross financial revenue and so was the income at the disposal of localities. At the same time, in October of 1980 measures to reform the administrative planning system were adopted, which stipulated that "guiding planning" should be taken for projects to be constructed with the capital raised by local departments and enterprises, and foreign investment borrowed and to be repaid by themselves; the control over the examination and approval of investments was relaxed and the scale of construction projects determined at the provincial level was expanded from under 10 million yuan to under 30 million yuan; non-production projects, regardless of size, could be examined and approved by each local department. All of these provided the structural conditions for grassroots units to expand rapidly their investment.

2. Bank credit autonomy.

In 1984 the central banking system was formed and it began attempting to replace the mandatory planning of loans with "indirect" macro regulations through the implementation of currency policy as required by a market economy. First, it introduced the margin allowance system allowing specialised banks to save more and lend more. However, the reserve system was not yet well established, so the specialised banks and the Central Bank shared same balancing accounts. The specialised banks took "remittance margins" as reserve funds, resulting actually in an unlimited supply of funds. At the end of 1984 it was announced that the loan balance of the specialized banks at the end of the year was to be taken as the minimum amount for the loan plan for the following year. As a result, banks were very active in granting loans to enterprises, thus leading to credit inflations. Even more serious, the investment autonomy granted to localities, the existence of the local branches of the Central Bank and the common interests shared by the Central Bank, specialised banks, local branches, local governments, local economies and enterprises all resulted in a mechanism, demanding from the grassroots level for more credit and currency supplies, and such demands were satisfied easily under the system of divided powers.

3. Autonomy in income distribution.

From 1984 to 1985 reforms began to expand the autonomy of enterprises and change the management of the wage system of enterprises. Besides stating that enterprises could make their own plans for a portion of production and sales, the reform measures also granted enterprises the autonomy in the distribution of their incomes, eliminated bonus ceilings and allowed enterprises, within a certain scale, to make their own adjustments of wages, and experimented in the system of linking wages with economic returns. This resulted in rapid increases in wages and bonuses. In the fourth quarter of 1985, the total wages of state-owned enterprises increased by 46 percent over the same period of the previous year, and this led to the so-called "runaway wages." In addition, due to the devolving of autonomy in expenditures, various types of expenses using public funds increased in large bounds and non-production outlays grew sharply (some under the name of dissipation cost, some as administrative fee and some as other expenditures). These were all important reasons leading to consumption inflation.

4. The adoption of contract system by enterprises accelerated the devolving of powers and profits.

First, the contract system was implemented in the state-owned enterprises nationwide in 1987. By the end of 1987 82 percent of large- and medium-sized enterprises had already adopted contracted responsibility system of various types in their operation. The significance of the contract system lies in fixing the total amount of tax on profits to be paid to the state (or the percentage of increase); the increased amount of profit became profits retained by the enterprises, this is to say that the government granted more profits to enterprises. From the perspective of operations, this was a step in further granting powers to enterprises. Especially in the early stages of the contract system, the content of contracts was comparatively simple; in principle the state had stopped interfering with all business operations of enterprises so long as they can guarantee to pay their taxes and fulfill the tasks of production.

After the implementation of measures like taxation on bonuses and wages and due to the increased autonomy of enterprises in expenditure, all types of disguised increases of bonuses and wages appeared, including issuing material objects. Of the total income of the workers and staff members the income in the form of material objects has increased proportionally year after year. Some studies indicate that in 1988 the proportion of income as material objects (not counting low rents and other factors) occupied one third more of the total income of the workers and staff members.

5. The new round of devolving decision-making power between 1992 and 1993.

Beginning from 1992 economic reform in China entered a new stage. On the one hand, non-government economy and the market mechanism developed further, on the other, the state-run economy went through another round of expanding the autonomy of localities and enterprises. Among these changes. The following two types of autonomy expansion had more significant impact on the instability of the macroeconomy and inflation.

(1) The complete freeing up of the right of examination and approval of project investments. This approval right of city governments extended to 30 million yuan, and 50 million yuan for provincial governments. This led to a great increase in the investments under local autonomy. For instance, some data showed that from January to May 1992, 82.7 percent of the new projects under construction invested by investors under the ownership of the whole people. Fixed assets investment increased rapidly; from January to May 1993 the fixed assets investment of the state-run department increased by 70.7 percent over the same period of 1992; a high speed seldom seen throughout history.

"Autonomy in direct fund circulation." This is an important right granted to local governments and enterprises allowing them to bypass the Central Government's measures controlling (regardless of whether it was direct or indirect control) credit and currency to directly raise funds from society at interest rates much higher than bank savings rates, thereby obtaining the necessary capital from society and making the government's currency policy lose its effectiveness. In 1992 the value of securities issued on the Chinese securities market totalled 128 billion yuan, of which 41 billion yuan were state treasury bonds, investment bonds of the investment corporations under the State Planning Commission were 12.7 billion yuan, enterprise bonds were 37.9 billion yuan, financial bonds were 25.5 billion yuan and stocks 10.9 billion yuan. The above listed are all relatively standard bonds. However, if the non-standard types of bonds such as internal stocks issued by enterprises, funds raised outside of plans and funds raised by selling registered permanent residence certificates are included, the total value, according to the People's Bank of China, was 220 billion yuan. By 1992 statistics showed that the amount of bonds was 410 billion yuan. Excluding the 25.5 billion yuan of financial bonds, the total amount of directly raised funds for 1992 was 194.5 billion yuan, accounting for 46 percent increased loans (422.8 billion yuan) issued that year by China's all financial organisations, including national banks, trust and investment firms and urban and rural credit unions. In 1991 the increased directly raised funds financing accounted for 12 percent of the total increased funds of 1991, and the figure jumped to 31.5 percent in 1992. Although this implies the shift in mechanism from bank savings to investment, however, it also shows that some effective macro-regulatory methods for currency were weakening.

The analysis above reveals that inflations occurred on numerous occasions since the 1980s are inevitably connected with the devolving of powers and profits within the state-run economy and the increase of autonomy of the grassroots units. A fact worth our attention is: as the autonomy of localities and enterprises increased from time to time, the speed of over-heated development of economy becomes ever faster and the inflation rate becomes ever higher.

(VII) The reason for the continued rise of the prices lies primarily in the insufficient competition

The new cycle of inflation which began in 1992 was brought about by a number of factors. Even though we cannot say that the excessive expansion of demand was the major reason for such a inflation, the picking up in demand was certainly one factor. This is to say, although the expansion of demand could no longer provide all conditions for inflation, however it remains as a necessary condition. In addition, there were also other reasons, including the monetization of the economy and transformation of the system, speculation and blind investment, the rise in cost following wage raises, the shifting of burden by enterprises during reforms in tax systems, etc. These reasons are certainly not independent of each other, but are mingled together, mutually related to and, conditions each other.

Beginning from 1992, the pace of price reform reached the highest level of the preceding dozen years. For years many economists have advocated that the price reform should be carried out at the time when the economy is relatively contracted, and that the adjustment in price structure can be realized only under the condition that the general price levels are basically stable. However, the cycle of economic growth and the cycle of reforms are almost always coincide. In a situation where the economy continues to rise, it is not only possible to abolish the price control, but has also been proved by facts that it will definitely lead to an overall increase in prices. The three years of reorganisation and consolidation from 1989 to 1991 let the opportunity slip by, so in 1993 and 1993 price reforms could not be put off any longer. The general prediction of society on inflation played a major function. For many years Chinese citizens and enterprises have formed a mode of prediction: economic growth are always followed by price rise; the announcement of price reforms actually means price increases. To make people understand the real situation of the large-scale increase in the total supply is not easy, but to foster a public opinion to resist price rise is even more difficult. The prediction of inflation in 1988 certainly served a purpose; but it was not a major reason, because at that time the total supply was far from being sufficient to meet the total demand. However, the situation in 1992 and 1993 was entirely different.

The rapid rise in wage costs also pushed up the overall price levels. The expenditure growth for wages of the state-owned enterprises was very fast, reaching a level of 30 percent in two years running. Following the implementation of measures to readjust wage structures government departments vied with each other for wage raises, which served as a constant factor for price rise over the past dozen years. However, due to the fact that in the past wages constituted only a very small proportion in the costs of production and also the fact that technology and labor productivity developed rapidly, therefore the function of the factor of wage increase was not obvious. At the present stage, however, the cost for wage raises plays a much stronger role pushing the prices up.

Factors of speculation start to play a major role. Since 1992, speculative activities in the commodities market, real estate and the financial market have spread all over the country. Various types of commodities and futures exchange markets developed rapidly, yet regulations were incomplete and speculative activities were rampant. For instance, prices of steel products in 1993 experienced the complete cycle of drastically rising, falling and rising again. As a result of speculation, grain prices also soared up; in some areas grain prices went up by 30-50 percent.

Blind fluctuations in the exchange rate played a vigorous function in driving up overall price levels; China already has a highly opened economy, and the value of imported goods represented one fourth of its GNP. Due to the fact that the proportion of the listed price of the foreign exchange kept dropping every year, the influence of the market exchange rate was extremely strong on the price levels of imported raw materials, semi-finished goods, accessory parts and complete sets of equipment.

The shifting of burdens by sellers in the reform of the tax system also quite obviously pushed the overall price levels up. First of all, the operation tax rose 3 percent to 5 percent; this was a move planned several years ago when the economy was weak. Owing to various reasons it had been held back not until when the economy had recovered a swift pace of development. The absence of necessary preventative measures made it possible for sellers to unite and push up prices at the same time. In addition to shifting the tax burdens, they also frequently scheme to gain extra profits.

Market swindling and seeking of huge profits also pushed price levels up. Because there was no sound market order or effective measure to protect consumers' rights and interests, in some areas, particularly in service industries, swindling in prices was seen frequently. Some operational units lacked a sense of self-restraint and pushed up the prices as they pleased. Organisations which had not separated government administration from enterprise management, including "markets," "centers" and "companies" run by the governmental departments, used their influence to monopolize the market in some areas so as to gain quick huge profits.

To sum up the above factors which have led to price increases, one can say that the problem lies mainly in the incomplete competition mechanism. This shows clearly that the market system has not yet reached maturity, and it is not because of implementation of reforms toward marketization.

(VIII) The direct relationship between inflation and the current system

The continual inflationary pressure that has plagued China since reforms began is mainly due to factors of economic structure.

1. The internal imbalance of the state-owned enterprises continually creates inflationary pressure.

Since reform began, the increase of wages of workers and staff members of state-owned enterprises have all along exceeded the growth of labor productivity, thereby causing the rise of costs which creates an immense inflationary pressure.

In a market economy, the situation in which wage growth greatly exceed the growth of the labor productivity cannot continue for a long time because it means the self-bankruptcy of enterprises. However, this situation has become the norm with China's state-owned enterprises. Pursuing the maximum income is a rational demand of everybody in a market economy. The problem is whether or not a mechanism exists to effectively coordinate and control the behaviors of all participants of a market economy, enabling the realization of interests of owners of all production factors. Otherwise, the holders of human capital will encroach upon state assets, as in the case of wage growth exceeding production. The holders of state assets, in order to prevent the loss of their interests and the possible inflation, adopt measures to withdraw powers they had devolved before. After this, human capital, through stagnating production and leisure, replaces wage growth. As a result, the economy shrinks; and this in turn will force the holders of state assets to carry out reforms devolving powers and profits. The situation described above becomes a cycle. Therefore, it can be said that before fundamental changes have taken place in the current enterprise system, inflationary pressure will continue to plague it.

In addition to the fact that wage increases outpacing productivity growth, which directly creates wage-induced inflation, based on the present financial system of the state-owned enterprises and the banking system, this factor also continually influence and induce inflations.

2. The subsidy-based financial system continually diverts inflationary pressure.

In the situation described above, a relaxed economic environment and the granting of powers and profits bring about the phenomenon of wages increasing faster than the productivity increases, and the encroachment upon the state assets inevitably leads to the hidden losses of enterprises; when the economic development is receded and the granted powers and profits are withdrawn, the losses of state-owned enterprises become the norm. The intensification of the deficit among state-owned enterprises since reform began was caused mainly by subsidies for the losses.

Readjusting financial imbalances can be achieved either through overdraft from banks or through issuing bonds (thereby switching the burden to long-term inflation); and the expansion in basic currency (by overdraft) or in future basic currency (by issuing bonds), either of which will intensify inflation.

3. A passive banking system uses price increases as a way of

easing inflationary pressure.

As described above, the effect of currency increases and the effect which imbalanced finances has on shifting the burden of the currency supply, both lead banks to giving out currency passively. Lacking a micro-basis, an independent banking system is nothing more than an idea. At a time when passive lending activity creates enormous inflationary pressure, the Central Government has to either tacitly agree to let prices rise in order to release inflationary pressure or adopt scale-control and other strong measures to restore balance.

4. The distribution mechanism based on rivalry with each other leads to structural inflation.

Under the present economic system the socialist distribution principle of to each according to his work is often mistaken as equal pay to equal amount of work done; however, this is in direct conflict with the distribution principle under a market economy—distribution according to the operation of each enterprise. Since labor, particularly the labor of employees, is to be accomplished during the process of production, regardless of whether the market direction of a certain product is correct or not or whether differences exist in the amount of necessary capital of each enterprise, the labor put out by employees is the same. This results in an income distribution mechanism of citing the case of others to suport one's demand for equal pay. Those who work in successful enterprises request that their income should be linked with the enterprises' profits while those who work for less successful enterprises demand that their income should be base on work hours. Since the latter case happens to conform to the socialist distribution principle of to each according to his work, therefore the demand is often satisfied. The formation of such a distribution mechanism tacitly has rationalized the fact that low efficiency enterprises get at least the average income, thus leading to structural inflation.

5. An incomplete market system produces profit induced inflation.

Since reforms began, the intense expansion of the disparity between people's incomes, numerous successful speculators and the influence they had created made people to spend more than they earn. The strong urge to enter a new consumer level, the incompleteness of the market mechanism and the expectation for higher income gave rise to improper competitions and seeking for exorbitant profits, thus leading to profit induced inflation. It can be said that the motivation to seek excessive profit and the disorder in the grain circulation system led to the large scale increases in grain price at the end of 1993, and also greatly increased the inflationary pressure during 1994 and beyond.

(IX) Chaos in the economic order intensified inflation

The top priority in opposing inflation is to establish a regular, effective new economic order. Economic activities of a nation or a region must be based on an established order and regulations, otherwise they will suffer from a state of disorder or even reach a point of utter confusion and chaos. This is due to the fact that economic activities must be carried out in an organized way according to order; the objective demands the participants of economic activities to exclude any subjectivity and randomness and their behaviors should follow the internal rules which exist in economic activities. China, in its 45-year process of socialist construction, had already had its fill of the pain of economic chaos. For a fairly long period of time after 1949, under the influence of the pattern of the former Soviet Union, China's economic order was not normal; this was expressed as an abnormal, ineffective economy, experiencing frequent leaps and setbacks. Between 1966 and 1976 (the "cultural revolution" period), the Chinese economy marched toward the edge of collapse, so even in the course of reform and opening up, China did not completely throw off the situation of economic disorder. The most obvious example is the chaos arose in the financial order during the second half of 1992 and the first half of 1993. The chaos in the financial order brought about foaming hot points in its economic development, giving rise to an overall price rise of production materials, real estate, stock, funding, service and foreign exchange. This is the inflation of 1993 brought about by chaos in the financial order. By 1994 this situation was changed to certain extent through a series of macro-adjustment measures adopted in the latter half of 1993. However, 1994 was a significant year tackling the key problems, when many major reform measures came out all at once; price reform actually bore the brunt of this. It cannot be denied that some mistakes had been made in terms of the choice of time, strength intensity and the way to implement these reform measures. Influenced by the chaos in the financial order in 1993 the circulation system also went into a chaotic state, thus spurring on the most serious inflation that had ever occurred in China since reforms began. The most prominent expression of this was in the loss of control over prices, the lack of norms for fixing prices and the chaos in the price fixing order. Only due to the overall balance in the country's total supply and demand, the improved endurance ability of the whole society and the general population as well as the government's macro-adjustment measures did China prevent strong repercussions and instability in society. Nevertheless, the problem should put all of us to attention.

China urgently needs to establish an appropriate, effective economic system, which should be capable of maintaining an order of sustained, steady and coordinate growth of its economy. Such an economic order does not manifest itself in excessive growth rate of economy nor in an overheated economy. Because an excessive economic growth rate easily causes imbalance in economy, which will bring about economic crisis or even political crisis. With this in mind, the viewpoint of a well-known Dutch economist is worth our attention. He believes that a national economy should maintain a growth rate next to a high-speed, because such a productivity is capable of maintaining an order enabling economy to grow effectively. Even though this type of growth rate will slow down the economic development somewhat, it can give confidence and hope to the people and avoid a great number of economic and social problems as well. This does not necessarily mean that the present rate of development of China's economy should be lowered down because for a developing country like China a high growth rate is absolutely necessary. Only when China's economy develops in a sustained, steady and coordinate manner or, to put it another way, when a normal effective economic order is established, will it be able for China to maintain a more reasonable speed of economic growth. Such a economic growth rate, though not very high, is sound and therefore feasible. Not only can it effectively control inflation, but also help the national economy enter a healthy cycle.

II. The Influence of Inflation on Society's Economic Life

(I) The inflationary situation is still severe

Since the mechanism leading to inflation is still functioning, the situation still requires our full attention.

1. The bait-and-hook type investment mechanism is still being used.

At present, there are almost no investment projects which do not exceed their budget. They usually exceed their budget by 40-50 percent, and some go over the original budget even many times. The reasons for exceeding investment budgets are many, for instance inflationary factors. However, the primary reason lies in the investment system itself. Currently, excluding a portion which is raised independently, the investment capital of local governments and enterprises mainly comes from bank loans. And bank loans, in the final analysis, are still state loans. Therefore, the interests from the investment primarily go to the localities and enterprises while the risks of the investment are left primarily with the state. Under such a situation, localities and enterprises naturally vie for investment and are active in going for more projects. This is the major reason for the scale of investment to get out of control repeatedly.

2. The mechanism of rivalling each other for more income and encroachment upon profits by wages is still functioning.

Since reform began, the proportion of residents' income in the national income has continued to rise, at a rate of almost one percentage point annually. Contrarily, the national financial revenue has fallen. This shows that the national income has already shifted into the pockets of the people; the mechanism of wages encroaching profits has been in effect all along. At the same time, the mechanism of rivalling each other for more income is also in effect. Reforms in the macro-economic system has not fundamentally touched these two mechanisms. Tax reform has touched upon the problems of income, but that has little direct connection with the vast majority of people. As long as these two mechanisms continue to function, the people's income will continue to rise. When the present wage mechanism continues to function in cities, the disparity between urban and rural areas also expands. This is a basic feature at the present stage in the income distribution system in China, not to mention the growing disparity between coastal and inland areas. These are potential factors contributing to instability in society.

It is worth noting that for a long period of time, the average growth rate of wages has been higher than the growth rate of productivity. From 1992 to 1993 the annual wage increase rate for state sectors was 15 percent and the annual rate of increase of total productivity was only 8 percent. Another piece of data shows that in the first half of 1994 the average income increase rate in cities was 37 percent, even excluding the influence of inflation, the actual income growth is still incredibly surprising. This is to say, for several years on end the average growth rate of income exceeded the growth rate of productivity, a situation worth our attention. On the one hand, this has strengthened the general inflation endurance ability so that when prices rise people's reaction was not too strong and the political danger was relatively small. However, this situation also has a number of negative influences, one of which is the rise in demand following the rise of income. From January to September of 1994 the commodity retail sales in Chinese society increased by nearly 30 percent, already a fairly high rate. The increase in income also causes production costs to rise, and this finally shifts to general price rise, although this shift takes a longer period of time. Under such situation prices will rise due to the increase of production costs. And the economy is receding and demand is sluggish, producers will have no choice but to put more into production costs to ensure a high price for their products. This leads to a stagnant inflation. On the other hand, within a period of time, it will weaken competitiveness. In joint ventures, wages increase fast, causing China's favorable position of low labor costs to disappear. Especially compared with countries close to China in southeast Asia, China's advantage of low labor costs will gradually be weakened. If this trend continues, China will lose its superiority in the competition.

3. The inverse pressure mechanism still exists.

Local governments and enterprises are constantly looking for ways to increase investment, and force local banks to grant more loans. If the bank refuses to do so, the bank's original loans will be lost. Another example is diverting circulating capital to fixed assets investment. When factories are faced with problems of keeping their production going and paying their workers, banks have to issue more loans to maintain stability and unity. If local banks run out of their planned allowance, the burden will be directed to higher level banks and finally the specialised banks will force the central bank to increase loans.

Approximately one-third of bank loans lent to state-owned enterprises have become uncollectable debts and bad debts. In order to meet the needs for circulating funds, it is necessary to continually add new capital. This becomes one of the main reasons why it is difficult to check the endless flow of bank loans. When specialised banks want to commercialise themselves, they are faced with the same problem of how to deal with bad debts and uncollectable debts. In addition to the reform of the ownership, this is another major problem affecting banks in their move towards marketization.

(II) Amply estimate the influence of inflation on social life and make effective control over inflation our objective for macro-control during rapid economic development

Accompanying reform and opening up and the rapid economic growth, the income of both rural and urban people has increased markedly and their inflation endurance ability has also improved. However, we cannot simply approach the problem by looking at average numbers because they have been pulled up by the high income of a few moneybags; the average figures often conceal the true situation of those poor households far below the statistical average. Not only do they have a much lower inflation endurance ability, they also suffer greater during price increases.

Reform is the impetus for economic development, and a developed economy will provide a solid foundation for social stability, which in turn serves as a prerequisite for reform and development. Both reform and development require a stable social environment. Economic stability is the foundation for social stability. The price rise is the barometer by which to measure stability.

In 1994 a relatively large number of reforms were carried out, and some of these were substantive reforms of a deep level. All these reforms, including the establishment of a macro-adjustment system for banks, tax reform, reform by using national debt to make up for the budget deficit, the establishment and improvement of the social security system, new adjustments of the prices of grain, cotton and energy resources, the change of the government functions, all require the support of the masses. The crux of whether or not these reforms can be implemented smoothly lies in whether the masses support them. If the prices run out of control and infringe upon the interests of the people, reforms will be affected. We must be clear-headed in handling this issue.

In the past dozen of years since reforms began, China's economy has experienced three cyclical fluctuations of takeoff —heat-up—overheated—readjustment. In addition, a smaller fluctuating cycle appeared at the peak period during the second fluctuation between 1984 and 1988. The economic growth rate dropped from 16.2 percent in 1985 to 9.1 percent in 1986, but the economy continued to grow fast after the small fluctuation all the way to 1988. Later, following three years of readjustment and consolidation, beginning in 1992, China's economy entered a new peak period of growth, currently it has kept an annual growth rate of about 13 percent for two years running. It seems that the development of a socialist economy also has cyclical fluctuations. Before fundamental changes are made in the traditional investment system, investment peaks, peaks in economic growth and peaks in price increases accompany each other (usually it takes the additionally issued currency about ten months to bring about an obvious increase in prices). If we grasp the economic cycle law and strictly control the scale of price rise during the peak period of economic growth, we can certainly ensure the peak period to continue.

In 1994 the inflation rate in China went up to over 20 percent. This was the third instance of inflation since reforms began; it was also the highest inflation out of the prediction of all people. Such a high inflation obviously had very bad influence on the economy.

Due to the high level of inflation, the actual living standard of a portion of the people decreased, contributing to the instability factors of society. In 1994 due to the quick increases in incomes (excluding the factor of price rise), the actual income of urban and rural dwellers increased by 7-8 percent; from January to September the income of city residents increased by 6.8 percent and that of the rural people increased by 10 percent. Therefore, it could be said that on the whole the actual living standard of the people did not go down. But the situation was uneven, especially among workers of state-run enterprises (which had stopped production completely or partially) who were unable to receive their full pay on time and also retirees whose retirement pension increased by a much too low rate to keep up with the scale of price increases. Hence, their life was relatively difficult. As a result, there was a strong reaction to the inflation this time. Objectively, inflation can result in the worsening of the situation in the redistribution of national income, thus leading to the widening of income disparity between different social strata and to the tensioning of social relationships. The results of a social survey show that at present, inflation has moved up to become the number one reason for dissatisfaction in society. And we definitely cannot rely on low interest loans to solve the problem of unemployment in cities and countryside. The basic method for solving this problem is to create more employment positions, and this can only be achieved when the productivity and investment efficiency of the whole society is increased. Inflation has led to irrational allocation of resources and decreased efficiency; therefore, inflation can only make the employment problem even more difficult to solve. Those whose income has increased faster than the increase rate of prices suffer less severely compared with those whose income has not increased as fast as prices and with their income actually decreased. Inflation has become a direct factor for brewing social contradictions and friction.

Inflation has made reform more costly and risky and seriously affected the smooth development of economic reforms; it also jeopardises the healthy operation of the socialist market economy. The excessive price increases, first of all, are to the disadvantage of the deepening of price reforms; many reform measures for price adjustment and for the relaxing of prices that should have been implemented as quickly as possible were forced to be postponed or cancelled. And this happened both in 1986 and 1988.

Inflation leads to an irrational allocation of social resources. Serious inflation interfere with price signals, making price signals become distorted and unreliable. As a result, the economy becomes all the more unstable; enterprises and consumers, unable to rely on price signals in judging the market price quotations, cannot come to any correct and timely decisions. Therefore people, funds and technology all move towards circulation areas and other non-production areas for speculation activities, resulting in a lopsided economic development. The price increase ratios for different commodities are different, causing distortion in pricing and commodity production. This can intensify structural imbalance and economic chaos, affect the effective distribution of social resources and bring about serious imbalances in the national economic development ratio. The result of all this is that the state has to pay an even higher price in order to control inflation.

Inflation put macro-controls into a double plight: on the one hand are urgent cries of the people, demanding the checking of inflation and the levelling of prices, on the other, enterprises are confronted with financial difficulties and the increasing seriousness of chain debt. Too much of tight control over bank loans and demand would push large- and middle sized enterprises into even graver circumstances and the economy into a low ebb or sluggishness. Economic reform as a whole would suffer from big setbacks. The relaxation of the control over banks would relieve the difficult facing of enterprises but the banks would have to increase the issuing of currency. This would lead inflation to move in a worse direction, making the society less able to absorb the burden. Finally, nothing could be done except pull the brakes on the economy, resulting in an even bigger economic shock.

High inflation is also unfavorable for the adjustment of the industrial structure. The imbalance in China's industrial structure is relatively serious, power industry, communications, raw materials industry, agriculture and other basic industries are weak, lagging behind in development. Over many years in the past much has been done to change the industrial structure. However, like the difficult situation in the adjustment of the total existing amount of assets, it is also very difficult to carry out any readjustment in processing industries, because they require less investments, go into production fast and bring about high profits. Although over-rapid price rises are usually brought about by the price rise in raw materials and power industries the price increases of the products of basic industries in general cannot keep up with the continual price increases of products of processing industries. This is decided by the characteristics of the basic industries and the basic products. Since the price of basic products concerns the overall economy, the adjustment in this area calls much greater efforts. Normally, the state would first relax prices of products of processing industries and then gradually free the prices of basic products. Up to now still a portion of basic products are under state planned prices. Although the prices of transport, electricity and oil, controlled by the state, have always been too low, they can only be adjusted slowly and bit by bit. As for the prices of processed products, they go up automatically as the prices of basic products rise. Moreover, the government's control over these prices compared with that over the prices of basic products is much weaker; they are basically readjusted by market prices. Due to the fact that basic industries require large investment, long periods of time from construction to production and slow circulation of capital, the investment initiative of localities and enterprises in basic industries has never been high. Therefore, in an overheated economy, basic industries are not the source of the over heating, but processing industries, stimulated by the rise in prices, expand fast in their scale of investment. Sources have shown that in 1993 China's fixed assets investment inflated quickly, an increase of nearly 50 percent over 1992, and during the first half of 1993 the proportion of the investment for power industry decreased by 8.8 percentage points compared with that of the same period in 1992. Viewing the situation in China an excessively rapid economic growth rate and excessively high rises in prices are not only disadvantageous for the adjustment of the industrial structure, but also add more difficulties to its adjustment. In the present grave situation in prices, the control over inflation is the objective call that concerns the overall national economy.

III. The Road Ahead for Inflation

(I) Inflation is a global phenomenon requiring conscientious research into and analysis of the reasons for its formation

The spectre of inflation is something which haunts the entire world and its shadow extends to every country. Very few countries have been spared from experiencing this monster. It varies in degree. According to a report in the US *Time* magazine published in August 9, 1993, the top ten countries hit by bad inflations in 1992 include former Yugoslavia 15,201 percent, Zaire 3,860 percent, the former Soviet Union 1,202 percent, Brazil 1,038 percent, Albania 226 percent, Mongolia 202 percent, Romania 202 percent, Zambia 191 percent, Cambodia (Myanmar) 177 percent and Sudan 114 percent. In November and December of 1992 the International Labor Office surveyed the problem of inflation in 94 countries and regions. The results show that the inflation rate in 60 percent of the countries and regions was lower than that of the same period in 1991. The inflationary rate of the majority of African and Latin American nations still on the rise.

Since inflation is a global phenomenon, it naturally attracts the attention of the governments of all countries and economists who explore its origins, make studies and formulate countermeasures.

In the West, there are many different schools of thought on the origin of inflation. One is the theory of monopolization; under free capitalism, inflation is caused by monopoly. Monopolized prices can stay high without coming down and inevitably create inflation. The second is the theory of monetary system. Under a metallic currency system, inflation cannot possibly occur, for excessive currency precipitates down and is stored up. If a metallic currency system is switched to a paper currency system, then excessive paper currency will inevitably cause inflation. The third is the school of government behavior. Keynes firmly advocated that the government should intervene in the economy. The government, ambitious for great achievements, likes to get involved in matters beyond its ability, and as a way out it has to issue more currency, which results in inflation. The fourth is the theory of inflation induced demand. When demand is too big (including both production demand and demand in daily necessities) and far exceeds the supply capacity of goods, price levels will continue to rise and inflation will be the final result. The fifth theory is inflation induced by the increased production cost. The production cost of a commodity is the basis and primary component in determining its price. A rise in production costs will naturally bring about price increase thus leading to inflation. The sixth is inflation induced by various factors. Inflation is a syndrome of a social economy, or the result of the joint effort of many mechanisms; inflation by no means can be brought about by one factor alone.

(II) China's economy is currently in a historical period of transition; a certain level of inflation is unavoidable and will exist for a long time

The current inflation in China is a syndrome caused by

various factors, including both demand and supply, macro- and micro-economics, as well as the overall imbalance in the economy and the transition of the economic system. Among all these factors that have brought about the syndrome the transition of the economic system serves as a factor at a deeper level. Therefore, it can be called inflation induced by economic restructuring. China's economy has all along had a deep-set desire for expansion and an internal drive to expand the scale of investment. This internal drive originated from the combination of the state political power and economic power under the former planned economic system. This power combination put the power for investment policy decision and the operation of funds under the hands of the government and there is no way to impose any tough financial restrictions on enterprises who need not to worry about paying the cost for using the state capital. Later on, even after the state has changed the practice of allocating funds to issuing loans, the restrictions through loan interest rates showed little effect and the situation was not fundamentally changed. As the Central Government granted more power to localities, their decision-making power for investment increased and the drive of the economic expansion also grew stronger. Almost all of the inflations occurred since the 1980s have been induced by the excessive growth of investment.

Experts point out that although it is true that the inflated demand for investment has led to an excessive growth of the demand for currency; however, the growth of the demand for currency in many cases is either directly or indirectly connected with the structural reforms. For example: —Reforms in the pricing system include both adjustments of price levels and structures and the switch in the decision-making mechanism for prices (from the state-planned pricing to market pricing). However, an adjustment in the price structures is always followed by rise in price levels, and the releasing of the state control over prices usually must experience the impact of price rises. In addition, before the releasing of the control over prices set by each particular industry, they all must go through several adjustments in price levels and structure. In recent years price adjustment and price relaxing were carried out successively in many industries, especially the relaxation of prices in 1993 for foodstuffs and services—the last two important areas. Naturally, this move has not only brought about price increases in these areas, but also imposed a new impact on the overall price levels. This is something as anticipated and it is also a price which reform must pay. These price increases will finally express themselves as an increased demand for currency.

—As the planned economy develops into a market economy, the process of monetization will speed up and a number of products and resources which in the past never entered the market has also entered the market in the form of currency, thus increasing the demand for currency. The development of the real estate market is a case in point. In the past two years, huge amounts of currency flowed into the real estate market following the opening up of the domestic real estate market. This naturally increased the demand for currency. It should be admitted that this demand for currency was a logical outcome in conformity with the demand of the monetization process. It is true that phenomena like speculation and the driving up of prices occurred in the real estate market. As a result, the demand for currency was exaggerate partially due to some artificial factors. Undoubtedly we should make distinction between the demand for currency following the development of the real estate market and the artificial demand for currency.

—Since the reform in the financial and banking systems had just begun and the currency market and securities market had just been established, the channels for capital circulation were chaotic. During the change from an old system to a new one, at least two grey areas appeared. One was that financial capital was moved to become credit and loans; many government organizations and public institutions used every means possible to lend their financial capital as loans to enterprises and corporations set up by themselves. The second was the industrialisation of loan capital. Banks and financial institutions used the loan capital under their control to illegally operate various industrial companies and even engage in secrities and real estate; there chaotic phenomena emerged, including random fund-raising, breaking of loans, arbitrarily raising interest rates and establishing financial organisations without permission. In 1993 the outflow of capital from financial organisations through inproper channels reached as much as 150 billion yuan. Not only did this disrupt the financial order, but also expanded the total demand for currency unnecessarily.

—Since 1992, the amount investment which China has imported directly from abroad has increased rapidly. The amount of foreign investment China had actually used in 1993 alone increased US$25.3 billion. From a long-term perspective, the use of foreign capital is conducive to an increase in supply, however, in the short-term it serves to increase overall demand (including imports). Moreover, the use of foreign capital requires Chinese currency as to supporting capital. Even if calculated according to a 2:1 ratio, the year of 1993 alone would need US$8-9 billion as supporting capital, equivalent to approximately 70 billion yuan. As all localities craved to attract foreign capital they seldom gave any thought about the supporting capital and even less about the pressure that has put on the currency supply.

The pricing policy worked out under the traditional planned economic system denies the existence of economic land rent, and the starting point set for the prices of farm and mining products was very low. Following the increase in production costs, the deviation between price and value becomes more and more serious; however, under the control of planning, prices remains stable and unchanged. And services are not even recognised as commodities; a number of important resources concerning the country's long-term development such as water, land and public housing, do not even have prices. An important task of the market-oriented reform is to make prices truly reflect the level of scarcity of the resources and to make the market mechanism develop its fundamental function in rationally allocating resources. According to this, the rise in prices brought about by reforms carried out in the price formation mechanism and the reforms to adjust the price structure became one of the features of the inflation in the transitional period. This is something no country in transition can avoid, and it is also the price to be paid by economic development.

Some experts point out that allowing a certain level of inflation was one of the characteristics and strong points of the moderately-paced reforms of the last ten years, and we must soberly recognise that in controlling inflation, we cannot be overly anxious for quick results. Moderate inflation is both an inevitable product of economic reform and the lubricant for the process of economic transformation. If we recall the bitter experience of accepting the conclusion that "the law of value is like a large school," then today we should strive to study and grasp the law governing the market economy through inflation. It is necessary to adopt resolute measures in order to control inflation to a certain level and make it fall.

Chapter 2
Inflation Control During Economic Development

I. China Must Maintain Rapid Economic Development

(I) The sustained rapid development of the Chinese economy will play a decisive role in the Asian Pacific. A flourishing Chinese economy has a great impact on the entire Asian Pacific's development of prosperity

As everyone knows, at present, the Asian Pacific is the fastest, most vigorous developing economic area in the whole world. And China is the part of the Asian Pacific which has most attracted people's attention and caught the admiring eye of investors worldwide. It has already become the hot spot of investment in the world. It is apparent that, with a population of 1.2 billion, China's economic development and the direction of its future development will have an influence and effect on all of East Asia, and on the whole world, which cannot be ignored.

In more than ten years of the reform and opening up, China has achieved economic development of world renown. Under maintained economic development from 1978 to 1993, China's overall national strength gradually increased; the average annual increase in the GDP was 9.3% or more, making it the nation in Asian, and even in the world, with the fastest rate of economic development.

Entering the 1990s, China's economic development went from a stage of shattering part of its old system into a new stage to completely establish a socialist market economic system. At present, the traditional planned economic system has already received a total blow, and the marketization process of the whole system deepens day by day. The singular public owned economy structure has already been destroyed and a flourishing pluralistic economy structure has already taken form. The speed of the non-state-run economy's development has been fast and its momentum intense, becoming a force spurring on the development of the Chinese economy that cannot be ignored. It has strongly catalyzed the development of the Chinese market and the formation of the market system. Following the prosperity of the commodities market, markets of important production factors, particularly the capital market and labor market, experienced marked corresponding development. The gradual completion of two national stock exchanges, the operation of the secondary market of treasury bills and the continued movement into foreign markets by large Chinese enterprises all revealed the first signs of life in China's capital market. In recent years, the amount of capital investment raised by enterprises has already surpassed half the total amount of the nation's fixed assets investment. This shows that in the process of allocating capital resources, the market has already begun to play a greater and greater role. According to statistics, at present, Chinese enterprises already rely on the market for approximately 85% of their primary resource supply; and the production and marketing of the vast majority of products is already decided by the market. Since reforms began, China has already freed up the prices of over 90% of goods step by step. According to the magnitude of value, the amount of industrial consumer items whose prices are adjusted by market forces has reached 95%, agricultural products 85% and means of production more than 80%. It should be noted that to a relatively large extent, China's micro-economic activity has already entered the market system. It is without doubt that all of this has set an excellent foundation and created the necessary preconditions for China's economy to take the first steps in establishing a market system at the end of this century.

As it walks towards the twenty-first century, China will work under the new socialist market economic system, and an economy which maintains sustained and stable growth will be an even more wealthy, vital, prosperous developing economy.

In the past ten years, at the same time that it concentrated its energies on developing the domestic economy, the Chinese government also unwaveringly carried out opening-up policies. From opening coastal areas on the east to the establishment of special economic zones; from riverside areas to the opening of border areas and inland areas. Presently, the entire nation has arrived at a new point of all-direction opening up to the outside. For more than ten years, China has continually maintained a positive development momentum in trade with other nations; the import-export turnover has increased at an annual rate of 16%. This speed is not only greater than the annual increase rate in the GDP for the same period, it is also greater than the speed of increase of trade worldwide for the same period. In 1993, the total volume of import-export trade reached US$ 198.5 billion, of which US$ 91.8 billion was of export and US$ 104 billion was of import. In international trade, China moved from 32nd place in 1978 to its present position of 11th. The total amount of world-wide export trade accounted for by China increased from 0.75% in 1978 to 2.5% in 1993. Concurrently, by the beginning of the 1990 China had already completed the shift from primarily exporting primary products to primarily exporting finished products. In 1993, the proportion accounted for by exported finished products to total exported goods rose to over 81%.

At present, China has already established trade relations with 220 nations and regions and has participated in many international economic organizations including the World Bank and the International Monetary Fund, UN. From 1979 to 1993, the total of approved direct foreign investment projects amounted to 174,000 and actual foreign investment totaled US$ 63.9 billion. In recent years, large foreign corporations and well-known transnational corporations investing in China increased substantially; the sphere of investment and joint venture type investments also increased in number and type.

During the final five years of this century, China will put its energies into establishing a more legally perfect foreign trade system with a relatively high level of transparency, fair in competition, and it will increase the scale of opening up to the outside. The fact that nations which have a closed structure have no way out, so China's development is inseparable from its cooperation with other nations in the world. To properly play its role as a large, developing socialist nation, China must throw off its undeveloped state. To realize modernization, in addition to relying on the hard work and creative spirit of the people, China must also step up measures of opening up to the outside, put great effort into developing trade relations with other nations, widely take part in international economic cooperation and exchange, and study and absorb mankind's outstanding achievements of civilization to the greatest degree.

Since the 1980s, in contrast to the stagnation of the Western nations' economies, the Asian Pacific economy has risen abruptly and become the economic growth center of the entire world. In the 1990s, the large scale inflow of international investment enabled Asian Pacific nations and local economies to maintain momentum for sustained economic growth. It is beyond argument that in the Asian Pacific, which is becoming the new economic growth center of the world, the southeastern coastal region of China and Hong Kong have become the nucleus of this center. The primary impetus pushing the economic development of the Asian Pacific forward comes from China, especially from the Guangzhou-Hong Kong economic zone made up of Hong Kong and areas of southern China. Within this economic zone, there are more than 3 million workers hired by Hong Kong businesspeople for production, assembly and manufacture of a large amount of export goods. The total number of these manufacturing industry laborers by far exceeded the number of laborers in Hong Kong itself and is actually more than half the total population of Hong Kong. Now, 90% of the Hong Kong manufacturing industry has already shifted to the southern China region. Every day 80,000 trucks filled with processed goods pass through the area on their way to Hong Kong, to be shipped from Hong Kong to countries all over the world. The region of southern China has already become the production base for Hong Kong. In addition, Hong Kong and southern China have already become a store-and-factory team, a symbiotic and interdependent relationship. Altogether, southern China adjacent to Hong Kong has a population of approximately 100 million. Each year this region experiences economic growth at the astonishing rate of more than 30%. Quite a few foreigners having visited this land, full of life and vigor, firmly believe that the economic region made up of Hong Kong and southern China will become the region most drawing the Asian Pacific's and the world's attention in the 21st century. It will become the new economic growth center of the Asian Pacific and the force sustaining that growth.

Hong Kong is the financial center of the Asian Pacific, the center of transit trade and the largest center of containerized shipping. In 1997, after Hong Kong returns to the mainland, the speed of economic integration of the two areas will increase even more. Due to factors involving China, post-1997 Hong Kong will not only be the intermediary and bridge by which China will walk towards the world and by which the world will enter China; moreover, in the process of taking on this intermediary role, it will also consolidate and develop its unique role in Asian Pacific trade relations and become the fortress and vanguard of Asian Pacific trade development.

From the perspective of cooperation between areas within the Asian Pacific, China, being the largest developing nation in the Asian Pacific, will have close trade connections with nations of the Asian Pacific and members of the Asian Pacific Economic Cooperative Organization. Among China's import-export trade, 70% of economic activity is with Asian Pacific nations and regions; 85% of foreign businesspeople who invest in China also come from this region. Because of this, looking at the matter from any perspective, the sustained, stable development of China's economy plays a decisive role for all of the Asian Pacific. The prosperity of the Chinese economy has a major influence on the prosperity of the whole Asian Pacific.

In the latter part of the 1990s, as the political and economic systems of the world tend towards diversification, the major problems of the present day remain peace, development and reform. Economic competition is gradually replacing military and political confrontation and conflict. Reform implementation, economic development and engaging with the rest of the world have become the road which all developing nations must follow. In a sixteen year process of maturing based on subjective and objective factors, China's reform and opening up has adopted the strategy of gradual advance extending from spots to areas. It is proved that in the process of switching from a traditional planned economy to a modern market economy, China's experience has been successful, and that reform has brought vitality to Chinese economic development. The prospering Chinese economy and its immense market of 1.2 billion people is attracting more and more investors of other countries. Moreover, in setting the establishment of a new system—a socialist market economy—as its goal, China's economic reforms have won the world's affirmation and approval. It should be noted that in the last ten years China's rapidly developing economy has not only set the foundation for the establishment of a market economy, it has also created the possibility for China's economy to join with the international economy. In the process of joining with the world economy, since China is the world's largest developing nation, its economic development and the direction it will take in the future will necessarily have a far-reaching influence on the economic development of the whole world.

First, China's all-direction opening up to the outside has already made China's market of 1.2 billion an important component of the world market. Undoubtedly, this has provided the conditions and opportunities for every nation and region to enter this massive market and to cooperate with China in every area of economic development. Under conditions of all-direction opening to the outside world, China will implement economic projects on an even larger scale and will merge with the world economic system at an even faster rate. At the same time, every nation will also richly benefit from trade cooperation with this nation, full of development potential.

Second, China is an economically under-developed nation with a population of 1.2 billion. The sustained, stable development of China's economy and the improvement and enrichment of the material life of its 1.2 billion people are both a great contribution to the world and to mankind. This nation's prosperity and stability, at a relatively large level, will influence the Asian Pacific's and the whole world's economic and social prosperity and stability.

Third, the Asian Pacific is presently the center of economic growth of the whole world, and China and Hong Kong form the center of Asian Pacific economic development. Therefore, the economic zone made up of southern China and Hong Kong will have a positive influence and play an active role on the economic development of the whole world.

In the final few years of this century, we will take market diversification as our objective. Through hard work, we will gradually make the Asian Pacific market our emphasis and the surrounding markets the sustaining force by which to reach a reasonable market structure balanced between the markets of developed and developing nations.

(II) Spurring an economy into a relatively fast pace of growth has strategic significance for any country. In the post-Cold War era, economy is becoming an ever-increasingly important factor in international relations. The speed of China's economic development must be dealt with in relation to the world's economy

At any given time and as far as any nation is concerned, the speed of economic development is a crucial problem. The problem of just how to spur an economy into developing even faster has strategic significance to all nations.

Just how fast any given nation can develop its economy is decided by a number of factors involving that nation, including economic factors, non-economic factors, domestic factors and international factors.

Since entering the 1990s, the economic growth situation of the whole world has been like this: the economy went through a period of recession. To look at the world's economy as a whole, during the four years from 1990 to 1993, the economy fundamentally came to a halt.

Why did this situation occur then? It was due to different types of nations, including the developed Western nations, the former Soviet Union and Eastern European nations, and even large developing nations, all meeting with less than ideal situations; of course, they each have their own character and their own circumstances.

The developed Western nations or the developed capitalist nations, from 1990 to 1993, experienced economic recession. This recession was led by America, England and other nations. The recession in America began in July 1990 and continued for three seasons, coming to an end in March 1991. This is not a long period of time, however, the grave problem is that after the recession there was no swift recovery. Instead, the recovery rose and receded in sluggish waves, lacking force all the way until the present.

While America was going through the recession, the economies of the continental European nations and Japan continued to grow, but when America had basically pulled through its economic troubles, the Japanese and European economies were successively hit by recession. To the present, they have still not gotten rid of the economic difficulty.

High unemployment and massive financial deficit put the developed industrial nations in a conundrum: in order to reduce unemployment, the financial administration must increase its expenses to stimulate economic growth, which will inevitably cause the deficit to become even greater.

In addition to financial deficit and serious domestic public and private debts, another problem worth our attention, involving the recession, is the financial and currency crisis.

Even though the economic recession experienced by the developed Western nations ended rather quickly, none of the problems mentioned above, including large-scale unemployment, huge financial deficit and massive amounts of debt as well as the breakdown of Japan's foam economy and the aftermath of the upheaval in European currency, is the one which can be eradicated in a short time.

On the other hand, the economies of the Western nations have not yet entered real economic depression. Since recession is of a cyclical nature, the end of a recession implies that the new period is the beginning of a turn for the better, while the governments of every nation adjust their economic policy and seek ways to control the financial difficulties. The rate of inflation of these nations was not high (1.5%-5.5%), which is beneficial for the spurring of economic growth. Hereafter, the international market price of petroleum and primary resources will not increase much, but will fluctuate more or less around the present levels; this is also beneficial for the economic growth of developed nations. The Western nations are currently working hard to develop high technology, pushing the growth of high technology industries and promoting new high technology products, increasing market competition.

It is estimated that, to the end of this century, the economies of Western nations will experience a certain amount of growth, but it will not be fast and it will limited to a yearly average rate of about 3%.

In their shift of direction towards privatization and a free market economy, the former Soviet Union and Eastern Europe (which, in the United Nations statistics, are referred to as countries whose economies are in a transitional period) have faced difficulties which were not expected, and, consequently, have entered a crisis. The nature of the crisis they face and of the cyclical recession experienced by the Western nations is completely different; some economists call it a system crisis. For several years, the economies of these nations have continually slid down.

Since China implemented reforms in 1978, its economy has literally flown forward at a furious pace and in the fourteen years up to 1992, the average increase in the annual GDP was approximately 9%, a seldom seen level in any country. In the past two years, the level of growth stayed at 10%; until the end of this century, the rate of growth can be maintained at 8-9%. This level of growth forms a stark contrast with the low level of economic growth among developed Western nations and the economic crisis facing the independent Soviet states and Eastern Europe.

However, when comparing China with other nations, particularly developed nations in their speed of economic growth we should perform a scientific analysis. Since we are a developing nation, we are not running on the same track as that of developed nations:

1. There are a number of developed nations whose economic scale is massive. For instance, in 1992 America's GNP was US$ 5.954 trillion and Japan's was US$ 3.6743 trillion, respectively thirteen and eight times China's GNP. So if America's GNP increases 1%, the actual increase in output value is actually equivalent to 13 times of an 1% increase in China's GNP Growth.

2. It should also be seen that China is a developing nation, so our economy still fundamentally relies on speed and quantity while the economies of developed nations relies on efficiency and quality. China's production growth relies primarily on continual investment for increasing production factors by large amounts, increasing capital, energy resources, primary materials and labor while very few rely on improving technology and management techniques. According to statistics, the amount of our productivity growth attributable to technological factors does not exceed 20-30% while among developed nations, the ratio is 60-70% or higher. If we only seek high speed growth and do not attach any importance on better results, this implies that the expansion in production is only at a low level, indicating waste and low efficiency in the major factors in production.

3. Since China is a developing nation, the structure of our GNP is different from that of developed capitalist nations. In developed industrialized nations, agriculture constitutes a very small proportion, for instance only accounting for 2% in America, England, Japan and other countries. In China it still accounts for 27%. The proportion of service in these nations is very high, in America 75% or more, in Japan 56%, while in China it is only 31%. In the structure of China's industrial sector, textiles, ship building, general machines, food products, leather, paper and other traditional industrial products still constitute a large proportion of the economy; new technology industries are still in a young stage. In the industry of developed nations, these tradition-

al industries no longer have any fundamental development; they primarily develop airplanes, spacecraft, micro-electronics, computers, fiber optics, advanced medical products, high-precision instruments, environmental protection products and other high technology products.

Due to the above mentioned factors, when comparing China with other nations, we must carry out a total analysis and cannot simplify things. China should not merely or blindly seek high-speed, it must maintain rapid growth and increase efficiency; it must strive for high-speed growth on top of a foundation of efficient results.

(III) In 1994, a series of reforms were implemented rather smoothly and the overall state of the economy was healthy. We must predict the effect of inflation precisely and, while speeding up reforms and development, effectively control inflation

Presently, inflation is at a scale that we can bear. In 1995, we should hold economic growth to a level of approximately 10% and, while maintaining a relatively high speed of economic growth, we must control inflation.

In recent years, macro-controls have brought about an improvement in the overall state of the economy, making our "soft landing" objective basically attained. Several of the important reform measures that have been put into practice one by one to obtain the goal of establishing a socialist market economy have, all in all, made smooth headway. A fundamental balance was maintained between supply and demand; for over 90% of consumer goods, supply was greater than demand or was balanced; there was no stampede to buy things as occurred in 1988 due to a shortage. The inflation in 1994 was quite different from those preceding it; it had a very unique nature, and many important economic indicators reveal that the economic situation in 1994 had already improved greatly over the first half of 1993.

Every year since 1979, the Chinese economy has grown at an average rate of 9.3% and the price of retail commodities has increased by 6.44%. For several years from now on, the Chinese economy will maintain a growth level at above 9%. In a period of economic transition, if the growth rate falls below 8%, industries will suffer losses, production cease, goods become overstocked, unemployment worsen, and the stability of society will become threatened. For the next one or two years, the economic growth rate should be sustained at 9-10%, only then can the positive development momentum of China's economy be maintained.

The major contradiction in China today is the problem of development; development is a hard fact. In the process of rapid, sustained economic development, inflation can arise due to a number of factors. We must, however, consider a major precondition. That is, if the economy does not grow and reform is not speeded up, from a long-term view, this can turn into the primary source of serious inflation and can make it quite difficult to solve the root of the problem.

The inflation which has emerged today has its origins in problems of a weak agricultural base and a lack in agricultural and side-line products supply, problems of low efficiency among state-run businesses and an inability to absorb price reform factors, problems of marketization of the economy not being complete enough and of receiving all kinds of restrictions. However, the major reason lies with the fact that reform of the system has not been thorough. The development of our economy still lags behind and its structure is not balanced in a reasonable way. Therefore, the method by which to solve the root of the inflation problem lies in reform and in development. We must give priority to solving the problem of inflation, but, at the same time that we speed up reforms and encourage development, we must also find effective means to control inflation.

In speeding up economic development, the emphasis should be placed on increasing the effective supply. Seeking stability while developing, we should use the development of production power to increase the effective supply and, through this, curb inflation. In developing, we must pay attention to adjusting and improving the industrial structure, lay emphasis on quickening the development of capital and technology-intensive industries, and assist fundamental industries which are expected in great demand in the future domestic market and currently dependent on imports, such as machinery, electronics, automobiles and important primary material industires. This can have the effect of killing three birds with one stone in controlling prices. First, going through scale expansion and high-level development of these industries will greatly reduce the disparity in quality, grade and technology that exists with foreign countries in these areas. Substantial drops in production costs will also produce reductions in excessively high prices. At the same time it will offset the part of influence on overall price levels that caused by the rise in fundamental living costs after reform. Second, as the competitiveness of the quality and prices of domestic products increases, domestic demand will switch from imported to domestic products, alleviating pressure on balancing foreign exchange and reducing the influence of a depreciated exchange rate on prices. Third, as we reduce the level of reliance on imports, when there are rises in prices on the international market due to supply-demand factors, we can then reduce or even do away with imports, and thereby reduce or avoid the influence of foreign introduced inflation on domestic prices.

Some experts believe that in more than ten years of reform and opening-up, a trend of stable growth exists in the Chinese economy. The average annual economic growth rate is 9.3% making China one of the fastest developing nations in the world. The potential for high-speed economic growth in China is huge.

First, China's industrialization is being urged on gradually: enterprises not owned by the state are developing rapidly, the potential for development in service industries is great and agriculture is developing steadily.

Second, Chinese economic reforms have contributed positively to the stability of the economy and to the promotion of development.

Third, resources exist in China to support economic growth: labor is plentiful and the quality of labor is improving all the time; a certain level of investment and savings is being maintained; there is a great possibility for the influx of international capital and technology; the technology level and productivity rate are continually going up.

II. Raising the Quality of Investment is the Crux of Controlling Transitional-Type Inflation While Maintaining Relatively High-Speed Growth

(I) In the process of guaranteeing effective investment growth, we must speed up economic development and solve the root of the inflation problem

In a certain period from now on, a large degree of China's economic growth will be decided by investment growth. There are sources that indicate from 1981 to 1993 the coefficient of relationship between the rate of investment and the rate of economic growth is 0.63. Approximately 60% of China's economic growth relies on investment growth. High investment inevitably affects the speed of economic growth. While attaching importance to good economic results, China must also pay close attention to investment. The primary problem at present is the low investment results that have been brought about by the high investment, but low output of state-run businesses. Therefore, the key problem is not whether or not to invest, but, while guaranteeing investment growth, to speed up reforms which can solve the problem of investment results.

Due to a number of factors, a certain level of induced inflation can always be expected to accompany high investment growth. All of the instances of inflation in China have reflected this fairly common problem. However, the problem is not in investment itself; in some areas, although investment increased very quickly, no serious inflation resulted from it. For instance, in Hainan, fixed assets investment in 1990 was 23.4% greater than the previous year, in 1991 it grew 28.4% and in 1992 90.8%; however, the retail price index for these years only increased 0.6%, 3.1% and 8.7% respectively; this is by no means an excessively high rate of inflation. Looking at foreign countries, when the economies of Japan, South Korea, Singapore and Hong Kong were taking off, the annual investment growth rate was at about 30% and the retail price indexes for these areas was below 5%. This shows that investment growth itself does not necessarily bring about inflation; the crux is that the investment system and the corresponding financial and banking systems must meet the economic demands of the market. These systems must also provide a certain amount of guidance to the structure of the investment demands, the source of the investment and its scope. Therefore, in looking at the problem of how investment demand brings about inflation, we must first recognize clearly where the crux of the problem is; this will be beneficial to the high-speed growth of investment.

1. We must strictly control the scope and amount of direct national investment, encourage and support investment in all areas of society and create a competitive diversified-investment body.

(1) National investment should slowly withdraw from average competitive spheres and move to fundamental areas, key sectors and public utilities, especially increasing input for basic facilities, to bring about the best possible results for national assets in a market economy. Investment growth and economic development in China have both received bottleneck restrictions originating from basic facilities and industries. This is related to China's investment structure being focused on processing industries and other competitive areas. Therefore, in improving the investment structure and adjusting the direction of investment, we must bring about the greatest results in investment.

By increasing the production output of society's capital, we thoroughly remove the hidden danger of inflation. It is important to work hard to reduce the shortage of basic products that leads to rises in prices. Fundamental facilities and industries are basic conditions which guarantee society's supply; if their development comes to a halt, it will be hard to fully exploit society's productive capacity and can lead directly to low efficiency of society's output and intensify latent inflationary pressure. Particularly in the nineties, pillar industries such as machinery, electronics, automobiles, and petrochemicals must be greatly developed, and this requires the support of basic industries and facilities, otherwise the good results anticipated by the large amount of capital put into these pillar industries will be difficult to develop to their fullest. So, on top of predicting the needs for fundamental facilities and industries, we must also anticipate future deficiencies in the supply of certain links and products, strengthen investment in these areas and improve supply. The focal point should be placed on loosening up restrictions on railroads and other transport; increasing the supply of coal, oil, natural gas, electricity and other energy resources; bringing information equipment to a more modern level including developing different types of information resources and making them more accessible; and increasing important primary resources especially the shortage in the productive capacity of iron and steel products.

(2) At present the proportion of direct national investment is great, accounting for approximately 60-70% of society's overall investment. However, since reforms of the investment system are not yet in place, results have been bad. According to estimates, on the same investment of 100 yuan, state-owned enterprises are only able to produce a profit of 2.7 yuan while rural enterprises produce a 7.2 yuan profit. From January to June 1994, the gross output of state-owned industrial enterprises only grew 5.3% while industrial enterprises with collective ownership grew 27.8%. It is obvious that the results of direct national investment are far and away lower than those of private investment.

(3) In order to control direct national investment, we must thoroughly solve the problem of soft budgetary restrictions of the investment system. First, we must execute a strict financial budget, strictly prohibit the indiscriminate allocating of loans or capital and approving of projects and stop the financial administration from lending complete support to banks. Second, we must strictly control extra-budgetary investment. Third, we must control the issue of currency and control the expansion of lending activities by banks. Fourth, we need to establish a corporate investment system and a strict investment responsibility system.

2. We must guide society's consumption funds to shift towards investment.

At present, there are the three most crucial problems:

(1) Reform of the housing system must be speeded up with the focus on selling public housing, on the basis of cost value. In this way, a portion of consumer wealth can be attracted to this area and decrease the reliance of housing construction on bank loans and, instead, bring about a cycle of self-reliance for housing capital.

(2) Staffs should be encouraged to buy stock in their companies. If the staff is willing, using their stock as the basis for a proprietary company could be considered.

(3) The investment scope for all kinds of businesses should gradually be expanded, and we should guide society's investment capital towards important investment projects thereby lightening currency pressure. First, all segments of society are encouraged and supported to invest in the construction of basic facilities. For example, in Hainan's process of accelerated development of the shareholder system, using shares for the construction of basic facilities, guiding the use of society's investment capital and unified remuneration provisions were implemented for investment in the construction of basic facilities, achieving notable results. Hainan's aviation, highways, electric power and other large projects have all adopted the form of a shareholder system. Second, we want to gradually broaden the investment scope of foreign investment firms and private enterprises; except for special areas, there should be no artificial restrictions. Third, for construction of the average basic facilities, the proportion of each side's investment should not become an artificial restriction. Among Hainan's shareholding companies, personal shares account for approximately 15%; in aviation, direct national investment only accounts for 4-5%. Over-emphasizing national control of stocks is both detrimental to the strengthening of this area of investment and also increases the burden on the nation.

3. We must gradually enlarge investment in all areas of agriculture.

A serious deficiency in agricultural investment is the major reason for a weak agricultural foundation, a lack of farm products, and by-products and rises in prices. In recent years, although overall investment in China has risen quickly, however investment in agriculture has gone down each year. According to surveys, around 1985, investment in the agricultural sector accounted for approximately 6-7% of overall fixed-assets investment; by 1990 this had dropped to 4.5% and by 1993 to 3.5%. A major reason for insufficient investment in agriculture is that the payback for such investment is relatively low. Even to this day, the problem of the scissors difference in agriculture product prices has not been solved. Although the government has attempted raising prices to solve it, this has quickly been offset by the price disparity sending prices to their former levels. At the end of 1987 in Hainan, the ratio of farmer's to city employees' incomes was 1:1.5, and by 1993 this proportion had already tilted massively to 1:2.72. Therefore, it is imperative to use unified methods to solve the problem of agricultural investment.

To increase investment in agriculture and increase the payback of this investment, we must integrate rural economic reform, especially the reform of the rural land right system, with the reform of agricultural prices. Where conditions make it possible, we must put out all efforts to integrate development of land, capital and technology. Mutually integrated methods like that of the reform of the shareholder system in Hainan where farmers provided the land and the scientific research department provided the technology, thereby cutting the costs of stocks for enterprises to provide the capital. These enterprises, using an agricultural shareholder system yielded excellent results.

4. Adhere to grasping the investment and the results at the same time.

Growth with no real improvement is the root of vicious inflation. China's economic development is still in a stage revealing high growth and high inflation, so to achieve the objective of high growth with a reasonable level of inflation we must maintain one hand on investment, one hand on positive results. As the economy continues to grow and the scope of investment continues to widen, we must shift from extensive economic development to intensive economic development. This includes lowering construction costs, reducing time periods required for construction, raising the return rate of investment, strengthening business management, raising product technology capacity, exploiting potential, reducing waste and turning loss into gain. We must use every method possible to start up and broaden the market for industrial products and use appropriate guidance to increase consumption and turn around the current insipid situation of the industrial product market as quickly as possible.

(II) There is a considerable distance between China's current investment system and the demands of a market economy. This means that effective control of the scope of investment, reasonable adjustments of the investment structure and ameliorating the investment situation all involve a number of difficulties and influence the chances of raising payback on investment

Beginning in 1979 with the launching of reform of the entire economic system, in the area of investment management, surrounding administrative simplification and granting autonomy were the release of restrictions on rights in making investment policy, opening numerous channels for capital, implementing the use of investment with remuneration payment, implementing reforms for inviting and submitting bids and of the responsibility system. All achieved a certain degree of success, however, these reforms were only the initial steps and, on the whole, a number of fundamental problems with the investment system had not yet been solved. Compared with the requirements for the establishment of a socialist market economic system, to make the market system play a fundamental role in the allocation of resources under national macro-controls, the current investment system is still quite different from playing that role.

1. The freeing up of investment policy decision rights does not mesh with the establishment of the investment body's self-restraining mechanism.

Many localities, departments and businesses take responsibility for profit but not for loss, therefore they invest irresponsibly. They exceed their district's or unit's need for economic development, employment and high level of consumption. Regardless of the possibility of collecting enough capital they start and expand projects, pursue high-speed development, greatly increase investment in processing industries, put large amounts of money into constructing high-level buildings, blindly play the real estate market and set up development zones, all of this further intensifies inflation of the investment scale and exacerbates the unbalanced investment structure.

2. After the release of investment policy decision rights, financial power and administrative power became unbalanced.

National investment is primarily put into key construction projects, such as energy resources, transportation, raw materials; investment by localities and businesses is primarily put into processing industries. As the amount of government investment in the proportion of society's overall investment decreased, the percentage occupied by local and enterprise investment increased rapidly. Particularly as key projects in energy, transportation and raw materials taken on by the government were not able to fulfill the national economy's development needs, many instances of repeated and blind investment in low-level projects and projects with low return could be seen. This exacerbated the deficiency in energy resources and transportation facilities and caused the structure of regional investment in the same way to tend towards unreasonable circumstances.

3. There is a lack of an authoritative, comprehensive control body and of effective regulation measures to manage and control investment activity.

Overseeing of investment is multi-headed, disperse, disconnected, inconsistent and without standards. Relations between different investment management departments have not been smooth, thus causing investment policy decision to divorce from the investment guarantee measures implemented; the proportion of investment directly controlled by the national budget to the overall investment has continually gone down and effective control and guidance mechanism for extra-budgetary investment and investment by the rest of society has not yet been established; control of investment still primarilly relies on the use of the executive branch and profits are distributed to parts devided according to administrative relationship, thus causing power, responsibility and interests to be disconnected seriously. As a result, either macro-regulations of the overall scale of investment or adjustments of the investment structure lack effective methods and proper conditions.

4. The legal system is imperfect.

In investment policy making, neither the investment behavior of investment body nor the investment control procedures of the government are standardized; the relationships between all areas of the investment world are less than smooth; the responsibilities, rights and interests of investors are not clear. The damage which faulty investment policy resulted in still exists. Regulations in the area between planning and construction are not sound and administration and supervision are weak. Add on the protectionism of some localities and we can see that competition conditions for inviting and submitting bids have not really come into place. Phenomena of enjoying employment guaranteed by the nation and, therefore, of loss and waste are still quite common.

Due to reasons related to the investment system itself, inflation in the overall scale of investment has occurred in certain investment spheres, projects under construction and newly opened projects increased in a too large number, and the investment growth rate becomes excessively high. When the investment structure is imbalanced, certain bottlenecked sectors and construction projects which society and the economy are calling for existing cannot collect enough investment capitals. Payback on investment is low, there is too much waste and there is an improper allocation of resources. If we want to solve these problems at their root, we must begin with reform, and only in deepening reform can these problems be solved.

(III) Create a risk-restriction mechanism for the investment body to prevent loss of control over the scale of investment

1. The special characteristics of investment-scale inflation

and this instance (1993-94) of inflation.

Investment-scale inflation, also called investment starvation, has occurred on numerous instances in China's socialist construction, almost like unrelenting symptoms of a chronic illness. It is like a specter, continually casting its shadow on those beneath and rending them laden with grief.

Of the three instances of investment-scale inflation that occurred under the traditional system, all were primarily brought about by an impulse at the central policy-making level to broaden investment and enjoyed support from the increases of the basic construction expenditure in the central financial budget. In a sense, they are relatively easy to correct. If the policy-makers ever realize the problem, they will cut an enormous part of expenditure on fundamental construction from the central budget with one fell swoop, the construction projects will be reorganized and re-prioritized, and restrictions will be used to achieve the target of reducing the scale of planned investment bringing down the scale of society's annual investment. Since reform and opening up began, the pluralization of investment bodies and investment channels has made curbing investment inflation much more difficult. Old methods such as setting loan quotas and requiring government examination and approval of projects are no longer effective in reaching lower planned targets. There is one theory that believes the crux of controlling the scale of investment lies in controlling the source of funds. However, currently the only capital directly under the control by the central government is investment from the central financial budget and the investment loans and capital borrowed from abroad are allocated in the national credit plan. In recent years these three parts of fixed-assets investment have not even accounted for 1/8 of society's overall fixed-assets investment. Therefore, even if the source of this capital was put under control, this would only really control 1/8 of the whole amount, and the control of the majority of funds would still remain weak and ineffectual.

In modern, developed nations with market economies, the government has no special organization to set and manage the scale of society's investment, nor does it have any fixed dates to reorganize projects under construction. Although there are times when investment is flourishing and times when it is stagnant, however, the big rises and falls associated with the period of free capitalism are no longer seen. Outside of the government using its financial and legal power to strengthen macro-controls, this is related, to a large extent, with the further improvement of the risk-restriction mechanism of enterprises and other economic bodies. This is especially true of the bank risk-restriction mechanism, which has been strengthened greatly through leage system building since the economic catastrophe of the 1930's. In these nations, when banks and enterprises invest, they pay close attention to whether or not they have adequate strength and show great concern for the level of payback. We should use this for reference.

In China, for a variety of reasons, there are a fairly large number of investors who frequently do not make an accurate assessment of their own resources when they are investing: they do not seriously consider the actual amount of capital they are capable of paying out (including follow-up capital) and of whether or not this capital is sufficient to support the smooth completion of the project; they do not seriously consider how great the profit margin will be after the project is completed and whether their project will appreciate even more. This is the root of why China's long-term investment inflation has yet to be solved. If this problem is to be fundamentally solved, appropriate measures must be applied.

Some experts believe that the outstanding characteristic of the economic fluctuations of 1993-94 is that just as the economy entered a period of high inflation, there was also a massive expansion in fixed-assets investment. Therefore, the inflation of 1993-94 was first and foremost connected with rapid price rises in investment articles and primary materials which are closely tied to fixed-assets investment. Only after a lag of three to six months did consumer prices enter the process of inflation.

In 1992, fixed-assets investment grew 42.6% over the previous year; this was the fastest speed of expansion in more than ten years. Compared with the two instances of inflation of the 1980's

(1985 and 1988), the investment growth rate was 3.8 and 19.1 percentage points higher respectively. The excessive growth in investment continued straight until 1993 when fixed-assets investment grew 50.6% over 1992. The total amount of fixed-assets investment for those two years was 109.2 billion yuan more than the total amount of the four years from 1988 to 1991.

Excessive investment caused investment results to worsen: dates set for construction projects were delayed and production costs for projects greatly surpassed the budgeted amount. Taking the construction of residences as an example, investment in residences grew 21.1% in 1992; however the actual area taken up by completed projects fell 9.6%. In 1993, even though investment in residences, like all other areas of investment, rose greatly, the area of completed projects still fell 1.6%.

The direct result of excessive investment was to release the trigger of latent inflationary pressure all at once. Moreover, the release initially appeared as rises in the prices of project-needed and production-needed goods and raw materials. Beginning in the summer of 1992, prices of production means (including raw materials and other project- and production-needed goods except equipment) continually rose. In April 1992 the buyer price index for production means was 4.9%, by September this figure had surpassed 10%, after March 1993, it surpassed 20% and from July to September it surpassed 30%. In little more than half a year's time, the prices for steel construction materials and some other important construction materials increased more than double.

When excessive investment appears during a period of high economic rise, this will lead to the overheating of the economy and cause norminal salaries to increase, thus leading to increased consumer spending. After the fourth quarter of 1992, the growth rate on the amount of retail sales of goods rose monthly. After this, inflation also appeared in the area of consumer prices; the retail price index rose from 5.7% in September 1992 to 6.8% in December and by March 1993 had reached 10.2%. This was the first time since the fourth quarter of 1989 that retail prices reached an inflation rate in two digits. The inflation rate has already increased while the controlled savings interest rate has not seen a timely increase so that in actual terms the interest rate has quickly become negative. During the second quarter of 1993, bank savings experienced zero growth and even showed a decrease in the overall amount, the amount of retail items on the market grew significantly and retail prices grew intensely. The retail price index was growing approximately one percentage point every month; in August it reached 15.1% and in the first quarter of 1994 it reached 20% more or less.

2. The risk-restriction mechanism for investment must be established quickly to ensure effective investment.

Investors must develop a sense of risk towards their own investment behavior. To this end, a property risk mechanism and an occupation risk mechanism for investment policy decision must be established as quickly as possible so that conscientious attention will be paid to hedging investment and to investment appreciation, and so that risk and the rate of return on investment will be taken into account. This is also a restriction preventing investors from exceeding their actual capacity to invest and from blindly investing.

Enterprises need to implement an occupational risk mechanism widely at the managerial level so that general managers will look after their company assets as if they were their own. This is to say that the salaries at the managerial level and the appreciation circumstances of the company assets (including appreciation brought about by investment) need to be joined together, the fate, status and honor of management must be linked with the life and death, success or failure of the company. This will act as an incentive for everyone to stay together through thick or thin, creating a situation where honor or humiliation is everyone's to share. The investment activity of companies should be the same as other operational policies: the ability or inability to bring about appreciation of assets should directly affect the careers and lives of the management.

Investment activity should be determined by the investment body itself; this includes the amount of investment, the choice of industries and the level of technology, etc. It is also up to the representatives of the legal body to take up responsibility for repayment of corresponding loans and debts and for appreciation of the investment. Naturally, in the course of making policy decisions, in order to make investment decision more scientific and to increase the reliability of investment returns, it is necessary to provide feasible research reports on construction projects and to carry out scientific proofs and appraisals. At the same time we need to seek the advice and predictions of related experts, although the final decision still rests with the investment body itself, thus bringing together rights, responsibilities and interests and putting more time limitations on investment decisions and increasing the sense of risk for the investment body.

In order to expedite technological progress and strengthen product development, the method of investment adopted is fundamental construction or technology improvement, renewal of equipment; it is up to the investment bodies to compare investment and output, cost and return and then, on the premise of striving to obtain the greatest appreciation of its assets, to make their own investment decisions.

For investment projects, when state-owned asset management corporations (including investment companies) are investing or when banks are giving out loans or promising certain amounts of capital, we should learn from the way the World Bank does things; we must investigate the credibility of investment bodies and evaluate the profitability of projects as well as the possibility of risk that comes with each investment. Only under the preconditions of having a fairly full grasp of the situation, guaranteeing appreciation of the investment and that interest on loans will be paid back according to schedule will capital be provided. When the risk is too great, providing capital should be rejected in order to guarantee the safety and liquidity of capital.

The government should use tax collection policy, depreciation policy, financial subsidies, interest rates, financial measures and the activity of the market to regulate the profit margins of certain industries and certain products and arrive at its own industry policy. The government should supply capital funds to the basic industry, pillar industry and bottlenecked industry, which need to be developed faster, through state-owned assets management companies and foster and support them through the development banks and long-term credit banks. This will also serve to attract capital from society. After the establishment of these projects, a manager must be located and it will be up to the manager to take responsibility for the protection and appreciation of the investment and for the repayment of loans. Correspondingly, employment-risk mechanisms must be set up.

(IV) The focal point of investment reform in China should be on profit restrictions

In the past, under the planned management system, the planned aspect in fixed-asset investment has always been stronger than in other areas in the relationship between planning and market forces, and the level of centralization of power has always been higher in the relationship between centralized and divided powers. Both of these set the stage for the characteristics of planned management to appear. In China's past, strict management targets were set for fixed-asset investment. The planning department took on the huge, difficult task of balancing the overall amount of fixed-asset investment for the whole society, achieving the most ideal investment structure and providing a reasonable distribution over all areas. Strict approval procedures must be implemented for investment projects. However, regardless of whether we are talking about controlling the overall amount of investment or improving the investment structure, the result always runs counter to our hopes. Almost every year, investment demand is greater than supply, and investment starvation has become the incurable illness of China's present economy. To shrink fixed-asset investment has become the cry most frequently heard and the magic weapon most frequently used by government to fix its economy. Forming a stark comparison to the large increase in overall investment is the insufficient investment in some basic industries and basic facilities that restricts the development of the whole economy. As far as managing fixed-asset investment, the following cycle tends to appear: free things up and chaos results, when there is chaos, investment pulls back; when investment pulls back, the economy dies; when the economy dies, restrictions are freed up, and so on. To the present day, nothing has been found to thoroughly solve this problem.

We have gotten rid of planned management for a large number of commodities and adopted market regulation; the result is that in differing degrees, for these products, demand is no longer greater than supply, but in many instances supply is greater than demand. It is apparent that the fundamental reason for the growth in demand does not have to do with the developed level of productivity, but with the management system. Under the planned management system of the past, investment planning and investment capital were entirely up to the government to set and arrange. The prices of products supplied to invested projects did not fundamentally reflect the relationship between market supply and demand, the risk of investment was entirely taken up by the government, and enterprises were the investment body in the name only: they did not have any real power over investment policy decisions, nor did they take the corresponding risk involved with investing. This necessarily leads every area, department and unit to compete for investment projects solely contemplating their own interests without receiving any restrictions arising from investment costs.

In a market economy, an enterprise is, by all means, an independent interest body, market prices are primarily set by the relationship between supply and demand, and the allocation of economic resources is determined by the market. If investment demand is greater than supply, the prices of investment products will rise, lowering businesses' estimated future profits and increasing the risk of investing. This forced businesses to adopt strategic policies of withdrawing, leading to a drop in society's investment demands and also inducing society's resources to flow towards industries and businesses with high estimated profits, ensuring that the best would get better and the inferior be filtered out. Due to a market risk whose dimensions are unclear and people with an inclination to save their currency, under market conditions, it is difficult for investment demand to grow, with it tending to show a slight deficiency.

Reform of the investment management system is an organic

component of the reforms of economic system and is intimately bound up with reform of the economic system. The success or failure of the reform of the investment management system is linked to the success or failure of the reforms of the entire economic system and, in the process of reforming the economic system, the investment management system reform is influenced by reforms of other aspects of the economy. Therefore, the content it encompasses is quite varied and goes in all directions. As far as the influence of the reform of the investment management system is concerned, the reform in the following several aspects, in particular, should be speeded up:

1. Speed up shifts in government functions.

In direct investment activity within the micro-economic realm, the government should gradually reduce its role or even basically backed out of the activities. The government activities of direct investment in the micro-economy and participation in market competition for profit exist and corrupt practices abound. The most notable effects are: (1) It is unfavorable for the establishment and perfection of a fair market competition mechanism. In playing the role of the overseer of society's activities, the government also becomes the architect and guardian of market order. If the government itself is investing largely in businesses and participating in market competition, then it is quite difficult to guarantee behavior of an objective and impartial nature, difficult to guarantee that all types of businesses are in a position of equal competition, and, therefore difficult to guarantee the impartiality of the market; (2) When the government invests directly, since there is no concrete-, direct-interest party, it is impossible to form any risk-restriction mechanism and easily results in a situation where attributing responsibility becomes difficult, investment returns are low, capital is seriously wasted and demand for investment grows. The social ownership and state ownership of theory, when they are actually in operation, lack any real responsible party. Their rights can only be exercised as representing a government official at some level. There is frequently a lack of effective economic measures over their activity, which is restricted basically by non-economic factors. Therefore, the behavior of decision makers is often not formulated over considerations of profit and loss, but is made according to a large number of non-economic factors. It is not uncommon to see companies use a large amount of government money on "scholarly exchange expenses" without blinking an eye. There are even instances of people seeking personal gain at the public's expense and of embezzling; (3) Excessive direct government investment in enterprises also easily brings about an unbalanced composition of the sources of the government's income and expenses, harmful to the balanced development of the whole society's economy. A government's income should be based on the society's overall economic development but not on the government's direct profits. If the proportion of the government's income taken up by investment in profit oriented businesses is too great, then this easily leads to the government's expenditures tending to favor gain oriented businesses and industries and to ignore science, education and cultural areas and fundamental industries and facilities, which are important to the nation's development in the long-term but which do not show outstanding profits in the short-term; (4) When the government over-invests in industry, its efforts become split, its agencies cumbersome and overstuffed and, in general, overworked. Items that should be looked after are ignored, it gets over-involved in unrelated areas, and ideal results are naturally difficult to achieve.

Of course, looking at things from the present, the likelihood of the government at all levels completely backing out of its direct investment activities in the micro-economic realm is not too high, however, investment activity should be reduced step by step, and, finally, the government should fundamentally withdraw. Excluding important projects related to the interests of the people and large projects which it is difficult to rely entirely on society to complete, the government should use its energies primarily on the establishment and protection of a market system, and its expenditures should primarily be used for important, non-profit enterprises or the long-term development of the economy, and for the perfection of the investment environment.

2. Clear-cut property right boundaries allow enterprises to

become real, independent investment bodies.

Chinese enterprises in the past, particularly state-owned businesses, although, participated as investment bodies in market investment activity, but, since their connection to property rights was unclear, their position as investment bodies was only nominal, with no reality behind it. The question of property rights for enterprises has been a difficult one since reform began. Compared with other aspects of reform, it is most closely connected with reform of the investment management system. When property rights are not clear, it is very difficult for the investment behavior of businesses to meet the market's requirement of taking a corresponding risk. They also lack the economic incentive to strive for appreciation of their investments. Enterprise investment activity must evolve into government investment activity. Regarding reform of property rights, in the past we primarily favored the division of proprietary and operation rights and expected the division of rights to solve the problem of business operational autonomy. In reality, the idea of separation of rights has its definite limits: operating rights must be founded on ownership. If ownership is not the basis for operating rights then the operating rights are necessarily limited. Therefore, reform of state-owned enterprises should shift from divided powers to linked powers. In a word, as long as the problem of property rights is left unsolved, it is also difficult to truly implement operational autonomy for enterprises. Enterprises are still state-owned enterprises, and it is still up to the government to invest; however, the trend towards short-term activities of enterprises is also quite difficult to curb, and it is even more unlikely to establish an investment management system which adapts to the needs of a socialist market economy. It is also unlikely that the function of the market mechanism will be exploited to its utmost potential in the realm of investment.

3. We should speed up the reform of the banking system as quickly as possible, turning them into autonomous, independent units and making them economic bodies responsible for their own profits and losses.

At present, a significant portion of China's investment capital comes from bank loans. But, when the system is so constructed that banks can rely on unrestricted support from the government, a large amount of the risk involved in investing, while passing through the banks, finally ends up on the back of the government. The risk which these nominal investors take is exceedingly small, and many people take the money borrowed from banks as though it would be a pity if they did not. The banks offering up the loan capital are also taking practically no risk at all. As affiliates of the government, banks have not become real independent, autonomous groups who are responsible for their own gains and losses. The bank loans granted through governmental interference continue to account for a large proportion of the total loans.

As far as perfecting the market mechanism, this is incredibly harmful to the strengthening of a investment-risk consciousness. The same is true for investors: if banks—one of the major sources of investment capital—are not subject to strict investment-risk restrictions, then the idea of developing the market's function as an investment regulator and controlling China's traditional investment starvation is nothing more than empty chatter.

(V) Measures to control the overall amount of investment must be appropriate and moderate

The crux of the problem at present lies in speeding up reform in order to solve the problems of investment structure and investment effectiveness at the same time while maintaining investment growth. If the level of restrictions on the amount of investment is too great, this will influence the economy's development. If there is no development, the problem of inflation is even harder to solve. Now, when means of production have come close to production cost-level prices, investment restrictions should be appropriately relaxed and investment increase should be carried out selectively. Otherwise, the negative results arising from the deficiency of a necessary amount of investment will influence the situation of the entire macro-economy.

Fixed assets investment is the starting point for economic growth; if an appropriate scale of investment has not been reached, the economy cannot possibly develop. At present, the economic recovery of a number of European countries has lacked real strength; the reason lies in weak investment demand. As discussed above, China has a flourishing investment demand which is the strongest moving force in her economic development. This in itself is a good thing; however, our problem frequently arises from investment being too vigorous and the scale of investment too great. In 1992, China's overall fixed-asset investment totaled 785.4 billion yuan, an increase of slightly more than 19% over the previous year. In 1993, fixed-asset investment already had broken the level of one trillion yuan, estimates place the increase between 45-55%. This contained a factor in price inflation, but, even if we exclude the price inflation factor, the increase in scale is still excessive. The growth in the amount of investment from 1991 to 1992 was 19%. This was due to putting through relatively weak control measures over the scale of investment during the preceding two years. This had recovery value for the economy, and it also set the stage for a large increase in the scale of investment for 1992.

While pushing forward relaxed economic policies under a precondition of strictly controlling currency issue, a feasible choice is: speed up the shift from saving to investing and adjust the expenditure structure of the government, enterprises and families so that a portion of consumption funds become investment funds. Presently, the value of the money that the people have deposited in all types of financial organizations and the cash that they have in their own hands is nearly equal to the GDP; however, the scope of their investment is quite narrow. They fundamentally strive for luxury consumer items or turn a large amount of their money into non-productive capital, such as stocks, making the demands of the capital speculation market too vigorous. Businesses, especially investment companies and government financial organizations, also put the vast majority of their investment capital into real estate and every type of stock market.

Why the growth rate of fixed-asset investment is difficult to control now? It has so happened because we have not yet arrived at the common understanding: to change China's underdeveloped conditions, develop the nation's economy, raise people's standard of living and achieve commonwealth, China must maintain rapid-speed economic growth, but this speed must be reasonable; it cannot exceed the actual bearing capacity of the economy, nor can it ignore the major restrictive conditions which have been set up. China's surplus labor force is incredibly large and the problem of employment is a major one. To increase employment, China must have a relatively high speed of economic growth. However, the relationship between inflation and unemployment is not necessarily the one in which one rises the other falls. China has experienced relatively rapid economic growth in the last two years and has also had a relatively high level of inflation; however, the circumstances of unemployment and semi-unemployment among state-owned enterprises have not improved remarkably. This shows that it is not a lack of investment that brings about unemployment, but a number of other reasons. On the other hand, there is an obvious connection between the over-heated economy brought about by excessive fixed-asset investment and inflation.

III. Reasonably Fast Economic Growth and Relatively Low Inflation Can Be Mutually Achieved

(I) Within the operations of a modern market economy, high economic growth and high inflation have no internal connection

First, the numerical boundaries of the high economic growth rate and of the high inflation rate must be made clear. In current academic circles there is not an accepted opinion, and, therefore, theory offers no clear-cut standard. Looking at the traces of the last fifty years of domestic and international economic development, if we perform a vertical and horizontal comparison of China's economic growth with the economic situation of the rest of the world and summarize an analysis of statistics of the speed of China's economic growth rate, then 1-3% constitutes a low growth rate, 4-6% constitutes a mid-range growth rate, 7-10% constitutes a high-growth rate and 11% or above, an excessively high growth rate. This kind of numerical delimitation fits China's real circumstances and is also relatively appropriate.

Academic circles also have different opinions on the question of delimiting what qualifies as a high amount of inflation. Some experts believe that according to China's circumstances, the following numbers can be used to delimit it: 6% should be the critical threshold value between low and mid-level inflation; 10% should be the critical threshold value between mid-level and high inflation; and 20% the critical threshold value between high and excessive (vicious) inflation.

If we analyze the state of the national economic activity for the ten-odd years of reform and opening up according to the viewpoint stated above, looking at the overall picture, the years between 1979 and 1984 was a stage of rapid growth and low inflation; the years between 1985 and 1987 was a stage of rapid growth and mid-level inflation; and the over-heated economy and excessively high growth rate of 1988 sent the mid-level inflation shooting into the high inflationary stage; the excessively high growth rate from the second half of 1992 to 1993 allowed inflationary pressure to intensify and quicken a large-scale increase in prices at the end of 1993 so that by Spring 1994 the rate of price increase had broken through the grim figure of 20%. Of course, the excessively high inflation was controlled right after it started up, but the level of price increase remained high and any impetus to fall looked relatively weak. This economic phenomenon brought about a certain kind of viewpoint which is considered as the objective rule of the operations of a modern market economy: the viewpoint holds that an unavoidable internal relationship exists between high economic growth and high inflation. Experts believe that high inflation is not the inevitable development trend of modern market economies in the contemporary world, and even less is it the objective rule of the development of the socialist market economy of contemporary China.

Looking at the historic tracks left by nations' and regions' economies which have experienced rapid economic growth since the end of World War II, high growth accompanied by high inflation has not been the economic situation formulated in those nations and regions. Even if this type of economic situation did appear in certain nations, it was only a temporary and relative phenomenon, and it is very difficult to prove that an internal and inevitable relationship exists between high growth and high inflation. On the contrary, avoiding high inflation and maintaining a relatively low rate of inflation during periods of rapid economic growth is entirely possible.

As everybody knows, the economic development of post-World War II Japan, previous to the 1973 oil crisis, was high-speed, even excessive, allowing the actual average annual economic growth rate to reach 11.2% during the 1960s while the average annual price increase rate was only 5.8%. During a period of rapid growth, Japan maintained an economic growth rate of approximately 10%. During this time the highest rise in the wholesale price rate was 1-2% and in consumer prices only 3-5%. This was the experience of Japan during a period of high-speed economic growth. By the 1970s, the average annual growth rate in Japan had dropped to 6% and the rate of price increase had risen to 9.4%. That is a situation of high growth and low inflation during the 1960s shifted to a situation of mid-level growth and mid-level inflation during the 1970s. Therefore, China has a number of papers written by scholars who quote the example of Japan during the 1960s and 1970s to prove assertions that high inflation necessarily follows high economic growth does not accord with reality.

The historic tracks left by the economic growth and inflation of China's economy in the ten-odd years since the reform and opening up also makes clear that no internal, inevitable relationship exists between high economic growth and high inflation (see table below).

Economic Growth and Inflationary Trends in China, 1979-1993 (%)

Year	Growth rate	Inflation rate	Year	Growth rate	Inflation rate
1979	7.4	2.0	1987	10.6	7.3
1980	7.9	6.0	1988	10.8	18.5
1981	4.6	2.4	1989	3.6	17.8
1982	8.8	4.9	1990	5	2.1
1983	10.2	7.5	1991	7	3.4
1984	14.5	2.8	1992	12.8	6
1985	13.0	8.8	1993	13.4	14.7
1986	8.3	6.0			

Data source: figures from related years in Chinese Statistical Almanac.

We can see several point from the table:

First, in the 15 years of reform and opening up from 1979 to 1993, there are seven years where the national economy experienced a high growth rate from 7% to 10.6%. The inflationary rate for six years is at a low level between 1.5% and 6%; one year has a mid-level rate of 7.3%, still a relatively low level of inflation. Therefore, we can assert that for the seven years of high growth and low inflation, high growth did not bring about high inflation.

Second, in China's economy since 1979, not only has the scale of fluctuations of economic growth been large, but the scale of fluctuations of the level of inflation has also been quite large. The lowest level of the former was 3.6%, and the highest level, 14.5%, a disparity of nearly 11 percentage points; the lowest level for the latter was 2%, the highest, 18.5%, a disparity of 16.5 percentage points. Although this is the case, for 15 years, the average annual economic growth rate was 9.3% while the average annual rate of inflation was only 6.4%. Therefore, looking at things from the perspective of these two annual averages, the economic state of affairs for these 15 years was one of high growth and low inflation.

Third, of the years from 1979 to 1993, 1984, 1985, 1988, 1992 and 1993 all had excessively high growth rates of 10.8% or higher, and yet high inflation only happened in 1988, 1989 and 1993. This shows that the possibility for high or even vicious inflation definitely exists in excessively high growth: if other conditions are present, then the majority of years with excessively high economic growth will cause this possibility to become reality. However, looking at China's situation during those three years, it can be said that the massive changes which appeared in the growth and inflation rates were special economic phenomena which occurred under unique historic conditions and also a kind of historic complication produced by a Chinese market in the process of reform and marketization, and definitely were not an inevitable trend reflecting the development of a socialist market economy.

(II) Four types of interactions between economic growth and inflation in nations across the world

The mutual relationship between economic growth and inflation in nations across the world from the 1950s to the 1980s can be used to delimit the world's modern market economies in the process of their development: during different periods and varying from country to country, there were four types of economic development targets and inflation targets, and together they form four types of economic models.

1. The high growth, low inflation, high effectiveness (high-low-high) economic model. As mentioned previously, Japan of the 1960s is the representative case for this model. This economic situation spurred Japan's economy to take-off rapidly, and, within a relatively short period of time, to become one of the world's economic powers.

2. The high growth, high inflation, low effectiveness (high-high-low) economic model. South Korea's economy from the mid-1960s to the mid-1970s went through a stage of high growth accompanied by high inflation. Especially newly emerging capitalist nations during the 1960s and 1970s, such as Latin American and certain Asian nations, which threw off economic backwardness in a short period of time and developed their economies very

rapidly, but commonly faced serious inflation which greatly restricted a rise in their economic effectiveness.

3. The low growth, high inflation, low effectiveness (low-high-low) economic model. Yugoslavia, Hungary and Poland are states representative of this situation. From 1980 to 1987, the average annual rate of economic growth for these three nations was 0.9%, 1.2% and 0.5% respectively while the rates of inflation peaked to 64%, 8% and 20%; this grave stagnant inflation phenomenon attracted the attention of the whole world.

4. The low growth, low inflation, high effectiveness (low-low-high) economic model. Since the 1980s, the economies of major developed capitalist nations no longer unilaterally seek high growth of the overall economy. Due to this, there has been an obvious trend for a drop in the economic growth rates of these nations; economic development has shifted from growth in the overall quantity to growth seeking quality results. Although they are in a stage of slow economic growth, the economy's effectiveness is high, causing developed capitalist economies to follow the path of the low-low-high market economy; this is a new characteristic quality of the development of modern capitalist market economies.

(III) At the same time that great efforts are put into controlling inflation, the relationship between controlling inflation and developing an economy must be handled properly

Inflation and economic growth are inseparable mates; any country in a period of high-speed economic growth will experience inflation, the only differences will be of degree; economists are in agreement on this part no matter what country they are from. But every nation has a certain level of tolerance for inflation, and China is no exception. In recent two years, the annual growth rate of China's GNP has been at 10% or above; this is a very impressive achievement, a figure which England, America and Japan simply cannot obtained. At the same time, inflation levels stayed high. Though people's ability to withstand inflation is higher than it was previously, however, sustained periods of high inflation is still difficult to stand. The side-effects of inflation are also very large: not only can it influence a nation's economic development, but it can also affect its political and social stability, and this cannot be looked upon lightly. Therefore, resolute efforts must be made to control inflation.

Without a doubt, adopting measures to control inflation will necessarily affect the speed of economic development, this is simply a question of degree, and it demands our full understanding. Generally, there are two ways of thinking about how to curb inflation: one is to bring about a rapid drop in its scale within a short period of time; the second is to bring it down slowly over a correspondingly, relatively long period of time. These two ways of thinking, or the two methods they employ, necessarily bring about two different results. For China, it is the latter method which should be adopted, the first slam on the brakes philosophy has too great an effect on economic development and is quite likely to result in post-depression symptoms. The results of applying this method in 1988 prove this only too well.

In the process of shifting from a traditional planned economy to a modern market economy, if China wishes to maintain high growth and low inflation, it must conscientiously address and solve the following set of fundamental problems.

First, the scale and speed of economic development cannot exceed the nation's financial, material and human resource levels, and it must coordinate with the capacity of China's resource environment system. This is one of the important characteristics and fundamental principles of modern economic development.

Second, the rate of inflation cannot exceed the rate of wage increase, otherwise the actual standard of living of the people will go down, influencing society's stability.

Third, the rate of inflation cannot exceed the savings interest rate, otherwise, people's savings will be pushed down, bringing about chaos in the economic livelihood.

Fourth, the rate of inflation cannot exceed the rate of economic growth, otherwise, the economy will break loose from a track of normal economic behavior, affecting the stable development of the economy and of society.

(IV) There has been a fundamental shift in strategy for spurring on the economy: choose a moderate level of economic growth

Now, more and more people are recognizing that the raising of the efficiency and positive results of economic activity is the foundation for maintaining a stable national economy and bringing about rapid, sustained and balanced development. In the past decade or more, rapid or excessively fast economic development was not established on a firm foundation of increasing efficiency and positive results, instead relied upon massive investment and massive consumption to sustain it, and it, in the end, forced the nation to print excessive amounts of currency to maintain this inefficient, low-result, rapid or excessively fast development. This substantiated both theory and practice that resolutely pushing forward a shift in the model of economic development, adhering to changing the traditional economic development model which primarily relies on increasing investment and consumption as its primary method for achieving development, and seeking low investment, and low consumption as a way for development are necessary to lay the foundation for the high productivity, efficient, high-low-high economic model.

In the macro-economy, a definite coordinated relationship exists between speed, price and employment. An overheated economy forms a high-speed, high-price and high-employment situation. When price increase exceed the ability of the people to sustain it, this problem should be dealt with. However, adopting a method of forcing down the speed to force down prices will force the macro-economy to enter a low-speed, low-price and low-employment situation. High inflation is the same as high unemployment, they both bring down the people's living standard. Therefore, they must be guarded against and controlled. We should pay attention to the fact that, in the present state of economic growth, the repercussions caused by insufficient employment and a sluggish market are no weaker than those caused by inflation. All of the most recent few instances of macro-adjustments caused a negative result of excessive unemployment at a certain level. The current social guarantee system, especially the unemployment compensation system, is not perfect, the salaries of workers and employees are still at a relatively low level, and its ability to support the population is weak, so when there is excessive unemployment, it is difficult for the masses to bear it, both mentally and economically. Therefore, in the present stage, we must control the speed of development at a moderate level. If we do not instantly find the best scheme for both zero inflation and zero unemployment, then we can seek a second-best plan which maintains a certain speed, a certain level of price increases and a certain level of employment, with controls of the rates of price increase and employment at levels that the masses are able to absorb. That is between an endurable rate of inflation and an endurable unemployment rate to locate a point of balance.

Some experts advocate that China's macro-control policy objectives should organically integrate anti-inflationary measures with measures to maintain a moderate level of economic growth, moreover to put designs for anti-inflationary measures within the overall framework of speeding up the establishment of a socialist market economy, and implement macro-economic management policies for restricting inflation while allowing rapid economic growth. This, probably, is the necessary conclusion made from China's present situation.

As everybody knows, China is a developing nation, and like all developing nations it faces problems of insufficient capital and an undeveloped micro-economic body with relatively low efficiency of operation. Under these conditions, there is an objective need to make rapid economic development and increased employment a prioritized regulatory objective of macro-economic policy in order to reduce the disparity that exists with developed nations. Just allow for the effective supply of abundant resources, then the full use of an as-yet untested production capacity and a quest for rapid economic development will be options for maximum improvement. And naturally, the lower the level of inflation, the better; no country wishes to see its economic accomplishments offset by inflation. However, looking at the economic development wake of the world's emerging industrialized nations, a low inflationary rate and a high rate of economic growth have become mutually exclusive goals, and it is very difficult to achieve both. In the cycle of economic fluctuations, economic growth is always followed by inflation; if inflation did not follow, then the positive period of economic growth might just be even longer, and the possibility for an effective, no-filler-routh rate might be even higher.

Chapter 3
Check Inflation Effectively and Deepen the Reform

I. Reform the Prices of Farm Products and Check Inflation

(I) Fluctuations in the supply and demand of farm and sideline products and pricing reform have a clear influence on inflation. The most salient feature of inflation in recent years is the fairly high rate of price increases in farm and sideline products

Before the reform, China had for a long time suffered from a short supply of food grains; there was no alternative to state monopolies for the purchasing and marketing of grains. The institution of the family contracted system of responsibility with remuneration linked to output aroused the enthusiasm of the peasants in production and grain output increased as a result. By 1984, the total output reached 814.6 billion catties (407.3 million tons), equivalent to an average of nearly 800 catties per head. It could basically meet the demand and provided the material premise for changing the system of state monopoly for purchasing and marketing. Beginning in 1985, the system of state monopoly for the purchasing and marketing of food grains was canceled and replaced by a system in which goods were purchased on contract and later by the system of selling and purchasing gains all through the market. As a result, economic growth in rural areas made a big stride towards the socialist market economic system.

In 1992, some regions relaxed their efforts to grasp the farm and grain production and turned their attention to the construction of development zones and real estate. It led to a big cut in useable farmland; also, large tracts of farmland were left uncultivated. Due to the compulsory apportionments made to the peasants, the use of signed paper slips instead of money for purchasing farm and sideline products and the price rise of the agricultural means of production, the peasants received almost no benefit from their grain crops cultivation. All this dealt a severe blow to the peasants' enthusiasm for growing food crops, and further increases in food grains production was limited. Moreover, chaos emerged in the circulation of food grains: in a rush, some economically developed but grain-efficient provinces sent people to the hinterlands to purchase food grains. As a result, the price of food grains began to soar in the autumn of 1993. The central government took measures to check the price rise of grain and strengthened macro-control over economic development at the end of 1993 and the beginning of 1994. The chief move was not to decrease demand, but to increase supply. The chief measure to increase supply was to sell grains from the state reserves. All state-owned shops were instructed to sell grains at the marked prices. The prices were reasonable and acceptable to urban inhabitants. This helped to increase their sense of stability, and the heat of rush-purchases cooled down. Market prices went down somewhat. However, the effect was not notable and the price rise was not totally stopped.

As the central government strengthened its macro-control over economic development and strictly controlled investment, the withdrawal of money from circulation was satisfactory, and the supply of some capital goods was greater than the demand. The price situation in the first half of 1994 was optimistic. However, beginning in July, the price of grains soared again. In some places, the price of the rice rose from 1.6 yuan per kilogram to 3.2 yuan per kilogram, an increase of 100%. It pushed up the prices of other commodities as well.

The source of inflation in China in recent years has been food grains. Therefore, to check inflation, China must first solve the problems in the production and marketing of grains and increase its grain reserves.

So far as the grain production is concerned, our country is

still deficient; the grain problem has not yet been solved. Feeding China's 1.2 billion people has always been of the utmost importance. As production and the consumption patterns of people have changed, the demand for food grains has become greater and greater. The population increases by 15 million annually while the cultivated land decreases by 15 million *mu* (1 million hectares) every year. The production and supply of food grains in China is potentially a grave situation: production is underdeveloped, supply is insufficient and the material foundation for stabilizing the prices is very weak.

So far as the market is concerned, the purchasing and marketing system in China is in a state of transition. The old system of state monopoly has been abolished, but the new market economic system has not yet been established. Under the system of state monopoly for the purchase and marketing of food grains, food grains were supplied to urban inhabitants according to fixed rations, and the channel for purchasing and marketing was single and simple; that is, except for the state departments, no organizations or individuals were permitted to poke their noses into the purchasing and marketing of grains. This maintained the stability of grain prices. This system has been abolished, yet the grain problem was not completely solved. In the transition to the new system, the material foundation for keeping the grain prices stable is still very weak. Under these circumstances, if the government relaxes its macro-control slightly, speculation on grains is likely to occur and lead to chaos in the circulation of grains, thus helping to push up grain prices. When grain prices soar, people cannot decide to forgo or delay buying them in order to boycott them. If the price of the color TV sets soars, people can do without them or delay buying them, and the elasticity of consumption can pull back the prices. It won't do absolutely with the grains. If you don't consume them, it means death. If you delay consuming grains, it means gradual starvation. The soaring of grain prices in recent years has been mainly caused by speculation.

So far as China's grain reserves are concerned, they are the material guarantee for the economic stability and political stability of the country. With grain reserves, the country will be stable, and without them, the country will be in chaos. Moreover, they are the reservoir for regulating the circulation of grains. In the past, when grains were plentiful, we put more into the reserves. When grains were in short supply, grains from the reserves were sold to people. When grain prices soared, we did not use an administrative means too much, but mainly sold grains from the state reserves. The reason why we could do it in this way was because we had grain to spare. If we did not have grains to sell, we would have had to use administrative means to check the rise of the grain prices.

In short, there are three essential links to keep the prices of the grains relatively stable: production, marketing and reserves. We must grasp the links firmly.

The rise in farm product prices has a clear influence on inflation. The rise in foodstuff prices accounted for 60% of the retail price rise in the first eight months of 1994, the rise in August alone was up to 67.1%. By the end of September, the prices of the three major grains had risen by big margins: rice by 84.7%, wheat by 48.7% and corn by 40.1% over the same period the previous year. The rise in grain prices pushed up the price of feed, meat, poultry and eggs. Therefore, the most salient feature of inflation in 1994 was the big price increase of grains, and other farm and sideline products, all directly influencing the daily life of the people.

(II) The quick and sharp rise of grain prices and its cause

Since China's total grain output again began to rise in 1989, and up till October 1993, the supply of grains in China was relatively abundant. During that time, market grain prices dropped once. After the natural calamities in 1991, market grain prices rose, but not by much. Comparing 1993 with 1990, the grain purchasing price index rose by 15.3%, but the index of retail grain prices in the street markets dropped by 0.1%. On the other hand, the retail price index rose by 22.8% during the same period, and the retail price index of agricultural means of production rose by 21.7%, the consumer price index of the inhabitants of the whole country was up by 26.2%, and the consumer price index of the inhabitants in rural areas was up by 21.8%—all higher than the increase of grain prices.

However, beginning in November 1993, grain prices in the street markets soared suddenly. Beginning on December 28, 1993, the State Council stipulated that all state-owned grain shops in urban areas must sell rice, wheat flour and edible oils at prices fixed by the government. At the same time, to check the price rise part of the government grain reserves was shipped to the regions where grain prices soared. In some urban areas, the government took restrictive measures to check the price rise in street markets, and some regions restored the use of grain rationing coupons among urban inhabitants. After these measures were adopted, the quick rise of grain prices was brought under control, but the grain price rising trend was still developing. By the end of March 1994, market grain prices throughout the country rose by an average of 37.3% over the previous year, unhusked rice by 47.0%, wheat by 8.6% and corn by 37.5%. By the end of September, the market grain price rose by 62.6% over the same period the previous year, and 39.8% over that at the beginning of 1994.

By the end of September 1994, the price level and increase margin of the three major grains sold in the street markets were as follows: rice was 2.41 yuan per kg., up by 84.7% over the corresponding period of the previous year, 49.7% over the beginning of 1994 and 6.5% over the end of August; wheat was 1.25 yuan per kg., up by 48.8% over the same period of the previous year, 31.6% over the beginning of 1994 and 5.0% over the end of August; and corn was 1.14 yuan per kg., up by 40.1% over the same period the previous year, 30.2% over the beginning of 1994 and 2.7% over the end of August. The rise in grain prices also pushed up the price of feed, meat, poultry and eggs. By the end of September, the prices of rice bran and wheat bran sold in the street markets were 0.67 yuan and 0.97 yuan per kg. respectively, up by 40.7% and 52.7% over the same period the previous year; the market price of pork was 12.54 yuan per kg. and hen eggs was 7.24 yuan per kg. up by 72% and 22.4% respectively over the same period the previous year.

The year 1993 was a bumper harvest year in China's grain production: the total grain output hit a record high of 456.44 million tons, up by 3.1% over the previous year. It seems difficult to understand why the grain price rose by such a big margin when the total grain supply increased notably, but it is not at all hard to understand after a detailed analysis was made. The chief causes for the big price rise of the grain are as follows:

One, grain prices were relatively low since 1990. Objectively, it was necessary to readjust the price parities between grain prices and the prices of other commodities. Therefore, the rise of grain prices contains certain reasonable factors.

Two, the structural price readjustment made by the government caused a cost push. The integration of double exchange rates and the raising of home-produced crude oil prices in 1994 greatly pushed up agricultural production costs, including the price of chemical fertilizers, diesel oil and plastic films for farm use. Agricultural production costs in August 1994 were 34.5% higher than in the same period the previous year. It should be said that the grain price increase in 1994 had been expected, but the large increase margin was beyond expectation.

Three, the grain market at the time was very imperfect, the circulating order was chaotic and the middlemen's charges were too high. All this not only pushed up selling prices, but also pulled up purchasing prices of grains. An important cause of this situation was the big disparity between wholesale and retail prices of the state-owned grain departments. The grains that were on sale in the state-owned shops were mostly purchased before 1993. The grain prices were low in 1993, the contracted price fixed by the government for unhusked late rice was 0.74 yuan per kilogram, but the retail price of the husked rice on sale in the state-owned shops was in general around 2.00 per kilogram. Now, the government has fixed the contracted price for the unhusked late rice at 1.04-1.08 yuan per kilogram. The percentage of rice after husking was 72-75%, and the rice chaff and bran left over after the processing are also owned by the state-owned grain departments. Calculated at the contracted price fixed by the government in 1994, the price disparity should be above 0.50 yuan per kilogram.

If the rice is processed by the peasants themselves, the cost will not be more than 0.05 yuan per kg, and they own the rice chaff and bran. For this reason, first, the peasants are not willing to sell their grains to the state grain departments, and second, it leaves much room for private grain traders to raise the market purchasing price of grains.

Four, the contradiction in varieties and quality of grains has become outstanding. It cannot be alleviated solely by increasing the total supply of grains, which would make it more difficult for the government to exercise control over the grain market. The contradiction is becoming a sensitive factor affecting the price fluctuations on China's grain market.

(III) The influence of the contradiction in the varieties and quality of the grains in the grain Supply on grain price increases

The contradiction of the varieties and quality of the grains has become more and more outstanding in the supply of grains, and has become an important factor contributing to the big rise in grain market prices towards the end of 1993. It should be noted that when market grain prices rose in November 1993, the government had not yet made its structural price adjustments. Therefore, the November price rise was mainly caused by the imbalance between the supply and demand for the different varieties of grains.

1. The imbalance between the supply and demand of the different varieties of grains.

The total grain output in 1993 rose by 3.1% over the previous year, but the output of unhusked rice decreased by 4.6%. The total rice output in 1993 was 177.7 million tons. This is not only below any year between 1989 and 1992, it is even 560,000 tons below the 1984 output. Therefore, the chief cause for the grain price rise in 1993 was not that the total grain supply was short, but that the composition of the grain varieties in supply was imbalanced. Comparing 1993 with 1984, the national population increased by 13.57% in the nine years, but the total rice output dropped by 0.32%. So the rice supply was inevitably short. In fact, the supply of rice has been short for three years, and the contradiction became suddenly acute only because the total rice output dropped too much (8.52 million tons) in 1993. The peak rice output was 189.33 million tons in 1990, and the output was under that level for three subsequent years. If the 1990 figure is taken as the base, the combined total of the decreases in the three years was 20.26 million tons, surpassing the amount of rice Japan produces in two years. Southern Chinese people eat rice as their staple food. Of the national grain consumption, rice accounts for 60-65%. This eating habit is extremely tough on rice supplies. Therefore, despite the increase in the total grain output, as long as the supply of rice is short, the whole grain market supply seems to be short, because no other grains can substitute for rice. Under normal conditions, rice output in China usually accounts for 42-45% of total grain output, but the percentage of rice dropped to 38.9% in 1993. Beginning in 1982, the Chinese people had 150 kg of rice per head, more than 170 kg in 1984, and around 160 kg in most of the other years, but 149.9 kg in 1993, lower than 150 kg for the first time in 12 years. It was precisely because both the percentage of rice output to the total grain production and the per-capita output of rice in 1993 dropped to the lowest in 12 years that the market price of rice rose ahead of others after the late rice harvest was put to market in 1993. After this, the prices of other grains rose one after another. Several times in the last ten years a drop in rice production led to a big increase in market-wide grain prices. Rice production dropped by 5.4% in 1985 and grain prices rose by 9.2% in the following year; rice output dropped by 3.0% in 1988 and the grain prices rose by 21.3% in 1989; and rice production dropped by 2.9% in 1991, but the grain prices increased by 24.3% the next year. When rice production dropped by 4.6% in 1993, it was not difficult to understand that the grain prices inevitably rose by big margins. Thus it can be seen that short supplies of rice have become a major and sensitive factor causing price fluctuations in the Chinese grain market. And it is obvious that the influence of drops in rice production on grain price fluctuations cannot be offset by increased production of other grains. The total rice production in 1994 was around two million tons less than in 1993; the possibility of a continuing rise in grain prices should be taken into full account.

It is true that total grain output in China has increased since 1989, but the composition of varieties and regional distribution for the increase is imbalanced. The increase in total production with the structural imbalance has, in fact, accumulated the fluctuations of the supply and prices in the grain market.

The growth of grain production in China in recent years is mainly attributed to the growth of dry crops in the northern parts of the country. Comparing 1993 with 1984, the total grain output was up by 12.06%, wheat by 21.15%, corn by 39.90%, soy beans by 57.84% and potatoes by 11.69%. Only rice was down by 0.32%. Ninety-four percent of the area sown to rice and 92% of the rice production in China were concentrated in the regions south of the Huai River and the Qinling Mountains, but of the 13 provinces and autonomous regions and Shanghai, in the south, Anhui Province alone increased rice production in 1993. All others decreased rice production.

The main causes for the drop in rice production in the south are: One, the area of cultivated land has decreased. Two, the price parity between rice and other grains is not reasonable. Both labor and the material costs for rice production are higher than those for wheat production, but the price for rice fixed by the government has always been lower than for wheat, and the price of early rice is even lower. The price fixed by the government for early rice in 1994 was 0.84 yuan per kg, and wheat was 1.08 yuan per kg. The price of early rice is equivalent to 78% of the wheat price. As the mobility of the rural labor power has been greater, and there have been more opportunities for jobs, peasants in the economically more developed areas in the south have shown less enthusiasm for rice production. Therefore, if no powerful measures are taken to prevent the decrease in farmland and no proper adjustments are made to the price parity between rice and other grains, it will be very difficult to restore rice production in the south.

2. On the contradiction between the quality of the grains and the channels of circulation.

In 1994, the government took measures to check the rise of

the grain prices, but as a whole, the measures produced no distinct effect. So two points of view began to circulate: One is that the quantity of the grain reserves kept by the grain departments of the government is not correct. The actual figure is not 40 million tons as announced. So the government does not have so much to sell to check the rise of the market prices. The other view is that the government grain departments are seeking benefits for themselves and have taken no serious measures to check the rise of market prices. As to whether the two views are true or not, we can only wait until the matter is investigated. However, the fact is that the contradictions in the quality and the composition of varieties are becoming more and more outstanding, the quantity of the grains reserves are not sufficient to check the market price rise. In China, since grain production is scattered, and operates on small scales in many areas, natural conditions vary greatly from region to region. The quality of grains also differs greatly and the degree of standardization is low. These conditions determine the different purchasing prices and different channels of circulation, and there is a great difference in the quality of grain on hand. In normal conditions, the wholesale prices fixed by the government are all lower than the market wholesale prices. In 1994, the wholesale price fixed by the government for early rice was 0.84 yuan per kg, while the market wholesale price was 1.20 yuan. The wholesale price fixed by the government for late rice was 1.04-1.08 yuan per kg, while the market wholesale price was 1.40-2.00 yuan. The wholesale price fixed by the government for wheat was 1.08 yuan per kg, while the market wholesale price was usually around 1.25 yuan. The wholesale price fixed by the government for corn was 0.64 yuan per kg, while the market wholesale price in northeast China producing areas was between 0.85 and 0.90 yuan. The disparities between the government wholesale prices and the market wholesale prices were so big that it was impossible for the government grain departments to purchase good-quality grains. However, most of the urban inhabitants would rather pay more to buy good-quality grains than save money to buy inferior grains because they had more income and the proportion of their spending on grains to their total expenditure on consumption was fairly small (the national average was 6.25% in 1993). This provided a chance for the private grain traders who could purchase grains at the market prices to expand their trade volume. Because the private grain traders knew very well that the government grain departments lacked good-quality grains to sell (rice in particular), they were not at all afraid that the government could sell grains from the state reserves to check the rise in prices of good-quality grains in the street markets. For example, the state-owned grain shops sold rice at the restricted price of 1.92 yuan per kg, but not many people went there to buy it. The private traders sold rice at the market price of 2.60-3.00 yuan per kg, but the trade was brisk. This shows that if the government continues to implement the policy of purchasing grains at low prices, the function of the state grain reserves have to be studied again. The government can get only grains of inferior quality at low prices. The grain so reserved can only be used for preparedness against war and natural calamities, and reliefs and to meet the basic needs of low-income earners. As for grains for feeds or for industrial use, the state grain reserves can play some role in checking the rise of market prices. But as for grains for human consumption, it is difficult for the state reserves to play the same role.

(IV) To check inflation, it is essential, first of all, to properly control the rise in farm product prices, make genuine and energetic efforts to grasp agricultural production, and increase the agricultural input in real earnest to ensure the ample and effective supply of farm and sideline products

The most salient feature of inflation in 1994 was the big rise in the price of grains and all kinds of farm and sideline products. Between January and August, price increase for foodstuffs accounted for 60% of total retail sales price increase. The prices of the three major grains rose notably, with rice, wheat and corn up by 84.7%, 48.8% and 40.1% respectively over the same period the previous year. The rise in grain prices pushed up the prices of feed, meat, poultry and eggs. Of the income of the Chinese wage earners, spending on the basic necessities accounts for more than one half. When the prices of farm and sideline products rises too much, the influence on the daily life of the people is very obvious. It should be seen that after stopping purchasing grains at low prices and canceling subsidies, the prices of farm products more truthfully reflected their values; or after the prices are fixed by the market, the scarcity and shortage of the agricultural elements are reflected. So the rise in farm product prices is an inevitable trend. There is still the foundation and space for continued rise. Therefore, there should be a common understanding from above to below that a country with a population of 1.2 billion must attach importance to agriculture as the foundation and take fundamental measures to slow down the speed and margin of farm product price increases.

It is essential to attach importance to the problem of the insufficient input in agriculture and increase the input in agriculture in real earnest. For many years, the financial input in agriculture was insufficient, and this has become a link blocking agricultural development. The proportion of capital construction investment in agriculture to the total investment in capital construction has kept on declining, and the price scissors in the exchange of industrial goods for farm products has been widening in past years. It is an objective fact that governments at all levels, especially in economically developed regions, attach greater importance to industry than to agriculture, and it is very difficult to change it. Therefore, it is necessary to seek unity of thinking and increase the input in agriculture, especially scientific and technical input.

Persist in giving first place to agricultural production in the development of the national economy so as to keep the steady growth of grain production. It must be seen especially that the level of the agricultural productive forces in China is still very low and is still in the state of a natural economy. When one family contracts to cultivate one hectare of farmland, it keeps a sufficient amount of grains for its own use and sells only the surplus to the market in exchange for other goods. This presents almost no essential difference to the rural economy before the reform or even in old China.

To the two inflations in China (1988 and 1993), the rise in farm product prices contributed 50-60%. It is obvious that the agricultural problem is the chief cause for inflation in China. The inflation of 1993-1994 was caused even more by agriculture. Raising grain prices is a measure taken by the government on its initiative. But why should the Chinese government always raise grain prices? Why should the influence of natural calamities on the prices of agricultural products in China merit serious consideration? Of course, in the light of the special features of domestic resources and of the stage of development, the rise in agricultural product prices is only natural. Our per-capita possession of agricultural resources is far below the world average level, and the relative scarcity of agricultural resources inevitably causes rises in China's farm product prices. Another cause was the relatively low prices of farm products under the old traditional planned economic system. With progress in reforms, the prices of farm products inevitably rose. However, another factor not to be ignored is that the low rate of technological progress in agriculture also causes a relative rise in prices. When the rate of technical progress cannot offset the influence of the scarcity of resources, it is inevitably manifested in price increases. Now the government has only to raise farm product prices to solve the problem, but it also faces the problem of parity return to normality in light of farm product price discrepancies. In the 1980s, it was also the government which took the initiative in raising farm product prices to regulate the industrial relations. At that time, when the prices of farm and sideline products were raised, agriculture benefited at least in the following one or two years and then the prices of other goods rose slowly to offset the benefit given to agriculture by the raised prices. This process has now become faster and faster. This compels us to consider an essential question. In order to fundamentally eliminate the influence of agriculture on inflation, we have to consider how to raise agricultural productivity.

(V) Strictly control the loss of farmland to avoid the fast drop in rice production in the areas along the eastern and southern coasts. Properly adjust the price of rice to be purchased under the contracted quotas so that the price of rice is higher than that of wheat. Truly solve the contradictions of the varieties and quality in the supply of grains

Because the consumption of rice by the inhabitants in the urban areas in China accounts for 60-65% of their total grain consumption, once the supply of rice is slightly short, the whole grain market seems slightly tight. However, the rice producing regions in the south of China have shown less enthusiasm in increasing rice production due to more profitable land use or opportunities that have come about as a result of economic development. Therefore, if no powerful measures are taken to control the decrease in farmland and no proper adjustment is made to the price parity between the rice and other grains, it will be very difficult to restore peak rice production in the south.

1. In view of the fact that the grain reserves of the government with relatively poor quality are unable to check price rises of good quality grains in the market, proper adjustment should be made to the prices of the grains to be purchased by the government under the contracted quotas.

The prices fixed by the government for rice to be purchased under the contracted quotas in 1994: early rice, 840-880 yuan per ton, and late rice, 1,040-1,080 yuan per ton, both lower than the price for wheat, 1,080 yuan per ton. It was evidently under the international market price level. If the price parities between rice and other grains are not readjusted and if the price of rice is not higher than that of wheat against the law of the international market, the production and purchase of rice at home will become more and more difficult.

2. Strictly control the loss of cultivated land.

In seeking economic development, the problem of protecting farmland under cultivation has become more and more outstanding. It is necessary to take powerful measures to control the loss of cultivated land and strengthen the system of compensation for reclaimed farmland; this will help avoid the fast and continuous drop in rice production in the economically developed areas along the eastern and southern coasts.

3. Appropriately encourage the increased production of rice in the north.

At present, the proportion of rice production in the north is not high, but there is a big potential for expansion. For example, Heilongjiang Province produced 23.5% more rice in 1993 than in 1990. The quality of the rice produced in the north is good, and is particularly good to meet the demand of the inhabitants in the northern and eastern areas. Therefore, to increase rice production in the north will greatly help to increase the supply of good quality rice to the north and east of China.

(VI) Properly extend the use of the international market to regulate the supply and prices of rice at home

Special attention should be paid to two problems at present. One, as the price fixed by the government for contracted purchase is obviously lower than the international market price, and since the local governments and grain departments have the power to make their own decisions, the rice producing regions have vied with each other in exporting rice regardless of the domestic demand. This is detrimental to maintaining a balanced supply of rice and stabilizing prices at home. Two, properly encourage the local governments of the developed provinces and municipalities along the eastern and southern coast with the exchange payment capacity to import a certain quantity of rice. Calculated at the current market price, the price of the early rice in the Pearl River Delta in Guangdong Province is 1,400-1,600 yuan per ton, and the prices of the high-quality middle rice and late rice are 1,700-2,400 yuan per ton. If converted to the prices of the processed rice, their prices should be 2,000- 2,300 yuan per ton, and 2,350-3,300 yuan per ton respectively. Therefore, as long as they have the exchange payment capacity, it is not economically disadvantageous to increase some rice imports.

(VII) The system of purchasing and marketing grains and cotton should remove restrictions on the purchasing and selling prices to accelerate major farm product marketization

Since the beginning of the 1990s, China has evidently accelerated the pace of reforming the system of purchasing and marketing grains. In 1991, the central government put forward the plan for "the local governments to make separate decisions for different regions and make progress province by province" to reform the system of purchasing and marketing grains. Guangdong Province took the lead in taking measures to remove restrictions on the selling prices of grains at the beginning of 1992. By the end of 1992, more than 30% of the county towns in China had removed the restrictions on the selling price of grains, and by early 1994, 99% of the county towns in China had removed the restrictions on the selling price of grains. By this time, the reform to remove the restrictions on the selling price of grains consumed by the inhabitants in urban areas had been in the main completed. The reasons why the reform was completed in a short time were: One, the supply of grains was plentiful and the prices fixed by the government close to market prices, and the removal of the restrictions on the selling prices had little influence on the whole society; and two, the governments at all levels had difficulties in balancing their revenues and expenditures, and the removal of the restrictions on the selling prices of grains could free the governments from the burden of the price subsidies for grains as soon as possible. However, in the light of the current situation, because the governments at all levels were anxious to lay down the burden of financial subsidies, the removal of the restrictions on the selling prices of grains was very quick. But the construction of the grain market lagged behind and no perfect grain market was formed after the restrictions on the selling prices were removed.

On the other hand, the government had removed the restrictions on the selling prices of grains for the inhabitants of urban areas, but had not removed the restrictions on the prices of grains to be purchased under contracted quotas from peasants. For example, the average price fixed by the government for the purchase of grains under contracted quotas in 1993 was 0.80 yuan per kg (including 0.08 yuan as the price subsidy for the agricultural means of production), and it was 1.04 yuan per kg in 1994 (the price subsidy for the agricultural means of production had been abolished). This created a contradiction: The restrictions on selling prices were removed, but the restrictions on wholesale prices were not removed, and the peasants found that they suffered losses. At present, the government purchases 50 million tons of grains from the peasants under contract. About one fifth of them are agricultural levies. In fact, the peasants sell only 40 million tons to the government. If the difference between the government purchasing price and the market purchasing price is 0. 2 yuan per kg, the peasants suffered a loss of 8 billion yuan at least in performing the contracts signed with the government.

In view of the big contradiction in purchasing grains, some local governments have begun to use administrative means to restrict the market purchase and circulation of grains in order to keep down the market wholesale prices so as to ensure the fulfillment of the contracted quotas for the purchase of grains at the price fixed by the government.

The low price fixed by the government in the purchase of grains has created many contradictions. For example, the peasants are unwilling to sell grains to the grain departments of the government; the government can only purchase inferior grains and find it difficult to exercise the function of checking the rise of the grain prices; if the disparity between the wholesale and retail prices is too big, too much of the benefit of the grain producers is withheld by the intermediate links; and the big disparity with the international market price is detrimental to the use of grains in the international market by the government to regulate the supply and price fluctuations of the domestic grain market. Therefore, in the reform of the system of purchasing and marketing grains, we must make up our mind to remove all restrictions on the wholesale and retail prices as soon as possible. As a transitional measure, we can first remove the restrictions on the wholesale prices for the 50 million tons of grains to be purchased by the government under the contracted quotas.

We should complete the examination of the qualifications for the private grain traders as soon as possible. At present, the private traders "rush headlong into mass action when there is a profit, and rush back when there is no profit." They do not take social responsibility for the supply of grains, but add fuel to the flame in the price fluctuations in the grain market. Private grain traders should be permitted to take part in the circulation of grains, but their qualifications should be strictly examined, such as their amount of circulating funds, their quantity of grain in stock and necessary facilities. Those without the set qualifications should not be allowed to trade in grain.

Open state-owned shops selling grains at flat prices. At present, the grain reserve system of the government is unable to check grain price rises, and particularly of good-quality rice, in the whole market. Therefore, it is essential to direct the policy target at ensuring the supply of the basic grain necessities to low income earners in the urban areas. Open governmental shops selling grains of inferior quality at low prices fixed and announced by the government to ensure the basic grain needs of low income earners. This will help to stabilize the psychology of the urban inhabitants.

Accelerate the separation of administration from enterprise management in the grain departments. The chaotic order in the circulation of grains has much to do with the non-separation of administration from enterprise management. The government should keep only a policy-making organ with an efficient staff to exercise the administrative function, and most of the state-owned grain organs should be turned as soon as possible into organs of business operations without any administrative function.

Accelerate the construction of grain circulating facilities, market facilities and information distributing facilities, and gradually perfect the grain market system in China.

Restrictions on the purchasing (wholesale) price of cotton should be removed step by step and the process of marketization for major farm products should be accelerated. At present, contradiction is acute in the purchase of cotton. If the government does not allow the prices of farm products to truthfully reflect their values, it will hurt the interests of the peasants and affect the supply. Because the circulating system has not been completely reformed, the intermediate charges and commissions are too high, the peasants do not get benefits, and the urban inhabitants pay the price. Therefore, after removing the restrictions on wholesale prices, the government should direct its policy target mainly at controlling the intermediate charges and commissions that affect the prices of farm products.

Persist in reforming the wholesale and marketing system, abolish the state monopoly for the purchase and marketing of grains and make the transition to the market economic system. This direction is clear and incontestable. In this transition, however, it is essential to avoid chaos in the circulating order. This calls for strengthened macro control. Theoretically speaking, to strengthen the state macro control on economic development is an intention contained in the subject of the socialist market economy. It is an erroneous theory that to practice market economy means to let things drift. The chaos in the circulation of grains at present is directly related to the guidance of this erroneous theory. The reform of the grain purchasing and marketing system now under way will determine reasonable grain purchasing and marketing prices in accordance with the law of value. It not only meets the needs of the peasants and arouses their enthusiasm for cultivating grain crops, but also gives consideration to the payment capacity of urban inhabitants. Maintain the grain department of the public economy as the main channel for purchases, and permit multiple channels to purchase and market grains. Practice proves that this is a successful strategy.

It is necessary to continue the state grain reserve system. In a vast country like China, it is very dangerous if there is not a fair quantity of grain reserves. The quantity of reserves should be appropriate. Generally speaking, it should not be too big nor too small. If it is too great, the cost of storage will rise and lead to waste. If it is too small, it is not safe enough. The factors taken into account are China's production capacity, importing capacity, growing demand and natural calamities.

To maintain the stability of China's economic growth and prices, it is essential, first of all, to attach importance to agriculture and the production, marketing and storing of grains. Otherwise, there will be a serious shortage in the grain supply, the circulating order will be chaotic and grain prices will soar. As a result, we will possibly be forced back to state monopolies for the purchasing and marketing of grains, and there will be a historical retrogression in economic reform.

II. Reform State-Owned Enterprises and Check Inflation

(I) The long-time low return of state-owned enterprises is an important factor for the low return from social capital output. To check inflation, it is essential to give prominence to the deepening of the reform of state-owned enterprises

The original idea was to force down some of the price indexes through macro control, but the results were not desirable. The chief problem was that the efficiency of state-owned enterprises was too low, and they find it very difficult to respond to macro control. The problem of everyone eating meals from the same big cauldron has been very serious for a long time. So the biggest contradiction in checking inflation is mainly the problem of state-owned enterprises. They find it very difficult to respond to inflation, whether it is demand-pull, cost-push, or structural inflation. Because demand-pull inflation calls for the control of money supply and demand. If the money supply is controlled, state-owned enterprises are the first to suffer. As a result, triangular debts increase, losses become bigger and products are overstocked. Cost-push inflation calls for the reduction of costs, but state-owned enterprises are absolutely unable to reduce or eliminate the cost factor. Structural inflation shows the rise of farm product prices, and this occurs in the early stage of economic growth in all countries, because the old prices of farm products were low and the peasants had to raise their labor productivity to eliminate the price scissors in the course of economic development. However, there are many restrictions in China if peasants are to raise the labor productivity. Price shifting is an inevitable trend. The experience of developed countries has shown that all farm products have experienced the process of shifting from low prices to high prices, and even today their domestic prices are far higher than their export prices. It is very difficult for China to avoid this tendency, but in other countries the rise of the general price level is not common, chiefly because their industrial labor productivity has risen quickly and the returns are good. The prices of industrial goods are not raised correspondingly, and may even be reduced so as to offset the rise of farm product prices and to keep the general price level from experiencing high inflation. This is a very important issue that we are now facing.

Our agriculture has come to the above-mentioned stage of growth. Moreover, in the past few years, we kept the prices of farm products quite low, with a big gap between industry and agriculture. This contradiction is now even more acute. The returns of state-owned enterprises are very low. If this problem cannot be solved, we are very likely to see a process of high inflation for a few years running. This will be a big problem. A real and quite realistic solution for inflation, apart from strengthening macro control, is to deepen the reform of state-owned enterprises, turning them into true enterprises that are subject to market competition and making independent decisions, performing independent business operations and assuming sole responsibility for profit or loss. We must change the long-time state of high input, high consumption, low output and low returns. These businesses, instead, must constantly raise labor productivity, constantly increase returns, put an end to the malpractice of increasing wages without having increased the returns, reduce money sedimentation, lighten the pressure of the whole society on the money supply, and rationalize their economic structure. However, the reform in state-owned enterprises has progressed slowly with quite a big degree of difficulty. Although we have thought out many ideas for reforming the state-owned enterprises since the reform started, the state of high input and low output has not at all changed in the reform of most state-owned enterprises. Two figures illustrate this point: One, over 70% of social funds, including investments in fixed assets and working capital loans, were given to the state-owned economy, but the state-owned economy accounts for only 20% of total economic growth. Two, according to specialists, one fourth of the profit in state-owned enterprises depends on improved efficiency and three fourths of it depends on increased capital input. The figures were also true in the Unites States in the 1940s. Therefore, if Chinese state-owned enterprises do not deepen the reform, or solve the problem of eating meals from the same big cauldron fundamentally, it is very difficult to really control inflation.

(II) The failure to set up the mechanism for regulating assets accumulation in state-owned enterprises has made many no-return and low-return credit loans continue to exist in the time of macro control

The changes in the commodities market are varied and diversified. The rise and fall of commodity producers is quite normal. It is one of the inevitable results of the optimum allocation of resources. However, the business management and operation system of state-owned enterprises is not suited to the rapid development of the socialist market economy in China. A chief manifestation of this is that state-owned enterprises cannot go bankrupt and the staff and workers have difficulty in moving to and fro. Since they cannot go bankrupt, the government cannot but instruct the bank to grant loans to the state-owned enterprises which suffer losses or have poor returns. In order to check inflation, the chief means for macro control is to reduce the money supply, and the enterprises are surely short of funds, and the demand for commodities is checked. As a result, more enterprises naturally suffer losses. In the first half of 1994, 49% of state-owned enterprises suffered losses, and 10% of them stopped production. As the number of state-owned enterprises with losses increased, more and more enterprises asked for "special treatment" from the government: even to the enterprises which have completely stopped production, the government also asked banks to grant loans and give financial allocations to ensure that these businesses could pay a certain percentage of wages. It can be seen that some expenditures used as a variable cost of production operations became invariable cost in the state-owned enterprises. This is obviously the opposite of the original intention to control the money supply. It resulted not only in increasing the money supply, but also in increasing the overstocking of products and the triangular debts among state-owned enterprises. The statistical figures between January and June 1994 showed the "overstocking" part of the total sum held by industrial finished goods throughout the country exceeded the "normal stock" by 30%, and a good part of it was held by state-owned enterprises. Of the 300 billion yuan on account at state-owned industrial enterprises within the budget, only 200 billion yuan are regular commercial credit, and 100 billion are irregular arrears.

The contradiction between the macro-control of the money supply and the system of business management and operations in the state-owned enterprises is also manifested in the lack of coordination between input and output. Since the beginning of 1994, the Chinese government has followed a policy of inclination in granting working funds loans to large and medium-sized enterprises, and the proportion of loans granted to state-owned industrial enterprises against the background of macro control of the total working funds rose by 8.4%. But the total output value of state-owned industrial enterprises in the first six months of 1994 rose only by 5.3% while that of collectively-owned industrial enterprises rose by 27.8%. The problem of high input and low output in state-owned enterprises is precisely the concentrated expression of this deep-level problem of not being able to adjust the assets accumulation and not being able to make the optimum use of the funds. The other implication of this phenomenon is that the output (or supply) is even weaker than the demand. Under the past macro-control, all enterprises received the same treatment whether they had good economic performances or not. Under the current macro-control, the enterprises with good economic performances can still obtain funds normally. This is a good improvement. However, the enterprises with poor economic performances can also obtain funds, although not enough.

(III) When the reform of state-owned enterprises enters the new stage, there must be a new idea. Start with defining the relations of property rights and make the transition to the modern enterprise system

After the goal of the reform of the socialist market economic system is set, the reform in state-owned enterprises has passed from the stage of giving decision-making power and part of the profit to the enterprises to the new stage of creating a new system. The reform must have its continuity, and there must be a new idea. That is, start with defining the relations of the property rights and make the transition to the modern enterprise system. The reform of the property rights system is the core and key of the reform of state-owned enterprises. It is essential to harmonize the relations of the property rights as a key to solve the realistic problems of the enterprises, to promote the separation between the administration and the properties and the separation between the administration and the enterprises, and to facilitate the adjustment of the structure of the state-owned properties and the structure of state-owned enterprises.

As to the system of property rights, some specialists have advanced the theory of three-level property rights, that is, state ownership, the property rights of the investors, and the property rights of the legal persons of the enterprises. The property right of the legal person of an enterprise is a comprehensive right, including material right, creditor's right, intellectual property right and the personal right related to the property right.

Some specialists propose that part of the rights to the state properties in the enterprises be transferred to the enterprises: One, on the basis of a certain percentage, and every state-owned enterprise is entitled to it; two, on the basis of the amount of investments in the fixed assets the enterprises made by raising funds and borrowing loans after the policy of state appropriations was changed to the policy of loans. If an enterprise has paid off its loan, it will receive a big proportion of property rights. This part of property is still state-owned property, but the returns from it belong to the enterprise.

To exercise a two-level ownership of state-owned properties —central and local. The properties invested in by the central government are owned by the central government, those invested in by the local governments are owned by the local governments, and the jointly-invested-in properties are divided in proportions. Two-level ownership is in fact a type of relationship between the representatives at different levels. Both the central government and the local governments are representatives of the properties owned by the whole people. At present, it is essential to settle the question of who represents the state-owned properties, establish the procedure for state property consignment, and standardize the current practical experience in the reform.

Some specialists have advanced the theory of the labor power property right. They hold that the laborers should not only get wage income, but also be entitled to the returns from the property rights to a certain degree; that is, turning part of the profit into shares for the staff and workers of the enterprises in their own enterprises. Such shares have their peculiar characters: they are non-transferable, non-tradable and non-inheritable. In reforming the corporate system, 10-20% of the property rights of the enterprises can be allocated to the staff and workers, including the managerial staff. The staff and workers of an enterprise hold the shares by group through their trade union and join the board of directors and the board of supervisors to create the foundation for the community of enterprise interests. The enterprise and its staff and workers fuse themselves into one body on the basis of their interests.

The question of the form of realizing the property rights should be solved through the corporate system. The reform of the property rights is to introduce the corporate system. They rely on each other. The transformation of the corporate system must be pre-conditioned by the settlement of historical and realistic questions, and be carried out together with the reform in the macro control system, a change of governmental functions, the social security system and the construction of the market system. It should not be done separately and singly. It must not become a mere formality nor the same old stuff with a different label.

Some other specialists argue that the corporate system cannot solve the fundamental question, especially the question of non-separation of administration and enterprise management. At present, only 20% of state-owned enterprises have the conditions and are willing to introduce the joint-stock system, and most of the enterprises that have small profits or are suffering losses do not have the conditions to introduce the joint-stock system. Some specialists note that if the government controls the holding companies, it can only solve the problem of product competition, but cannot solve the problems of land, property right and capital competition. The enterprises under a holding company may have slow reactions to the market, limited power to make independent decisions and find it difficult to give play to the market function in eliminating or upgrading the products.

As to the measures to reform the property rights, some specialists propose the idea of reorganizing the liabilities of the enterprises, namely, turning the fixed assets loans and the circulating funds loans (equivalent to 30% of the fixed working capital of the enterprises in normal operation) into debts for reorganization and turning the bank credit into shares. The organs undertaking to reorganize the liabilities of the enterprises should not be the state's special banks because it not only violates the principle of separating the business between the commercial banks and the investment banks, but also will abet the bank's mechanism of soft restriction on the enterprises. The financial institutions controlled by the bank should be entrusted to reorganize the liabilities of the enterprises, such as trust and investment corporations, stock companies, and state property holding companies.

Other specialists argue that when the current bank system and enterprise system have not been fundamentally changed, turning the bank credit into shares is nothing more than the replacement of a "lord" or even an additional "lord." Neither the banks nor their holding financial institutions have a better ability than the enterprises themselves to manage them. Because of the closer relations between the banks and the enterprises, it is even more difficult to solve the problem of the soft budget restriction on the enterprises.

To make the reform of the property rights, apart from ensuring the normal operation of the properties of the legal persons, it is also essential to do the property trade. It is necessary to accelerate the establishment and perfection of the property rights market to promote the movement and reorganization of the state-owned properties.

(IV) The reform of state-owned enterprises should be flexible and be made in different ways. Alleviate inflation pressure in the course of optimizing state-owned enterprises and improving the results of state-owned enterprises

The actual conditions in Chinese state-owned enterprises are complicated. Different measures should be taken in the light of the different conditions in the different enterprises. The modern enterprise system should have different forms of organization for the properties and different ways of business management. It is necessary to respect the creative work of the entrepreneurs, staff and workers. The enterprises should have the power to choose their own forms of organization and business operation.

Classify the existing state-owned enterprises and adopt different ways of reform for the different types of enterprises. In the first category are a small number of medium-sized and small state-owned enterprises which have suffered losses for a long time, whose assets are not enough to offset their debts, whose technologies and equipment are outdated and whose products are unmarketable. These enterprises shall go bankrupt. In view of the fact that the complementary conditions for the bankruptcy of state-owned enterprises are not yet ripe, the government must be very cautious with bankruptcy. In the second category are the large numbers of small state-owned enterprises which should be turned into enterprises not owned by the state through reforms, transfer, leasing and selling. In the third category are the general medium-sized state-owned enterprises which can be transformed into enterprises with mixed ownership in the form of joint ventures or through the grafting of foreign investments. In the fourth category are the large state-owned enterprises and a number of medium-sized backbone state-owned enterprises which shall be transformed into standardized companies and establish the modern enterprise system in accordance with the Company Law. This category is the center of the reform in Chinese state-owned enterprises.

In market economic conditions, the government should take into consideration the overall interests, integral interests and long-term interests of the national economy; readjust the structure of the properties of state-owned enterprises; gradually withdraw state-owned properties from general fields of competition; concentrate state-owned properties in basic industries, essential fields and public utilities to show the irreplaceable positions of state-owned enterprises; and give full play to the leading role of state-owned enterprises. The general competitive state-owned enterprises should be gradually turned into private-owned ones through participating stock, joint operation, transfer, auction, bankruptcy and annexation.

In the transformation under the company system, full play should be given to the role of the joint-stock system. Limited-liability companies and state-owned companies with exclusive capital are easy forms of organization for the transformation, but because their shares cannot be easily transferred, the administrative structure of their legal persons is not very strict and the scale of business operations is limited. Their role in the reform of the state-owned enterprises is limited. In the course of practice, tremendous efforts should be made to solve the problem of unstandardized transformation of the joint-stock system and especially the unstandardized behavior of the government so as to reform the joint-stock system in its true sense.

(V) The reform in state-owned enterprises involves all aspects of the economic system. It is necessary to energetically

push forward complementary reform in state-owned enterprises, and especially to establish a perfect and effective social security system

Some specialists say that the central question regarding the reform of state-owned enterprises is the reform of the macro control system of the enterprises, namely the reform of the investors of these enterprises and their macro-administrative level. Concrete ideas for the reform of macro-control in these enterprises are: (1) Re-establish the administrative system and structure in charge of state-owned properties, including the setting up of a commission for the administration of state-owned property under the State Council; separate the functions of social and economic administration of the government from the functions of state-owned properties; establish a unified system of jurisdiction and administration of state-owned properties, and establish a structure of multi-level ownership and multi-level administration. (2) Re-establish the system of operating state-owned properties. Separate the functions of administration of state-owned properties from the function of their operation by setting up special intermediate organs for investments in the state-owned properties. (3) Re-establish the macro-control system for the state-owned enterprises. Gradually abolish the industrial departments of the government. The general economic functional departments of the government are not allowed to interfere with the enterprises. The administrative organs of the government for state-owned properties only have direct relations of management and supervision over the investments with the intermediate operational organs, and are not in direct contact with the business operating enterprises under the intermediate organs.

In practice, most of the subjects of the state-owned properties operations are the old industrial departments in charge or the head offices of industrial corporations, making it very difficult for business-operating enterprises to have their independent property rights and independent legal person status. The subjects of the state-owned property rights should be the legal persons of the enterprises, and they should be entrusted directly to operate the enterprises.

The separation of administration from enterprise management is the key to the creation of the modern enterprise system. The relations between the government and the enterprises should be reversed, and it should be stressed that the government should serve the enterprises. An important aspect of the separation between government administration and enterprise management is to solve the problem of the leadership system of the enterprises. The leaders of the enterprises should not be appointed administratively, nor should the system of administrative ranks be applied to them. The chairperson should not be concurrently the general manager. The relationship between the chairperson and the general manager is not the relationship between the leader and the led. They are both authorized and entrusted to exercise their respective functions and powers in accordance with the Company Law and the regulations of their corporation. The directors should be diversified. Apart from the representatives of the investors, they should also include representatives of the specialists and scholars in society. This should become a system. Selection of senior managers is most essential. It is necessary to establish a system of registered managers. Professional managers should all be registered and given the title of "entrepreneur" according to the required qualifications (education, professional background, managerial rank and accomplishments).

An important pre-requisite for the reform in state-owned enterprises is to establish a new type of social security system and setup, remove the heavy social burdens from the state-owned enterprises and solve the practical problems the state-owned enterprises face. At present, it is necessary to further accelerate the reform of the social security system and labor wage system and the reform of the housing system to create a comfortable external environment for the smooth reform in state-owned enterprises. It is necessary to promote the reform of the social security system. It can be considered that the reform of the social security system shall be introduced in advance under the conditions of earnest study, wide publicity and gradual implementation. And on this basis, work will be done to encourage the survival of the fittest state-owned enterprises. The program for the reform of the social security system should lay emphasis on old-age retirement and unemployment insurance, and at the same time, positive efforts should be made to promote the reform of the social security system for the medical service and industrial injuries and establish a multi-level social security setup.

III. Reform the Banking System and Check Inflation

(I) Make a full appraisal of the tremendous impact of the current banking system on inflation and adopt a stable monetary policy

An important cause for the rise of prices arising from the current banking system is the over-supply of money in circulation. The main factors for the non-economical over-supply of money are:

1. The turning of credit funds into finance caused by the financial deficit. The financial overdraft from the bank between 1981 and 1993 accounted for 31% of the market money in circulation. According to estimates by the department concerned, the financial overdraft from the bank, bank loans, potential losses of enterprises that should be subsidized but not subsidized, and policy subsidies on account make up 30% of the total bank stock.

2. The monetary deficit caused by the credit balance. In macro-economic terms, the modern enterprise system has not yet been established and this has, to a large extent, decided the soft restriction on the "father-son" relations between the government and the enterprises. Affected by delayed reform, state-owned enterprises are clearly not accommodated to the market and have suffered large losses. In order to help them out of difficulty, the government increased loans to large and medium-sized enterprises amounting to 150 billion yuan in September and October of 1993 alone, and added several dozen billion yuan of emergency loans to the enterprises with losses in the first half of 1994. From the micro-point of view, an enterprise has only benefits if it can

get more funds from the government and does not have to bear any risk. Once it loses, the loans are on credit, and it does not go bankrupt. This gives rise to the impulse for the blind expansion of the capital demand. According to the estimates made by the department concerned, 21% of the combined amount of money supplied in China between 1984 and 1993 had no material guarantee. The big increase of money in circulation led to serious inflation in 1988, 1993 and the first half of 1994.

3. The credit crisis makes the credit funds "inventory" critically ill. Because of the chaos in the economic and financial order, the credibility between the banks and the enterprises, among the banks, and among the enterprises has hit an all-time low. As a result, 40% of the remainder of the bank loans to the enterprises have become bad debts, creating three big financial shortages for loans for agriculture, loans for major construction projects and loans for large and medium-sized enterprises. According to the figures from the departments concerned, of the 2,600 billion yuan of credit assets at present, only one third is in circulation, and two thirds of the circulating funds' loans have been disabled or become immobile. In order to ensure the supply of normal, basic funds to the enterprises and the balance of credit funds, the government has been obliged to increase the supply of money.

Inflation is in essence a monetary phenomenon. The pressure of 1993's inflation was caused chiefly by the over-supply of money in 1990-1992. It is absolutely necessary to accelerate the reform of the banking system, and to give full play to the role of the banking system in regulating the money supply. The central bank should follow a relatively independent monetary policy to regulate and control money supply. Accelerate the reform of the commercial banks system and create the self-restriction mechanism of the commercial banks as soon as possible.

To avoids big rises or falls in the economy and serious inflation, a stable monetary policy is needed. For this reason, the relative independence of the central bank must be guaranteed. As the administrative money department, the central bank must have a very high authority and be able to withstand pressure from the government and enterprises in implementing the monetary policy.

(II) Accelerate the reform of the banking system to promote the marketization of banking

The important changes and problems in the transition to the marketization of banking in China in the past ten and more years:

1. The change from budget to banking finance has made the role of bank loans more outstanding in production and investment.

Before 1979, the People's Bank of China in China's single banking system played the roles of the central bank, commercial bank and bookkeeper at the same time. The Ministry of Finance was charged with appropriating most of the production and investment funds. It allocated the operating capital (circulating funds) to state-owned enterprises according to fixed quotas. Investment funds for fixed assets were also allocated by the Ministry of Finance according to the quotas fixed by the State Planning Commission. The bank issued only small and short-term loans for extra-quota production funds to state-owned enterprises. Even limited credit activities had to closely follow the credit plan of the government. The budget and credit plan of the government guided the capital flow. In its bookkeeper role, the banking system recorded all financial accounts, but did not think about the risks and returns from the loans. Under the central planned economic system in China, the role of the banks in the allocation of financial resources was passive and limited, and tended to serve the economic policy of the government.

The economic policy adopted after 1979 evidently changed the mechanism for the allocation of financial resources. The single banking system has been divided into one central bank (the People's Bank of China) and four state special banks: (1) the Industrial and Commercial Bank of China, mainly issuing short-term loans to industrial and commercial enterprises in the cities; (2) the Agricultural Bank of China, providing services to agriculture, industry and commerce in rural areas; (3) the People's Construction Bank of China, mainly handling long-term loans for key investment projects; and (4) the Bank of China, handling foreign exchanges and providing credit to the import and export enterprises. All these special banks are still strictly restricted by the credit plan, industrial policy and administrative interference. However, the current contracting system of responsibility has given the special banks the power to choose the borrowers of the loans and to use part of the surplus of their gains. Besides, there are some other newly-established state-owned commercial banks, such as the Bank of Communications, the CITIC Industrial Bank, the Guangdong Development Bank, the Shenzhen Development Bank and the Fujian Reconstruction Bank. The urban credit cooperatives and rural credit cooperatives are cooperative financial organizations between the banks and the non-bank financial institutions. They have supplied impressive commercial loans to the rapidly developing urban collective and rural enterprises.

With the rapid change and expansion of financial institutions, the control over funds is obviously scattered. As a result, the central government has concentrated fewer and fewer financial resources while individuals, enterprises, local governments and departments have increased their shares of financial assets. In the years between 1972 and 1978 before the reform, budget funds used for production and investments increased from 3.78 billion yuan to 5.82 billion yuan at an annual rate of 9%. During the reform between 1978 and 1991, they increased from 5.82 billion to 9.34 billion yuan at average annual rate of 1.2%, far slower than in the previous six years. This clearly shows that the role of the budget is fading in production and investment.

Because budget funds don't have to be repaid and loans must be paid back to banks, the annual increase in the loans of state banks can be compared with the annual budget funds of the government for production and investment. In 1972, the loans of state banks increased 320 million yuan, 1.87 billion yuan in 1978, and 28.78 billion yuan in 1991. The annual rate of increase of the loans was 81% from 1972 to 1978, but it was 110% from 1978 to 1991. This clearly shows that bank loans have become more and more important in production and investment.

The increases in budget funds and bank loans reflect the new funds China has poured into production and investment every year. Of these funds, budget funds and the shares of banks decreased from 92.3% in 1972 to 24.2% in 1991. This decrease was even more obvious in the operating capital. In 1972, 57.5% of the expansion of the operating capital came from the budget, and it dropped to 26.3% in 1978 and 0.6% in 1992. Now, the operating capital of enterprises comes mostly from banks.

In raising production and investment funds, the main cause for the decrease of budget funds and the increase of bank loans is the rapid shift from the planned system of the Chinese economy to the market economy. The proportion of state-owned enterprises to the total industrial output value dropped from 84.9% in 1972 to 77.6% in 1978, 54.6% in 1990, and 48.1% in 1992. The rapidly growing enterprises not owned by the state, such as collective enterprises in the cities and rural enterprises, are competing more and more fiercely with state-owned enterprises for funds in energy, transport, communications, imports and exports, and farm products processing.

2. Credit control faces new problems.

It is necessary to review the experience of direct and indirect monetary control. Before 1978, China exercised direct monetary control through the central credit plan. The deposits and loans of banks, and the money in circulation were all designated by a general and well-coordinated credit plan, which, at the same time, decided the total volume of credit and the structure of credit distribution. So banking institutions only exercised the account book function of the central planning authority.

After 1978, the reform of the banking system began with the restricted decentralization of the right to use loans and deposits to the local branches of the People's Bank of China. Each branch was given a fixed quota for the deposit/credit balance. Some branches were deposit balance branches, namely branches where the deposit quota exceeds the credit quota; and others were credit balance branches. The fixed quotas were used to ensure that the combined deposit and credit balance were concentrated for the convenience of overall arrangement of loans, thus the total credit volume could be put under control. Under the deposit and credit balance plan, the branches could increase loans if they had more deposits. The surplus funds of the deposit balance branches were transferred to the credit balance branches to make up for the deficit. At the beginning, the transfer of deposits among the branches was regulated by the head office of the People's Bank of China administratively without credit/debt contracts. This was possible in the early years of banking reform when the funds owned by the head office and the local branches were not separated.

After the People's Bank became the central bank in 1984, the ownership of the funds was divided among the People's Bank, the special banks and their branches. The special banks only had to deposit the deposit reserves and extra-quota reserves in the People's Bank; when funds were needed, each branch applied for loans to the People's Bank. In this way, in principle the People's Bank controlled the total sum of loans to the other banks in principle. The People's Bank could also decide the percentage of reserves and the interest rate of loans issued to the other banks. Theoretically speaking, the People's Bank could perform the following functions: (1) Controlling the loans of the central bank issued to other banks; (2) Adjusting the interest rate of the loans from the central bank; and (3) Changing the rate of the deposits reserve to control the total credit and money supply. However, since the banking system in China is not yet perfect, the standard instrument of monetary control is not always very effective.

The central bank in China still relies on the credit plan (specifying the ceiling on the increase of the loans for each bank) to control the total credit and money supply. Theoretically, the credit plan can easily limit the total sum of loans, but in fact it was not so simple. The special banks with ample deposits could issue loans on the basis of the loan quota, and deposit the surplus funds in the People's Bank as their liquid extra-quota reserves to get the interest, or put these funds into the market of the same trade to get the market interest. The other state banks without sufficient deposits but having made loans above their quotas would ask the central bank to make loans, and their best excuse was often that the loans were used for the policy loan projects.

The central bank always met the request for policy loans under the pressure of the government.

In 1991, the assets on the balance sheet of the central bank included: The policy loans directly issued by the People's Bank accounted for 4.9%, the loans from the central bank to the other banks totaled 66.6% (mostly policy loans). Also, gold, 1.2%; exchange reserve, 12.4%; government loans, 14.9%. Of the liabilities, financial deposits accounted for 14.1%; deposit reserves 20.2%; extra-quota reserves 26%; circulating cash, 35.9%; its own capital, 2.4%; and profit 1.4%. It can be seen that the loans taken by the special banks and the government from the central bank were the principal sources of the credit expansion. It was necessary to pay attention to the high reserves of the Chinese banking institutions. It was closely related with the strict credit control policy. The state banks accumulated extra-quota reserves because they did not have loan quotas. Such high reserves weakened the role of the rate of reserves in controlling the total credit volume and money supply, because the changes in deposit reserves reflected only the change of part of the extra-quota reserves to deposit reserves, and would not produce outstanding results in the credit control and money supply. Under the credit control system, high reserves (liabilities) could not be easily lowered by reducing the loans (assets) of the central bank. This was because the banks with extra-quota reserves would not obtain loans from the central bank, but those without extra-quota reserves would still obtain loans from the central bank. The assets and liabilities of the central bank would continue to expand because of this. When the credit scale was controlled and the money market was tight, it would be impossible for the banks to turn the extra-quota reserves into actual loans, but when the control was relaxed, the extra-quota reserves could easily lead to credit expansion.

3. The state banks have made improvements, but are still unable to suit the requirements of the market economy.

The reform in the operation of the state banks is similar to the practice of the agricultural and industrial systems of responsibility. The core of the responsibility system is the decentralized operations and the retention of a portion of the profit. The banking reform has separated the limits of power of the state banks for assets and liabilities from the accounts of the central bank, defined the rate of cost and the quotas of portions of profits they keep, given the limited initiative in the allocation of funds and the power to make decisions on the readjustment of interest rates and internal organization, the use of the portion of profit kept by the banks, the appointments of managerial personnel and staff. The portion of the profit kept by the Industrial and Commercial Bank of China under the 1983 stipulations was 12%, the Bank of China was 3%, and the Construction Bank was 12.6%. Of the retained portions, 60% can be used for business expansion and 40% for the bonuses and welfare of the staff. The profit after deduction was turned in to the central government as its budget income (62%) and distributed to state banks as new funds (38%). These measures have greatly stimulated the branches of the state banks to expand their business and meet competition.

However, in spite of these policies, the banks are still owned by the state and still have many non-profitable obligations. They are obliged to follow a strict interest rate and credit plan and are subject to the control of industrial policies. In this way, the competition among the state banks is called non-price competition, such as setting up branch offices in large numbers, giving souvenirs intended to win savings depositors, and flexibly selecting partners for loans and projects.

The state banks are in a dilemma with regard to the competition for funds. On the one hand, in response to market demand, they would rather make more loans to profitable enterprises owned or not owned by the state in order to get a greater portion of the profit that they can keep. On the other, as rooted in the traditional planning system, they have to obey the industrial policies and the credit plan and increase loans to highly risky and unprofitable projects. The state banks have almost monopolized the banking business. Except for urban and rural credit cooperatives and some foreign bank offices, China has no banking institutions not owned by the state. So the state banks have to meet the financial demand of both state-owned enterprises and enterprises not owned by the state.

4. Non-bank monetary institutions play a positive role.

The rigid banking system and the higher demand placed by the state departments and non-state departments for the monetary regulation have led to the mushrooming of non-bank monetary institutions, including trust and investment corporations, the Chinese People's Insurance Company, finance companies, short-term loan and leasing corporations and stock corporations. Sometimes, urban and rural credit cooperatives are also regarded as non-bank monetary institutions.

Non-bank monetary institutions have very close ties with the state banks. Many trust and investment corporations were set up by the state banks at the beginning. The urban and rural credit cooperatives usually have administrative and banking relations with some of the state banks. However, non-bank monetary institutions are more sensitive to profit and are less restricted by the credit plan and other regulations. They have more flexibility than the state banks. Because local governments are in charge of many non-bank monetary institutions, their activities are greatly affected by the policies of the local governments. Non-bank monetary institutions vary greatly in flexibility. Moreover, both state banks and non-bank monetary institutions are not private organs, urban and rural credit cooperatives are collectively-owned, and other non-bank monetary institutions are mostly run by the central government or local governments. So most of the banking institutions are undoubtedly protected by the government from going bankrupt. As a result, they care for profit far more than fear risks. Non-bank monetary institutions have weakened the monopoly of state banks for issuing loans and receiving deposits, and look particularly important in supplying funds to the more marketized departments not owned by the state.

5. The order has to be perfected for the financial market.

In China, the money market includes the commercial bill discount market, inter-bank short-term funds market, foreign exchange market, and government and enterprise bonds market. All these money markets are still in the initial stage of development. As far as the volume of transactions are concerned, the same-trade markets, the government bond market, and the foreign exchange market are the most brisk. Compared with loans from banks, the direct loans for production and investment issued through stock and bonds are still in the stage of development.

The money market is very important for the reallocation of funds between the banks and non-bank monetary institutions. The inter-bank market of the same trade has played a great role, but it is also chaotic, as both the banks and the non-bank monetary institutions can do business in the same market. The interest rate and the volume of assets transactions are decided by the market through consultation. This gives encouragement and provides conditions for getting large and frequent short-term funds needed in long-term investment projects. Many state banks have surplus funds, but they cannot increase loans as limited by the loan quota. They can get considerable interest income from the market of their own trade. Not restricted by the credit plan, some non-bank monetary institutions can accept high interest for funds, because they can invest the funds with even higher profit in departments not owned by the state, such as rural enterprises, real estate, foreign exchange transactions and stock. This shows that the inter-bank market has become the main channel for the flow of funds from state-owned departments (usually linked with policy loans) to departments not owned by the state (the main target for business loans).

6. Savings, investment and the stability of the macroeconomy.

The rapid expansion of the banking institutions, money market and financial assets has created tremendous pressure on the macroeconomic situation in China. The rate of inflation in China was around 10% in 1985, 1988 and 1992, but it was low compared with the growth rate of around 30% for the money and quasi-money (M2). There are two aspects of vital importance in interpreting the relative stability of the macroeconomic situation in China. First, in the past ten or longer years of reform, the Chinese economy has become a more and more commodity-oriented one in the course of changing the old planning system to the marketized mixed economy. And the growth of a very great part of the money supply has been absorbed by the non-state sectors and market transactions. Second, the high volume of savings has supported the high volume of investment during this period. They each account for 40% of the GNP.

It is worth noting that on the one hand, personal savings both in urban and rural areas have increased rapidly, but on the other hand, only a very small part of these financial assets have been invested by individuals directly. This is because of the government monopoly on savings deposits and investments. In 1993, about 70% of fixed assets were used for state-owned departments, and the government also exercised strict control over the stocks of direct private investments and enterprise bonds. The dual monopoly on savings and investments has ensured that the state bank has control over the main body of social funds. If the Chinese state banks can effectively turn savings into investments, the huge gap between personnel savings and personal investments will not become a serious problem. Unfortunately, the state banks are not very successful in putting the huge volume of personal savings into profitable investments. At present, about one third of the state-owned enterprises cannot repay bank loans because of their losses.

The change in the ownership structure of the Chinese economy is significant to the banking system. Because of the growth of the economy not owned by the state, the proportion of the disposable personal income to the GNP rose from 45.2% in 1978 to over 60% in 1994. A good part of it has become personal financial assets. Of all personal financial assets, about 70% are savings deposits, the others include cash, government bonds, other bonds, foreign exchange, stock and insurance. Personal savings deposits are very sensitive to inflation and interest rates, and may create pressure on the stability of the banking system in China. However, more fundamentally, how to effectively regulate these personal savings deposits and use them for competitive investment projects will be the key to rapid development of the Chinese economy and the stability of the macroeconomy. The "key" is not to lock the "tiger in cage," that is, don't keep family savings deposits in state banks, but use them in the proper place.

7. Policy loans.

Policy loans are usually established more on the basis of government policy than on the basis of profit and risk. Because of the serious interference from the government, they do not have the same profit as from business loans. However, under the planned economy system, planned mandatory loans are a better solution than distributing all funds through the budget. Marketization and the growth of the economic sectors not owned by the state have weakened the importance of direct policy loans to overall economic development in China. The policy mandatory loans have evolved into a tool to provide funds to the shrinking or stagnant state-owned departments, support the purchase of farm products, and control the prices of the import and export goods.

Policy loans should be helpful to the gradual and orderly change of the Chinese economy. They play an important role especially in subsidizing the investment projects supported by the government and the prices of the farm products and import and export goods. However, the rate of development and productivity of the priority projects supported by the state are quite low, and moreover, many policy loans have been transferred, or become bad debts.

While China is developing the market economy, the tool of policy loans is tremendously affected by underdeveloped private banking institutions, the immature money market and the rapidly developing market economic activities, and at the same time also affected by the decentralization of the decision-making power of the central government to the local governments and the local monetary institutions. Therefore, it is very difficult for the central government to exercise close supervision and control over the waste and transfer of funds in priority departments and projects.

Specialists in this field have analyzed the influences of policy loans on the Chinese economy.

First, policy loans are related to the overexpansion of credit during the period of reform. The policy priority loans are one of the main sources of credit expansion of the central bank. It is precisely the latter that has led to the overexpansion of credit in the national economy. In recent years, about one third of the total volume of credit of the banks were policy loans, and most of them were provided by central bank credit.

Second, because of the credit expansion and the distorted use of policy loans, policy loans in China have exerted important indirect influence on non-priority departments. For example, rural enterprises have never been priority departments of the state and have seldom had subsidies and loans. However, by raising funds themselves and soliciting loans from money institutions, they have been developing rapidly. Against the will of the central government, funds have been flowing to them through all channels. The proportion of loans made to them to the total sum of loans in the state banks rose from 2.2% in 1979 to 6.1% in 1984, and to 8.5% in 1991. It has kept rising in the last two years. However, the loans only reflect the lawful flow of funds to rural enterprises, non-state owned departments which have the greatest vitality. The continuous rise in the proportion of rural enterprises to the total fixed and circulating capital funds shows that some of the funds have not been distributed through lawful channels.

Third, the rapid development of non-priority departments (such as rural enterprises) have increased the supply of commerce and services, and alleviated the pressure of inflation caused by the credit expansion. However, over-relaxed credit control has led to the actual negative interest rate forced down artificially. The artificially low interest rate stimulated many state-owned enterprises (priority) and rural enterprises (non-priority) to make "irrational" investments. As a result, the capital efficiency of both has greatly dropped. The interest and tax rate of the total assets of the state-owned enterprises dropped from 24.0% in 1978-1983 to 19.1 in 1985-1991, while that of the rural enterprises dropped from 30.6% in 1978-1983 to 19.2 in 1985-1991.

(III) Accelerate the reform in commercializing state banks and turn them into enterprises, harden the credit restriction mechanism and marketize bank interest rates

The progress has been slow in the commercialization of state banks and managing them on a business basis. The banks still use administrative means to control the loans on the administrative orders and are in operation with deep negative interest rates for loans. The questions of the hard restriction mechanism and the system of responsibility for the risks of the banks have not yet been solved satisfactorily. Therefore, it is necessary to accelerate the reorganization of the state special banks so that they operate in the property structure and organizational structure of an enterprise and manage their business independently, assume responsibility for gain and loss, bear their own risks and compete with each other. The state commercial bank which is too big to do business effectively shall be divided into several banks. Administrative interference from the government in the affairs of the commercial banks shall be removed.

Give full play to the lever of interest rates to regulate the macroeconomy, stabilize money, control the investment scale and check inflation. Bank interest rates should be readjusted in light of the supply and demand of the market and macroeconomic policies. The current interest rates for state bank loan are lower than the inflation rate, and have twisted the market, thus creating an opportunity for corruption and rent-seeking acts. The bank interest rates should be raised properly, the anticipation of inflation by the society should be changed, and the efficiency of using social funds should be improved.

The proportion of loans to the economy not owned by the state should be increased and the use of bank credit funds should be optimized. The high growth of the Chinese economy has been created by the economy not owned by the state to a large extent, but state-owned enterprises have used 80% of the bank loans with poor returns from the input and output. The direction for loans and the structure of loans of the commercial banks should be changed. Loans should be refused to the state-owned enterprises with long-time poor gains, whose assets are not sufficient to offset the debts and which have no future, so as to force them to make reform or reorganization. The proportion of the loans to the economy not owned by the state should be increased so as to support the still faster growth of the economy not owned by the state, thus promoting the growth of the whole economy.

IV. Accelerate the Process of

Marketization and Check Inflation

(I) Marketization promotes economic growth

In the process of marketization, with the introduction of the competition mechanism and the stronger fluidity of the production elements, the economic subjects decide the allocation of the resources in the light of the changes of the market situation. In this way, the allocation of resources is optimized and the labor efficiency raised, thus promoting fast and stable growth of the economy.

Before the reform, the growth rate of the Chinese economy was relatively slow. The average annual growth rate of the national income was 6% between 1952 and 1977. The obvious accelerated growth rate of the Chinese economy after the beginning of the reform shows that marketization has promoted the development of the Chinese economy.

(II) The process of marketization gives rise to the long-time cost push and causes inflation

The structure of the price parities of Chinese products and production elements is irrational. The process of changing to a market economy track is also a process of rationalizing prices. The rationalization of the relative prices inevitably brings about structural changes in prices, which is manifested in a long-time cost push, thus causing the rise of the general price level. This is the risk that must be run in the reform.

However, inflation in the process of changing the economic track is by no means caused by marketization. The defects of the current economic system and the unfulfilled part of the reform are the main causes for inflation when changing economic tracks. At present, in macro-terms, the weaker control ability is manifested in the overgrowth of the money supply and the insufficiency of financial functions, and in micro-terms, the business operation mechanism of the enterprises has not yet been fundamentally changed, which is manifested in raising wages among enterprises. Both inevitably give rise to large financial deficit in public departments and inflation.

The process of marketization will give rise to a long-time cost push and cause inflation, mainly manifested in the following aspects:

1. The introduction of price reform has led to the rise of prices of farm products (grains, cotton and others) and primary products (crude oil, natural gas and electricity) as well as the prices of services.

2. Change the financial system of the enterprises, introduce the manufacturing cost method, raise the rate of depreciation, include wages and bonuses in the cost and include the interest of the investment in the fixed assets in the cost. The real cost will increase the cost of the products.

3. The wage reform of the government functionaries will bring along a rise of the wage level of the enterprises and lead to the rise of the cost of the product.

4. The integration of double exchange rates will cause a rise in the cost of import commodities and the products made of imported raw or processed materials, and thus give rise to certain price increases, although custom duties will have been reduced.

5. The reform of the tax system as a whole has not increased the burden of the enterprises, but some enterprises have had their tax burden increased and others have had their taxes cut. Because of the toughness of the prices, and especially in the conditions of high inflation, the enterprises with small tax burdens will not lower the prices of their products and the enterprises with increased tax burdens will transfer the price increases, causing cost push and a certain degree of price increase.

6. Price reform, the integration of exchange rates and the tax reform have improved the allocation of resources and the financial foundation. This helps to check inflation to a certain extent, but the results will be perhaps evident after some time.

(III) China's reform and process of marketization have gone through four stages

China's process of marketization has gone through four stages:

The first stage was from the end of 1979 to October 1984. The reform began in the rural areas, and the contracted responsibility system with remuneration linked to output proved successful; the turnover of profits to the state was replaced by tax paid by the enterprises to the state; a system of responsibility for local finance was introduced with the local governments receiving more revenues; and appropriations were replaced by loans in capital construction. The average annual growth rate was 8.8% during this period.

The second stage, was from October 1984 to September 1988. The reform shifted its stress from the rural areas to the cities, and the enterprises increased their vigor by practicing different systems of responsibility for business management; restrictions were removed on the prices of most farm products, industrial consumer goods and means of production not covered by the state plan; and the decision-making power was enlarged for the enterprises and local governments. The average annual growth rate was 10.9% during this period. The rate of inflation was 18.5% in 1988.

The third stage was from September 1988 to the end of 1991. In light of economic overheating, serious inflation and economic disorder in the development of the economy, the central government decided to improve the economic environment and consolidate the economic order in three years or longer. As a result, inflation was checked, the general retail price index dropped to 2.9% in 1991, and the average annual economic growth rate was 5.4% during this period.

The fourth stage was from the end of 1991 up till now. The market has played an increasing role in regulating the economy, the scope of planned economy has gradually diminished, restrictions have been removed on most of the prices, and macro and micro reforms have been in full swing. The average annual economic growth rate was 13.5% during this period, but with a fairly high rate of inflation.

The monetization of the Chinese market has accelerated, the reform of prices has been mainly completed, the mechanism for the formation of prices by the market has taken shape, the prices of basic services are being rationalized and have progressed very fast, the integration of double exchange rates has been completed with the emergence of a flat exchange rate facing the pressure of revaluation. The relative wage level is fairly high, but the pressure of restricting the rise of wages in the state-owned departments is limited. The problems left behind in price reforms are mainly: land, funds, housing rent, and part of the charges for public utilities.

In the initial stage, the reform was intended to remove some restrictions from the traditional system or to make it flexible and decentralize part of the power and introduce the market mechanism, thus arousing the potential and enthusiasm of the laborers and clearly increasing the benefits of the majority of the people. To establish the socialist market economic system and completely abolish the yoke of the old system, it is essential to readjust the interests of all sides, but with a very large degree of difficulty. The reform has entered the stage of assaulting the fortifications.

(IV) Structural contradictions have emerged in the process of marketization and the process of monetization in the course of changing the economic track, and have considerable impact on structural inflation

The money supply climbed high in recent years and did not lead to inflation, but why did it lead to high inflation in 1994? Obviously, it is not sufficient to analyze the current inflation only by citing the general features of changing the economic track. It is also necessary to analyze the special features at specific times in the stage of changing the economic system track. Now, a new and distinct feature is: Structural contradictions have emerged in the process of marketization and in the process of monetization, and this has considerable impact on structural inflation.

The process of monetization turns the articles which should have been commodities, labor and services into commodities through the transactions with money as the medium. The process of marketization calls for the universalization of market prices and the further growth of the economy not owned by the state, but this process is still going on and is far from being finished.

One of the important reasons why the process of monetization is faster than the process of marketization is that the huge income from the money supply in the process of monetization is supporting the demand of the reform, thus alleviating the conflict of interest. Moreover, it helps the central government to exercise macro control. Two important aspects of the process of monetization have been realized: One, the tremendous expansion of the money supply, and two, the universalization of the commodity scope, such as the flourishing of the real estate market and the development of the stock market. But this can be realized only when policy permits. The most fundamental feature of the process of marketization is the formation of a price through the demand and supply of the market. To a certain degree, in the process of changing from a planned economy to a market economy, the change of the mechanism for the formation of a price and the corresponding price rise will have certain impact on macro stability. Therefore, the control from the administration is understandable.

The gap between the process of monetization and the process of marketization has an influence on inflation. When the process of marketization is insufficient and the process of monetization is too quick, the money supply will be too large and give rise to the pressure of inflation. When the process of monetization is not sufficient and the process of marketization is too quick, it is impossible to lead to an overall price rise. Take the current inflation for example, the index of retail prices of the same comparisons all exceeded 8% in the last 18 months. In the light of the current system, the causes are that the process of monetization is quick while the process of marketization has been sometimes quick and sometimes slow, and it has even halted in some new and important fields (such as the stock market and the real estate market), with the money pushed out of these fields, thus giving huge pressure to the retail price index.

Two or three years ago, specialists suggested that different ways of selecting assets be exploited to "reduce the pressure and divert the flow" of inflation, and facts proved that it was possible. When we look at this now, the process of diverting the flow is in essence a process of monetization involving more commodities and services in the exchange with money as the medium. In the past year or longer, because of our control over the real estate market and stock market, the spontaneous forces of marketization were blocked, and the funds that were put into these fields began to be pushed out. This increased the pressure on the social retail prices. In other words, the role the diversification of assets played in "diverting the flow and reducing the pressure" of inflation has been reduced. Still further, what corresponds to monetization is the economic issuance of money. The increase of the money supply is caused by the increase in the demand for money. Therefore, it has no pulling effect on the prices. But the process of marketization brings about a huge change in the economic structure, a huge change in the subjects of investment and a huge change in the relationship between supply and demand. Therefore, the process of marketization, as a systematic reform, has influence on inflation.

(V) Promote economic development and check inflation in the course of accelerating marketization

Price reform and the process of marketization have become factors for inflation because of the influences of different factors. We should differentiate the different situations to solve the problem of inflation arising in the process of accelerating marketization.

—Marketization of the prices is not brought about in a single day. Rationalization of prices and perfection and improvement of the market competition mechanism require a long process. In the process of changing the economic track, the rise of the general price level caused by rationalization of prices is inevitable.

—Influences of all artificial factors in the course of price reform leads to a rise in price levels, and it plays an important role in the given conditions and period. This should draw keen attention.

—Marketization of prices does not always directly cause the rise of prices. In the condition of full competition, the standards of some prices will fall and gradually become reasonable and stable.

1. Marketization of prices cannot be put under administrative control, nor violate the principles of the market economy.

(1) Encourage the formation of reasonable price standards in competition and reduce the non-market factors as much as possible. Only in full competition, can a reasonable price system be formed. For example, Hainan Province started grain price reform in 1988. By May 1991, it had replaced the government-fixed purchasing and selling prices of grains with government-guided prices and led the country in introducing identical purchasing and selling prices close to the market prices, allowing the prices to float within a given range. In fact, there were no longer any restrictions on grain prices. After the restrictions were removed, the average market grain prices not only did not rise, but dropped by around 21% as compared with before the reform. There were no fluctuations in the prices of non-stable foodstuffs made of grains, nor were there any grain shortages, rush purchases or fraudulent purchases. This state of affairs remained until 1993.

(2) The macro control over prices must be based on full competition and the marketization of prices, and only this can the stability of prices ensure. The current price reform in China is mainly manifested in the readjustment of certain categories of price standards by the government. The price readjustment is made by administrative means, not by the market spontaneity. The artificial price readjustment often gives rise to the price chain reaction and brings up the general price level. In 1993, for example, the government raised the purchasing prices of farm and sideline products by 13.4%, and then the prices of industrial products, especially of the agricultural means of production, also rose. As a result, the prices of the agricultural means of production were up by 14.1%. Not only the original purpose of the price adjustment of the government was not achieved, but it led to serious inflation. In the process of the marketization of prices, the government must strengthen supervision and administration over the market prices, but the administration must not become artificial interference in the competitive and reasonable prices of the market. The setting of the price limits must be based on the price

market.

(3) It is necessary to prevent the influences of artificial factors and anticipation on the prices. The inflation in 1993 had much to do with the indiscriminate raising of prices, monopolizing prices and speculative factors. It also had something to do with people's anticipation of inflation after the price reform was announced. It is necessary to take measures to stop and control all artificial factors. Moreover, when every reform is made, full preparations must be made and preventive measures taken to prevent chain reactions from the reform. Full publicity should also be made to show the ability and confidence of the government in controlling inflation, thus helping eliminate anticipation by the people.

2. Accelerate property transactions. In the process of marketizing property rights, promote the adjustment of the capital structure and the effective allocation of social resources to make the most of social capital, especially state-owned capital, play a greater role and promote economic growth.

The large-scale sedimentation and low utilization ratio of fixed assets in state-owned properties in China have been a common problem. In 1993, the utilization ratio of the overall processing capacity of the national processing industries was only 60%. The enterprises which suffered losses for many years and whose properties were not sufficient to offset the debts also accounted for a large percentage of the state-owned enterprises. This part of the state-owned capital not only did not yield any results, but created artificial losses and increased the financial burden of the state. The serious losses and little profit of state-owned enterprises also constituted an important factor for inflation. Only by accelerating the marketization of the property rights and promoting the reasonable flow of state-owned capital, can state-owned assets preserve and increase value and yield profit. Standardized property rights markets should be established under a strict system so as to gradually promote property right transactions.

3. In the process of accelerating marketization, seek the optimum results of the state-owned properties, and solve the

problem of inflation in the course of adjusting the structure of state-owned properties.

The growth of investment and economic development in China are both restricted by the "bottleneck" of the infrastructure and the basic industries. This is largely because China's structure of investment and structure of state-owned assets are mainly concentrated in the processing industries and the general competitive fields. When too much investment is put in the processing industries, the rate of growth of the processing industries rises by big margins which energy, raw and processed materials, transport, communications and other basic industries find hard to bear, thus pulling up the general price level because of the serious imbalance of supply and demand. Therefore, strengthening the construction of infrastructure and basic industries to solve the "bottleneck" problem requires maintaining a sustained, fast and stable development of the national economy and using measures to check inflation.

The overheated investment in the Chinese economy is manifested mainly in businesses in the general marketplace. But the investment in basic industries and public utilities is quite underdeveloped. Therefore, in the light of the long-run interest and the overall interest in the development of the national economy, state-owned assets should be withdrawn from businesses in the general marketplace, and be transferred to basic industries, key departments and public utilities to achieve optimum results for state-owned assets. Businesses in the general marketplace should be left mainly to investment by the economy which is not owned by the state, including private and overseas investment. This is beneficial to accelerating economic growth and to controlling inflation.

V. Anticipation and Checking Inflation

(I) The relationship between anticipated inflation and general inflation, and the law of evolution

The main causes for anticipated inflation are: (1) The price increases in the past, which followed big moves in reform, have given rise to anticipation among people: Reform is a synonym for price rises. The moves taken at the beginning of 1994 also gave rise to an anticipation of inflation for lack of sufficient publicity. (2) While improving the banking order, the circulating order should also be improved. The acts of raising prices indiscriminately or in disguised and covert forms in some regions was not effectively stopped, helping to increase people's anticipation of inflation. (3) The incorrect press view of linking economic growth absolutely with inflation also helped people to increase their anticipation.

Such anticipation manifested in the prices since price changes are isolated from the direct foundation for actual supply and money supply and leapt to a fairly high point of anticipation which surpassed the proper price level, giving rise to the anticipated price rise and inflation.

Anticipated inflation is different from general inflation. General inflation is the process of sustained and overall rise of prices caused by the imbalanced supply of money and the changes in real economic life. Anticipated inflation refers to the price fluctuations caused by people's anticipation of inflation. Anticipated inflation is different from general inflation in the time and space of influence. There is no need to turn pale at the mention of inflation.

But the two of them are also linked. General inflation is the basis for the action of anticipated inflation. If there is no seedling of inflation, it is difficult for anticipated inflation to function. More important, the influence of anticipated inflation has its limitations in time and space, but it should be seen that if anticipated inflation does not draw our attention and is not stopped in time, it will also lead to and aggravate general inflation and the price fluctuations will become a process of sustained and overall rise of prices. Once the anticipation becomes part of common awareness, it will make inflation a reality and promote its development through the behaviors of the enterprises and individuals.

The behaviors of the enterprises: One, accelerate the purchase of raw materials (to avoid the purchase of raw materials at higher prices in the future), thus increasing the demand of the whole society for raw and processed materials; two, hoard products to sell them when prices go up, thus leading to a short supply of goods in the whole society. As a result, the contradiction between supply and demand aggravates the price rise, thus giving rise to inflation in its true sense caused by the changes in the supply of money and the supply from the enterprises.

The behaviors of individuals: On the one hand, they do not like to have money in hand and turn the money into a demand for real commodities, thus increasing the total demand. On the other hand, they force enterprises to increase wages on the pretext of inflation, thus increasing the production cost of the supply, blocking the growth of supply and bringing about inflation caused by money in its true sense and changes in the supply and demand of enterprises.

Moreover, the development of anticipated inflation will also make general inflation induced, by its appearance, in a more complicated form; changes in supply and demand in real economic life lead to and accelerate inflation in real life. On the other hand, it will turn demand-pull inflation into cost-push inflation, and stimulate price rises mainly through the cost-push channel. In the domain of money, on the one hand, it forces money to circulate more quickly and increase the speed of circulation, thus increasing the amount of money in circulation. On the other hand, it leads to the sedimentation of money in the form of materials, thus causing a universal shortage of funds.

(II) Control anticipated inflation by choosing the right medicine for the illness

Money policy is a demand control policy. When the causes for inflation are credit expansion, more money is issued and there is an excess of total demand. A tight money policy is immediately adopted at the beginning of inflation and, by controlling money supply, it can alleviate inflation and bring the economy back to a balanced cycle. When anticipated inflation occurs, the causes are partly shifted to total supply, namely cost-push inflation, and the money policy looks powerless. Either a "loose" or a "tight" policy does not work. If the money policy is "loose," inflation continues and becomes even worse. If it is "tight," the price level does not drop, but production becomes stagnant or even declines. So money policy must concentrate on how to avoid anticipation of inflation if it is to produce a good result. Once anticipation becomes anticipated inflation, care must be taken to avoid the mere use of money policy in macro control.

The concrete measures to cope with anticipated inflation are as follows:

1. Remove the foundation for anticipation and strengthen leadership over publicity work.

Some time ago, some so-called authoritative views printed in the press on the inevitable link between fast economic growth and inflation fostered the anticipation of the people, and misled them into rush purchases. Therefore, two concepts have to be cleared up: Reform does not mean price rises, and fast growth does not necessarily bring inflation.

In the course of reform, the readjustment of the price control system and the readjustment of price parities do give rise to some price changes. However, in fact, the true implication of the reform is to establish a market mechanism and competition mechanism for the allocation of resources, and this will check price rises. In the course of development, money supply increases and demand expansion will bring pressure on prices. But in fact, money investments can be absorbed in the course of reform as the economy is monetized and marketized. The pressure of demand expansion on prices in opening the economy can also be neutralized, and the demand itself can also be balanced naturally by the restriction of the supply cost.

2. Consolidate the circulating order and make great efforts to prevent anticipation from becoming anticipated inflation.

The key to the development of anticipated inflation from the anticipation is the inducement given by the indiscriminate raising of prices; when there is anticipation, prices rise if the anticipation grows effective in inflation; therefore, the anticipation has been confirmed, or the anticipated idea has developed into realistic action. The reasons why it is possible to raise prices indiscriminately or take the lead in raising prices are: one, the existence of a monopoly in the industry, and two, there is a separation of the market. Otherwise, in highly competitive industries or in the inter-linked markets, the raising of prices by one factory or by one market is sure to be shattered by other factories in the same industry or by other markets. So we must firmly investigate and deal with the acts of raising prices indiscriminately and at the same time oppose monopolies, set up a competition mechanism within each industry, improve the circulating system and establish a unified market. When necessary, it is appropriate to establish proper reserves to regulate the supply and demand of the market and to check the rise of prices. An important aspect is to make great efforts to consolidate the circulating order. Before control measures are perfected, we should not open too many futures markets at one time. Before the information network is completed and the competition mechanism is perfected, we cannot allow the unavoidable wrongly anticipated prices to mislead the society.

To consolidate the circulating order is not retrogression, but a necessary adjustment on the journey towards a market economy. We should not look forward to establishing a market economy in one day, nor could we allow all people to know all about the market economy and standardize their behaviors in accordance with the "game rules" of the market economy in one day.

3. Exercise strict income control and prevent anticipated inflation from evolving into cost-push inflation.

Once cost-push becomes the leading factor for inflation, there will be the evil consequences of stagnant inflation. If anticipated inflation is to be stopped from becoming cost-push inflation, it is essential to exercise strict control on income while strictly controlling the rise of prices. One, collect income tax on the wages of enterprises with overseas investment strictly according to law with no exemptions. Two, regulate the wages of the state-owned enterprises strictly in accordance with the principle that the increase of wages must not be higher than the growth level of labor productivity. Three, make great efforts to reduce the staff of government organizations.

Of course, while exercising strict control on income, give subsidies and reliefs to low income earners so as to raise their capacity to bear the price rise.

4. Prevent the consequences of stagnant inflation and work hard to raise and ensure social supply.

During times of anticipated inflation, a money shortage exists. Even if the policy of tightening the money supply is not adopted, there is also the danger of stagnant inflation. Therefore, it is necessary to properly increase the money supply to the key supply departments.

(III) Non-economic factors, such as unstandardized administrative behaviors and artificial driving up of prices, have important influences on inflation. It is necessary to adopt measures to eliminate the negative influences of the non-economic factors on stimulating inflation

High importance must be attached to the non-economic factors related to inflation, which include administrative monopoly, artificial driving up of prices and anticipation. It is of great importance to make a concrete analysis of the influences of these factors on inflation and formulate a corresponding policy and eliminate the negative effect they have on the normal operation of the economy. At present, sufficient consideration should be made regarding the negative influences on the process of economic reform by administrative monopoly factors that have existed in the traditional socialist planned economy system for a long times and a solution be found for it. Enact the Anti-Monopoly Law to reduce the administrative monopoly factors, which promote an irrational allocation of market resources and unfair competition in the economic order, and check inflation caused by the market monopoly. The administrative monopoly factors caused by the unstandardized behaviors of government interference must be scientifically controlled. It is necessary to correctly define and restrict the factors for inflation caused by the unstandardized administrative interference of the government by enacting corresponding administrative statutes.

Be fully aware of the arduousness in the marketization in China, establish a normal circulating order according to law, and prevent artificial driving up of prices from developing insidiously into acute inflation. We should educate the broad masses through meticulous organization and propaganda work and improve the market environment. At the same time, we should take powerful measures to strike blows at lawbreakers who drive up prices, and kill inflation induced by price increase resulting from the driving up of prices in its embryonic stage. Strengthen the administration for industry and commerce, keep market prices stable, correct the wrong idea that "no price control is needed for the market economy," and create conditions for the gradual establishment of a good market environment in which the market decides the prices.

Intensify the analysis and study of the consumption mentality and anticipation of people of all strata, enterprise groups and government organizations, and establish a scientific macro-control system. The People's Bank of China announces the target of the money supply at regular times, and starts work to set and announce the target of prices and the target of the policy of checking inflation at regular times. Organize specialists and research institutes to make investigations of the social consuming mentality and anticipation through different channels, at different levels and in different forms, and make the investigation results known to the public from time to time. Try our best to provide accurate information to government departments on the consuming mentality and anticipation, help the government and the public to coordinate their actions toward inflation, remove unnecessary misunderstandings and distortions and form a healthy and mature anticipation in society. Deepen the reform of the statistical system, strictly observe the Statistical Law, ensure the seriousness, independence and scientific character of government statistics, and ensure the impartiality and rationality of the statistical figures related to checking inflation.

(IV) The government makes known its position to influence public anticipation

The government should firmly and clearly make known its position to show its determination to control inflation, and rely on the trust of the people in the government's ability to control inflation to help the inhabitants make stable anticipation of future price changes, thus stabilizing their marginal propensity to consume and ensuring a normal spending on consumption so that the inflation rate will tend to go down steadily.

Otherwise, if the government keeps on vacillating on its position on the question of development and stability, it will lose the trust of the people in its ability to control inflation, and with the marginal propensity to consume up and down, consumptive spending high and low, and the inflation rate rising and falling at two-digit-figure levels, the economy will be in danger of an acute inflation.

Chapter 4
Control Inflation Effectively in the Course of Opening the Country Still Wider to the Outside World

I. Appropriately Appraise the Influence of Overseas Investment on Inflation

(I) The big inflow of international capital into china and the big alteration in the inflow and outflow of capital

1. The big increase in the inflow of capital. The main cause for the big inflow of capital is the quick increase in the actual use of foreign capital, which was 36.77 billion U.S. dollars in 1993. Investment from outside China continued to rise in 1994. By August 1994, direct overseas investment came to 20.4 billion U.S. dollars. China has become a hot spot for the circulation of international capital.

2. The big alteration in the inflow and outflow of capital. The net outflow of capital was 0.25 billion U.S. dollars in 1992, and the net inflow of capital was 23.47 billion U.S. dollars in 1993.

3. Big statistical errors and omissions on the international balance sheet. The 1993 figure was minus 9.8 billion U.S. dollars, mostly outflows and runaways.

(II) Inflow of capital has both positive and negative influences on the Chinese economy

The large inflow of international capital has both positive and negative influence on the Chinese economy.

1. The inflow of capital has promoted economic growth. The capital inflow into China is manifested in the increase in the

direct use of foreign capital. The investments have been used in basic industries and other industries, and they will play a positive role in the economic growth of our country.

2. The capital inflow can be used to make up for the trade deficit. The increase of the net capital inflow will encourage China to use these capital funds to import foreign machinery and equipment in large quantities and cause trade deficits. However, the trade deficits will be made up for by the surplus of the capital projects. In 1988 and 1993, the balance of international payments fitted with this growth pattern.

3. The capital inflow may lead to a relative surplus of the national currency and foreign currencies and consequently cause overheating of the economy and the appreciation of the national currency.

4. When the actual amount of the foreign capital imported is bigger than the relative demand of the national capital, the resources cannot digest and utilize it. This will cause capital outflow and runaway, thus resulting in the loss of resources. The meteorological analysis of the economic growth and the use of foreign capital shows that if the foreign capital imported in 1993 was fully used, the economic growth would be around 25%, but the actual economic growth rate was 13.4%. This showed that half of the foreign capital imported was not fully used.

Therefore, considering the positive and negative influences of capital inflow on the Chinese economy, we must correctly estimate the ability of our country to use the resources effectively, utilize foreign capital reasonably and prevent evil influences on the economy by foreign capital imported blindly in the course of development.

The large inflow of foreign capital leads to a large input of RMB to match it, thus affecting the macro-control. The unprecedented inflow of foreign capital gave rise to the unprecedented input of RMB. According to the estimation by the department concerned in our country, to draw one U.S. dollar of foreign capital, eight to ten yuan RMB is needed to match it. This showed that in 1993-1994, dozens of billions of U.S. dollars flowing into China each year demands hundreds of billions of RMB yuan.

China is now eager to import foreign investment, and the demand for RMB arising from the import of foreign capital is usually supported by the government when possible. As a result, it would undoubtedly weaken the dynamics of macro-control.

(III) Make still greater use of foreign capital to promote the steady development of the Chinese economy and effectively control inflation

Since the beginning of the eighties, the process of integration of the world economy has been quickened. It is clearly demonstrated in the following aspects: The growth rate of direct international investment has exceeded that of domestic investment, the growth rate of transnational banking transactions has exceeded that of domestic banking transactions, the overseas economic activities of the transnational corporations have continued to swell, and the international circulation of capital and technology has been greatly facilitated by the development of electronic computers. Therefore, whether in developed countries or in developing countries, the import of foreign capital has become an important condition for the sustained development of the economy.

So far as developing countries and regions are concerned, there are two aspects that merit attention: One is a high rate of inflation accompanying the import of foreign capital, as seen in some Latin American countries with long years of social upheaval; the other is the large import of foreign capital without serious inflation, such as in Singapore and Hong Kong. Singapore and Hong Kong both have economies built mainly with foreign capital, and a decisive factor in their economic growth is how much foreign capital is invested. However, as large amounts of foreign capital has been pouring into Singapore to achieve a two-digit economic growth, the price rise rate has less than 5%, and in Hong Kong, the price rise rate has been lower than the economic growth rate while foreign capital has been continuously imported. It is thus clear that there is no inevitable relationship between the import of foreign capital and inflation. In some countries, such as the United States, the inflow of foreign capital has been used as a means to control inflation. What has happened on Hainan Island is also representative. In the three years between 1990 and 1992, Hainan used nearly one billion U.S. dollars of foreign capital, but there was no big change in the general index of retail prices.

1. Encourage more foreign businessmen to make direct investments.

In Singapore, direct foreign investment accounts for the overwhelming majority of the capital inflow. Although Singapore has also drew loans from the World Bank, the Asian Development Bank and the Overseas Economic Cooperation Fund of Japan, Singapore has always believed that any loan with attached conditions is not as beneficial as the direct investment. Between 1975 and 1984, direct foreign investment accounted for 97.7% of the long-term net capital flow into Singapore. Hong Kong also adopted the method of using direct foreign investment, and the Republic of Korea has also begun to gradually increase the proportion of direct investment by foreign businessmen. It is thus clear that these success stories can be used for reference.

Indirect foreign investment (such as government loans) is accompanied by the problem of matching national currency, and it would to a certain degree increase the demand for national currency, while direct foreign investment can reduce the pressure on the national currency supply. Take Hainan as an example: between April 1988 and August 1994, it imported foreign investment amounting to 3.19 billion U.S. dollars, of which indirect investment was 0.63 billion U.S. dollars, accounting for 19.57%, and direct investment came to 2.56 billion U.S. dollars, accounting for 80.43%. Between January and September 1994, the foreign investment came to 568 million U.S. dollars, and only 200 million U.S. dollars demanded the regulated RMB to match it, accounting for 35.7%, while 64.3% of them were investments in kinds. To encourage and draw direct foreign investments can help reduce the demand for the regulating RMB arising from indirect foreign investment, but also help to reduce the proportion of foreign capital in the use of the regulated RMB. Moreover, direct investment pays more attention to its operation efficiency. Foreign businessmen demand the maximum profit from the minimum cost. As long as the direction of investment is reasonable, it will not greatly affect inflation in China although a small part of it is turned into consumption funds. Therefore, we should boldly encourage more foreign capital to pour in, direct foreign investment in particular, with a posture of opening the country still wider.

2. Open more fields to foreign investment, use more foreign capital and use it in a still better way.

Large foreign companies and consortiums usually tend to make large investments in big projects with stable returns. Judging from foreign investments made in the last two years, foreign businessmen are more interested in major infrastructure building projects. We should make the best use of this situation to guide our work, adopt a still more open policy, and abolish the man-made restrictions in some fields and the unnecessary restrictions on the controlling percentage.

It is necessary to give more guidance to foreign businessmen in the direction of industrial investments, and combine the direction for foreign industrial investments with the readjustment of the industrial set-up and the long-term strategy for the development of the national economy. It is necessary to institute a different policy of inclination. Foreign investment projects in the basic industries, infrastructure, and projects with high or new technologies should be given preferential treatment in credit and taxation. A still more lenient policy should be made for foreign investment in energy and transportation projects.

3. Encourage and support overseas investment in the export-oriented projects.

One of the goals of using foreign capital in China is to promote the development of foreign trade. A realistic choice for trade development is to utilize comparative advantages and to achieve comparative benefits, but judging from the demand for long-term development, a consolidated foundation for trade benefits must be established on the basis of constantly readjusting the structure of the comparative advantages. At present, the volume of imports and exports of the enterprises with foreign investments in China accounts for nearly one third of the national volume of imports and exports. This is a very encouraging achievement. As long as we persist in pursuing the policy of using foreign investments in export-oriented projects, we will certainly strengthen the international competitive power of the Chinese products and promote the stable development of the Chinese economy.

(IV) Give national treatment to foreign-invested enterprises as soon as possible, and gradually bring foreign investment policies in line with international practices

It is very necessary to attract foreign capital through preferential policies in a given period of time. With the accelerated transition to the market economy in China, there must be equal competition between foreign invested enterprises and domestic enterprises. If we still lean too much toward preferential policies for foreign invested enterprises, it is very unfavorable to the formation of market economic environments. To give national treatment to foreign investment enterprises is a successful international experience in drawing foreign capital. Proceeding from our own reality, we should give national treatment to foreign invested enterprises as soon as possible and gradually make it a law.

While encouraging the inflow of foreign capital, enough attention should be paid to the problem of capital outflow. At present, capital outflow is very serious. It is estimated to total more than 200 billion U.S. dollars. The government should make a long-term and definite policy regarding capital flowing out through different channels and properly restrict the capital outflow so that the capital outflow will be legalized and standardized.

Necessary restrictions should be made on foreign investments in speculative fields. Encourage and support the direct investment in export-oriented projects. Great changes in the inflow and outflow of foreign capital will give rise to economic fluctuations.

In the next two years, the flow of foreign capital into China may decline. Therefore, the policy readjustment must be done very carefully. The competition of neighboring countries for foreign capital is very acute. They are all trying every means to attract foreign investment. The economic revival in Western developed countries will also aggravate the contradiction of supply and demand for international capital. Moreover, since the growth in the wages of Chinese labor forces, the staff and workers in joint ventures in particular, has increased, the comparative advantage of low labor costs in China will soon disappear, thus weakening China's competitive power with the neighboring countries for foreign investment. Therefore, we cannot be too optimistic over the import of foreign capital, and our foreign investment policy must be relatively stable and must follow international practices.

(V) The international comparison on the strategies of importing foreign capital

The international economic pattern is changing, the tide of the times is also changing, and there are big differences among countries. Therefore, the strategies and policies for the use of foreign capital have varied from time to time and from country to country.

In the fifties and sixties, the developing countries in the high tide of national liberation and national independence adopted an unwelcome or even a negative attitude towards the capital of developed countries. In the late seventies and in the eighties, developing countries acquired a new understanding of the role of foreign capital and began to import foreign capital in a limited way. At present, when the former Soviet Union and East European countries switched to the market economic system and began to attract large amounts of Western capital, it became an international tide to import foreign capital. In the late eighties, when some developing countries met with debt crises, people again cast doubts on foreign capital. Of course, this time the doubts did not lead to the simple negation of the role of the foreign capital, but to the analysis of the causes for the different results of using foreign capital in the developing countries and to the self-examination of the strategies and policies of importing foreign capital. The most representative of them was the discussion on the different results of importing foreign capital in East Asia and Latin American countries.

Being debtor nations all the same, East Asian countries (with the exception of the Philippines) have shown high growth and low inflation, while the growth in Latin American countries has been slow and their inflation rate rose sharply. In the six countries of Argentina, Brazil, Chile, Mexico, Peru and Venezuela, the average growth of their GDP was 4-5% in the seventies, and in the first years of the eighties, the economic growth became negative. On the other hand, the inflation rate was 40-50% in the seventies, and the average value of the inflation rate in the six countries rose as highly as above 130%. Obviously, it was typical impeded inflation. The situation in East Asia was much better. Impacted by the international economic recession and the oil crisis, the foreign debts in Latin American countries met with crises, forcing the creditor nations or creditors to make rearrangements for debt clearance periods. There were no debt crises in East Asian countries and their economic growth was great. Indonesia, South Korea, Malaysia and Thailand all achieved a growth rate of 6-7% in the seventies and eighties while their inflation rate dropped from 15% in the seventies to 6-7% in the eighties. They have experienced a tendency towards strong economic growth.

Compared with East Asia, South Asia imported much smaller amounts of foreign capital. Of all debts in Asia, more than 70% have been owed by East Asia. The ratio of foreign debts and exports in South Asia is similar to that of countries in the western hemisphere. As capital funds were limited, South Asian countries adopted similar methods used by the countries in the western hemisphere, such as controlling imports under the pressure of international balance. They did not or had no power to increase their exports, thus exerting an unfavorable impact on their economic growth. India is a representative South Asian country in importing foreign capital. In the long periods of the sixties and seventies, India had relied on domestic bank savings and used remittances from the overseas Indians rather than owe debts related to imported foreign capital. When the pressure from the international payments increased, it adopted policies controlling imports and investments and reducing state expenditures and money in circulation, and adopted a replacement policy of selected imports for a fairly long period of years. Its foreign debts were limited to preferential loans. This strategy freed India of the pressure of foreign debts, even achieved a surplus of foreign exchanges, and maintained its economic stability. But its economic development greatly lagged behind the East Asian countries which boldly imported foreign capital. Therefore, in the early eighties, India also began to relax the restrictions on foreign investments, relaxed the control over imports, and increased loans from foreign commercial banks in addition to the preferential loans. This played a positive role in accelerating India's economic development.

It is worth noting that South Korea placed more importance on foreign loans than direct foreign investment. This had something to do with its own resources and market conditions, and also with its attitude of vigilance against direct investment by Japanese companies, for historical reasons. Singapore has operated differently. The foreign capital it has imported has mainly been direct investment. Moreover, in developing its export-oriented economy, direct foreign investment has likewise played a very big role.

African countries have not achieved good results in importing foreign capital. Although African countries did not import much foreign capital and had a low debt payment rate as compared with East Asian and Latin American countries, its long, slow economic development and economic difficulties had much to do with their lack of courage and ability to use foreign capital.

Why have different countries shown different results in importing foreign capital for economic development? There are many reasons. Some specialists have compared and analyzed the reasons for the gains and losses in East Asian and Latin American countries. Superficially, the Latin American countries met with debt crises, seemingly because the global impact in the eighties had exerted a greater influence on Latin America, and in the debt structure, Latin American countries had a greater percentage of loans with variable interest rate (the U.S. commercial banks raised the interest rate), and they borrowed more loans than East Asian countries. Detailed analysis found the above-mentioned suspicions and conjectures unfounded. The comparable index signs for the analysis of the causes of the debts in the two categories of countries were close to each other except for the notable difference in the ratio of debts and export volumes. In Latin American countries, debts were three times export volumes while in the East Asian countries, debts were only 80% of export volumes. This shows that good trade export is the foundation for the ability to repay debts. Restriction on imports alone, instead of expanding the exports to balance the international payments, over exaggeration of the role of the import replacements, and reducing the role of the export guidance are harmful to the use of foreign capital in developing the economy.

(VI) The strategy of importing foreign capital with the acceleration of development as its center and the marketization, legalization and internationalization of the Chinese economy as its goals

Since China decided to establish the system of socialist market economy in 1992, the importing of foreign capital has gained unprecedented momentum. The actual figure of foreign investment was 19.2 billion U.S. dollars in 1992, of which 11.3 billion U.S. dollars represented direct investment by foreign businessmen, surpassing foreign loans for the first time. It accounted for two thirds of the foreign capital imported in the year. The amount of foreign investment continued to grow at a high speed in 1993, and the actual figure came to 26 billion U.S. dollars, of which 18.8 billion U.S. dollars or 70% represented direct investment. As a result of the large imports of foreign capital in these two years, foreign capital increased its influence on China's international balance drastically and also increased its influence on China's economic development in the 1990s in an unprecedented scale. The problem of administration over the importing of foreign capital and the enterprises with foreign investments has become quite outstanding. Especially since the plan for the major reform of the economic system was adopted in 1994, the influence of the role played by foreign capital in the economy over the course of the reform brooks no underestimation. All this has made it a pressing matter to readjust and formulate a new strategy and policy for importing foreign capital.

Obviously, the Chinese strategy for importing foreign capital at the present stage must, from the angle of the socialist market economic system and the development plan for the end of the century, further answer the major questions of why, how much and how to import foreign capital, of where and how to pay it back, and how to make the transition to importing foreign capital according to international practices, how to strengthen the macro-administration, supervision and control so as to prevent major errors, and how to prevent the foreign investment from leading to inflation.

The administrative department in charge of foreign investment has put forward the proposal of "readjusting the strategy for importing foreign capital," and this has been accepted by many specialists. But as to how to understand the new strategy, different people have different views. Some specialists hold that the new strategy is to shift from quantity to quality, from small projects to major projects, and from a primary form of foreign investment to a higher form of foreign investment.

Others propose that China's strategy for importing foreign capital in the 1990s should be to continue to use foreign capital positively and effectively with the central task of accelerating China's economic development and the goal of promoting the progress in the marketization, legalization and internationalization of the economy.

To import foreign capital at the service of the sustained, stable, healthy and fast development of the Chinese economy is the central point of importing foreign capital. To achieve the goal of economic development in the 1990s, China needs a large amount of capital funds, sophisticated technologies and advanced managerial expertise. The gap between domestic savings and investment, and the gap between the earning and spending of foreign exchanges are to be filled up through the use of foreign capital. The use of foreign capital is in fact an ahead-of-time spending beyond the reach of the present national power, and the need of the strategy of providing an economic jump-start and catching up with and surpassing developed countries. Japan and South Korea have made the full use of foreign investment to achieve fast economic growth. To underline the import of foreign capital at the service of economic modernization and economic development is to prevent the use of foreign debts as a constant means to make up for the financial deficit and the imbalance of international payments, and to prevent the use of large foreign funds for non-productive purposes. Such things have happened in China in recent times and in Latin American and African countries. It resulted in a debt crises and economic stagnation.

To import foreign capital for the marketization of the Chinese economy is a special feature of China's strategy of importing foreign capital, different from other countries. China has imported foreign capital, not only at the service of its economic growth, but also at the service of its reform of the economic system and for the establishment of the socialist market economy. While importing foreign capital, it also introduces international practices of economic operation, the spirit of the legal system, the basic rules under the market economy, and the macro-managerial expertise and micro-operational mechanism which will help to promote China's economic reform. In fact, the development of the economy with foreign investments is placing a higher demand on China's banking system, financial and taxation systems, investment system, foreign trade system and market system. It is promoting the establishment of China's socialist market economic system and promoting China's effort to administer the economy under a legal system. The use of foreign capital in restructuring state-owned enterprises has played an unestimatable role in China's microeconomy.

To import foreign capital to promote the course of legalizing the Chinese economy is likewise unignorable. China has issued many laws and regulations concerning the importing of foreign capital. But some of them can no longer fit in with the importing of foreign capital and administration over the economy with foreign investments, and some can no longer suit the need of administering over the large-scale import of foreign capital. There are still many laws and regulations to be formulated on this issue. Foreign loans should be borrowed in accordance with internationally recognized laws, and this calls for the identity of our laws, the laws concerning the international banking in particular, with international laws and regulations. Thousands of overseas businessmen come to make direct investments in China, and the economy with foreign investments has constantly increased its role in the Chinese economy. This has asked us to administer them by law. Administration by law is an important means to clear up the opaqueness of the policies, an important means to solve the difference in policies that exist among local governments, and an important means to do away with the unlawful acts of foreign businessmen. Therefore, while we are stressing the importance of market guidance for the import of foreign capital, we should put more stress on the importance of administration by law.

To import foreign capital to internationalize the Chinese economy is to raise the importing of foreign capital to the new height of transcending export orientation and the export-oriented economy. It is impossible to import foreign capital without the cooperation of an export orientation strategy, because only by increasing the volume of export, is it possible to solve the problem of paying debts during a time of high-speed development. It can be said that the policy of importing foreign capital must be coordinated with foreign trade policy. Without a correct foreign trade strategy, there will be no successful results in importing foreign capital. However, it is not enough to talk of export orientation. It is not merely a question of trade to increase the ability to pay debts under the condition of ensuring economic growth. There are still many non-trade fields for earning foreign exchanges, such as tourism, international cooperation, etc. Therefore, it is important to develop the export-oriented economy, but this alone is not enough. What is more stressed by the export-oriented economy is the internationalization of the domestic market, not the integration of the domestic economy and foreign economies. It does not touch upon the question of the two-way flow of capital, nor upon the question of participation in the international division of labor and the international market (the international financial market in particular). To import foreign capital is absolutely not merely for the sake of developing industry, but to link with the international financial market and to participate in the operation of the international financial market. In face of the new situation of the link between the Chinese economy and the world economy, it is necessary to set the goal of importing foreign capital to promote the internationalization of the Chinese economy.

(VII) The key at present is to handle well the relationship between market orientation and macro-control in importing foreign capital

We should increase our understanding of the importance of market orientation in importing foreign capital. Market orientation is quite important to the importing of foreign capital, and even more important to the direct import of foreign capital. Domestic resources rely on the basic regulating role of the market, and foreign resources also rely on the basic regulating role of the market. Large investments by foreign businessmen should be guided mainly by the signals of market prices. It is up to the enterprises to analyze the market and make their decisions and up to the foreign businessmen to take the risk in making decisions and business operations. The responsibility of the government is mainly to improve the market situation to ensure that the market mechanism operates normally and the market signals are not distorted. Do not make any rigid rules for the direction of investment for medium-sized and small projects imported by non-governmental organizations, but trust the guiding role of the market and believe that the market will allocate resources to where they are most needed, although the process may be slow. The nationwide change in foreign investments to big projects and major facilities in the last two years is mainly attributed to the role of market guidance, not to the preferential treatment given by the government in this respect. It is precisely because of this that we should shift the preferential policy guidance to market guidance in importing foreign capital. In the early years of importing foreign capital, preferential policies did play a big role in attracting foreign investments, but today, it has become the joint voice of enterprises of all categories of ownership to give national treatment to enterprises with foreign investments. The preferential treatment to enterprises should not be given through the financial channel, but through the market. Only by producing according to market demand is it possible to achieve more profit. The gradual shift in the policy of inclination to the policy of national treatment shall become a major feature of importing foreign capital at a time when China is changing its track. The transition to national treatment should be gradually achieved for products made with foreign investments. In the transitional period, no new preferential policy shall be adopted for enterprises with foreign investments. When conditions permit (chiefly, when the international community understands and the foreign businessmen accept), some of the preferential policies with little impact on foreign investment can be abolished, but this should be implemented with special caution.

There will also be a reassessment of the composition of the sources of foreign capital when we treat it according to the principle of market orientation. For example, a larger proportion of medium- and small-sized capital investments from Hong Kong and Taiwan as well as from overseas Chinese is normal and has more advantages than disadvantages. Modern history tells us that the investments from overseas Chinese have many advantages to the development of the Chinese economy: We don't have to fear their control over the Chinese economy, nor to take their risk. China has more labor power, more village-run enterprises, greater pressure for employment, and a great domestic market. The medium- and small-sized investments from Hong Kong and Taiwan can play their irreplaceable role. The reason why China has much greater achievements than Russia and East European countries in economic reform is the inseparable participation of China's unique economy with investments from the Chinese living in other countries. Transnational companies have many advantages over the medium- and small-sized overseas businesses, such as their advanced technologies, scientific management and strict observance of the laws, but their power to interfere with the Chinese economy brooks no underestimation in the future. Therefore, our policy should be a policy of taking in everything. We should not play down too much the role of the medium and small capital investments, nor just see the advantages of the transnational companies to us. If all regions compete with each other for investments from transnational companies, and all Chinese enterprises vie to set up joint ventures with a small number of transnational companies, it will imperceptibly raise the cost of cooperation, and this is not beneficial. Therefore, we should give equal treatment to all sources of foreign investments. It's quite unnecessary to regard the investment from transnational companies as the only means for the strategic shift in importing foreign capital. It is more advantageous to treat it as commonplace and use the market to guide it.

The other aspect of correctly handling the relationship between market orientation and macro-control in importing foreign capital is to formulate more laws, regulations and policies in this respect. The inadaptability of the administration over foreign investments must be changed: the present situation of importing foreign capital on an especially large scale must be shifted to administration by law and to effective indirect macro-control.

China has promulgated more than 500 statutes concerning foreign affairs and signed investment protection agreements with 55 countries, thus laying down the foundation for the administration over foreign investment by law. However, it is still necessary to improve and perfect the existing statutes and abolish the outdated statutes in accordance with the new system of the socialist market economy. It is necessary to formulate new statutes, standardize the business activities of enterprises with foreign investments and stop all acts that harm China's economic sovereignty or violates international laws.

In order to strengthen indirect macro-control over foreign

investments, we should establish a unified and efficient administrative system and an administrative organization that meets the demand of the socialist market economy. It is necessary to solve the problem of making policy decisions by many departments and the incoordination of different policies in this respect. It is suggested that a national foreign investment policy coordination body be set up to coordinate the work of the different departments concerning the administration over foreign investments, to coordinate the policies concerning the administration over the direct investment by foreign businessmen and to coordinate the policies concerning the loans from and credit to China. It is necessary to strengthen statistical work, and supervision and control over foreign investments and strengthen the administration over the direction and results in the use of foreign debts by the government and over the importing methods and debt composition. It is necessary to predict and prevent possible debt crises with a high degree of alertness. It is necessary to solve the problem of attaching importance to examination for approval and ignoring control, and work out new rules for examination and approval, rules for assessment, and methods of supervision in accordance with the new situation.

To strengthen indirect control, it is necessary to make a distinction between the policy concerning the governmental import of foreign capital and the policy concerning the non-governmental import of foreign capital. As to the non-governmental direct import of foreign capital, it is necessary to strengthen the macro-administration on the basis of giving full play to the role of market regulation, and supervise their definite liabilities and responsibility to repay them. As to joint ventures and other forms of foreign investment established by large or medium-sized state-owned enterprises, it is necessary to exercise administration of different forms on the basis of making clear the ownership of the property rights and protecting state-owned property, and exercise direct administrative management through the government departments concerned. In the administration over the indirect import of foreign capital, it is necessary to follow different policies towards the different debtors. As to the governmental import of foreign capital, it is essential to truly strengthen the administration and exercise direct control. We cannot borrow a large amount of money merely for the micro-results in disregard of the total ability to repay debts and the total balance of the economy of the country. Strict control must be exercised over the projects guaranteed by the government. However, we should give a free hand to the projects with foreign investments established by enterprises which are not owned by the state and take their own risks, and exercise administration over them by law. In importing foreign capital, different policies should be followed for direct and indirect foreign investment, and the administration over governmental import and non-governmental import should also be differentiated. Generally speaking, the policies of inclination we now follow should be used as an internal means of administration for governmental projects with foreign investments, with a stress on projects using government-to-government loans in the indirect import of foreign capital.

Exercise good control over the enterprises with foreign investments according to law. Start with the improvement of the market and legal environments, provide the external conditions for the solution to the problem of losses in the enterprises with foreign investments (the enterprises with real losses). Formulate statutes concerning the enterprises with foreign enterprises, such as laws and regulations in compliance with the international practices concerning products, forms of distribution, procedure of investment, foreign exchange accounts and control over imports and exports so that there are laws for most of the companies and businessmen to observe and it can also help to prevent a small number of overseas businessmen from preparing false loss statements.

Further increase the number of domestic fields for foreign investment. Permit foreign businessmen to use their industrial property (patents and trade marks), special technologies and other invisible property as their capital investments, further open the market, handle matters according to international rules, and use foreign capital to reform and improve the environments for investments. For example, encourage foreign companies to invest in transport facilities and other infrastructure projects. In importing foreign capital, it is necessary to discover and study new forms of investment and joint investment, permit experiments in new form of joint investment that can have a big influence and attach importance to the results of the practice. On the other hand, we must be cautious. When there is no successful experience or opinions differ greatly, be careful to avoid making precipitous decisions. A classified list should be prepared for industrial investments that are under the terms of prohibition, restriction, permission and encouragement. However, the composition of foreign investments will be optimized mainly through market regulation. Continue to encourage overseas businessmen, including businessmen from Taiwan and Hong Kong, to make investments in China. The policies will not make restrictions on the scale of investment and technological level, but will guide and encourage overseas businessmen to enlarge the scale of investment and raise the technological level. By improving the environments for investments, we will encourage more and more big companies and transnational companies to make investments in China.

Attain the goal of macro-indirect administration by setting up intermediary organizations, such as accounting offices, lawyer's offices, auditing offices and consulting offices.

(VIII) Accelerate the development of capital-intensive and technology-intensive industries to reduce the influence of linking the tracks of domestic and international markets on the domestic price rise

As a result of opening the country wider and wider to the outside world, the process of linking the tracks of the domestic market and the international market has gradually speeded up. This is an unignorable factor that effects price rises in China at present.

The price differences between domestic products and foreign products are divided into three categories: farm and sideline products, common labor, daily necessities, the prices of which are far lower than the international prices, obviously having the character of welfare supplies; the domestic prices of capital-intensive and technology-intensive products of the heavy and chemical industries, such as motor vehicles, machinery and equipment, are far higher than the international prices, among them, passenger cars and some equipment, which are five times higher than the international prices, some even ten or several dozen times higher; the domestic prices of labor-intensive textiles and light industrial products are between the above-mentioned two categories, mostly under the international price level.

In recent years, China opened itself wider and wider to the outside world, the total volume of imports and exports at present accounts for as high as 40% of the GNP, the number of commodities controlled by quotas and other measures has been decreasing constantly, and most of the commodities are being imported and exported freely, helping to link the tracks of the domestic market and the international market. When international prices are higher, domestic products flow out; and when domestic prices are higher, imports increase. Judging from the three categories of commodities, as the tracks of the domestic and international markets link together, the prices of basic daily necessities and services in China are bound to rise year by year. Moreover, since the prices of these consumer goods and services are less and less controlled, price increases are sure to be quicker and quicker. The prices of export farm products, semi-finished products, resource commodities, light industrial products and textiles will be pushed up as a result of reduced domestic supplies. The prices for imports of machinery, equipment and other technology-intensive products are tougher. Large imports will lead to acute shortages of foreign exchanges and the fall of the exchange rate of RMB, thus becoming an important factor for inflation in China. In the last two years, RMB has been depreciated by more than 30%. In other words, the prices of these imports have risen by more than 30% in terms of RMB. China's volume of imports accounts for one fourth of its GNP, and attention should be paid to this factor regarding inflation in China.

Accelerate the development of capital-intensive and technology-intensive industries to reduce the influence of linking domestic and international market prices on price increases in China. The stress will be laid on accelerating the development of machinery, electronics, motor vehicles and important raw and processed materials for which there will be a great market demand in the future and most of which are imported at present, so as to replace the imports. This will mean killing three birds with one stone in controlling prices. One, the development of these industries in China will help the products of these industries to greatly shorten the distance between them and the foreign products of the same type in quality, grade and technological level, cut down production costs considerably, thus reducing high prices, and at the same time offsetting part of the influence of the rise in basic living expenses on the total price level. Two, as domestic products increase their competitive power in quality and price, domestic demand will shift from imports to domestic supply, thus alleviating pressure on the balance of foreign exchange and reducing the influence of the depreciated exchange rate on the prices. Three, as a result of reducing the reliance on imports, we can reduce or stop imports when the international market prices rise because of short supply, thus reducing or avoiding the influence of imported inflation on domestic prices.

II. Tighten the Exchange Control and Gradually Effect the Full Convertibility of RMB

(I) Fully estimate the direct influence of the exchange rate fluctuations and exchange reserve on inflation, and adopt measures, including the issuance of government bonds, to reduce the pressure of foreign exchange on inflation

The inflation in 1993-1994 was directly related to the major change in the foreign exchange: One, the blind fluctuations in the market exchange rates in 1993 greatly pushed up the general price level. In early 1993, the regulating market exchange rate was 6.8 yuan RMB/1 U.S. dollar, but in the middle of the year, the bexchange rate rose blindly to 10 yuan RMB/1 U.S. dollar. After the government adopted measures, the market exchange rate dropped quickly. However, the radical fluctuations of the exchange rate affected people's confidence in RMB and led to the price rise. Moreover, the prices of imported goods have found it difficult to fall back to their original level after they rose as a result of the exchange price. Two, after the double exchange rates became a single rate in 1994, the government reduced the exchange rate and RMB was depreciated, thus greatly increasing the cost of production for the imported means of production, machinery and equipment and pushing up the prices. Three, the foreign exchange reserve at present is too big, and as a result, the money supply also increased greatly. The money supply for the exchange reserve now accounts for 67% of the newly-increased money supply, thus increasing the pressure of inflation.

As a result of the reform and opening, the Chinese economy has grown swiftly, and many foreign investors have suddenly realized that China is a very big potential market. Beginning in 1993, large amounts of foreign capital flowed into China. The actual flow of foreign capital into China in 1994 alone equaled to more than half of that in the developing countries. It was only second behind the United States as compared with the developed countries. Such a big flow of foreign capital has had a tremendous influence on China's macroeconomy.

Generally speaking, large foreign capital inflows influence inflation through the following channels: First, as a result of the increased foreign investments, the demand for domestic raw materials and labor will lead to a short supply at home and increase inflation pressure. Second, as a result of foreign capital inflow, if the government decides to increase the trade deficit, it will help alleviate inflation, because large imports will ease the short supply. Third, if foreign exchange reserves increase swiftly, there will be the pressure of money appreciation, and more importantly, it will increase the money supply of a country. In many countries, the money supplied can be bought back by the government by issuing bonds, but it will lead to an interest rate rise. In China, we adopt the method of increasing the exchange reserve because of the favorable balance of trade, but we have not withdrawn the oversupplied money, nor have we withdrawn it enough through the issuance of bonds. Fourth, when a large amount of foreign capital flows in, there is also a great demand for domestic capital funds to match it. This also exerts a great influence on the demand for domestic currency. Fifth, the large inflow of short-term capital is very likely to create a foam economy.

A traditional idea has prevailed for a long time: that both a favorable balance of trade and an increasing exchange reserve are good things. But there must be a limit. If the trade surplus is too big and the reserve is too large, we should also pay attention to their unfavorable influence on the economy. A developing country like ours should adopt the policy of unfavorable balance of trade, not the policy of favorable balance of trade. Fast economic growth calls for the inflow of resources. However, from the angle of goods, a favorable balance of trade essentially means the outflow of goods. Countries like South Korea and Thailand maintained an unfavorable balance of trade for a very long period of time, because with a large favorable balance of payments, there is no need to limit it to the large favorable balance of trade. Strategically speaking, a favorable balance of trade restricts our economic growth, and causes the loss and shortage of resources. As a counter measure, we can maintain a high exchange reserve. At the same time, we must issue bonds to recall the increased amount of money. However, it is very difficult to issue bonds at present, and therefore, it is not feasible. Strategically, it is now a good time to increase imports, and it will help us to join GATT. Now all kinds of pressure are urging us to practice free trade and accelerate exchange reform. Since we have a large exchange reserve, we can accelerate our foreign trade reform, reduce trade barriers, increase imports and increase the inflow of resources into our country. Another better choice is to encourage the outflow of capital. Of course, we cannot encourage the outflow of capital in a short time, but in fact we have had large amounts of capital flowing out every year. This can be seen clearly on the capital balance sheet. It's better for the government to make a long-term and definite policy for the standardization of capital outflow than to allow enterprises to flow capital out covertly to no avail by paying a high tuition fee. Moreover, the outflow funds should be spent on production projects. China's investment in other countries is an inevitable road to take. The development in the "four small dragons" shows that it is insufficient to open the market of developing countries merely through trade. Only through trade with funds, that is, setting up factories with investments and bringing our finished products, semi-finished products, raw materials and processed materials to them, can we break open the market of the developing countries. This is welcome to them. Just as many developed countries have joined the Chinese market, it was impossible for them to join it merely through trade. They must rely on investment to help it. To reduce the risk, China should also do the same. The government should give detailed considerations to the question of investments in other countries.

The blind fluctuations of market exchange rates drastically pushed up the general price level. The Chinese economy is now widely opened, and the total value of import commodities has accounted for around one fourth of the GNP. The price level of imported raw materials, processed materials, semi-finished products, parts and accessories, and complete sets of equipment has been greatly influenced by the regulating market exchange rate. In early 1993, the regulating market exchange rate was 6.8 yuan RMB/1 U.S. dollar, but it rose to 10 yuan RMB/1 U.S. dollar or even higher in the middle of the year as a result of the unfounded anticipation at home and the press rumors abroad. The exchange control administration provided wrong information, ignored the fact that there was a net outflow of capital for years on end, and stressed that the exchange rate rise was due to domestic economic growth and the imbalance of the market supply of foreign exchanges. This could only aggravate rush purchases of foreign exchange. The central government adopted macro-control measures, and the market exchange prices fell quickly as a result. However, the prices were held steady. The prices of some imported goods did drop, but it was almost impossible for them to go back to the previous level.

Put an end to the large net capital outflow as quickly as possible. First of all, see to it that the foreign exchange reserve in the bank does not increase. Strict control must be exercised over capital outflow projects, bank transfer deposits and the purchase of foreign negotiable securities in particular. A practical policy should be made concerning the investment outside China, and blind investment should be restricted. Carrying large sums of foreign currencies out of the country should also be limited. At the same time, encourage foreign currency loans and investments at home.

(II) The government should adopt a policy to stabilize exchange rates and avoid blind exchange rate fluctuations and appreciation of RMB

It is necessary to maintain the exchange rate at a reasonable level so as to ensure that RMB will be fully convertible. Usually, when domestic inflation is higher than in other countries, the exchange rate is expected to drop. However, the exchange rate in China has risen at present. Once China returns to GATT, the fully open market may give rise to the appreciation of RMB in a given period of time. The appreciation helps to check inflation in a short period, but from a long-term point of view, it is detrimental. It will increase the production cost of exports and give rise to the pressure of exchange rate fluctuation, encouraging domestic capital funds to flow out, and in the end lead to a drastic drop in the exchange reserve or the depreciation of RMB.

(III) Accelerate the establishment of a unified exchange market and gradually effect the full convertibility of RMB

The regulating exchange market should be merged with the inter-bank exchange market. If the two markets cannot be merged for the time being, we should gradually abolish the regulating exchange market. It is necessary to greatly develop the inter-bank exchange market.

It is necessary to effect the full convertibility of regular accounts and remove the restrictions over the exchange supply to non-trade projects. Accelerate reform in the banking system, strengthen and improve the functions of the central bank, establish a developed commercial bank system, fully develop the capital market and exchange market and accelerate the establishment of the international financial center so as to absorb foreign capital flow and deposits.

III. Make Full and Good Use of International Exchange to Regulate Supply and Demand at Home

(I) Make use of the favourable condition of the present exchange reserve to properly increase imports, and use international exchange to regulate supply and demand at home

When the international balance of payments and the exchange reserve are very strong at present, we should think of reducing the import restrictions to regulate the domestic market supply and demand. Fundamentally speaking, inflation is caused by the contradiction between supply and demand. To use the international exchange to make up for the shortage of the domestic structural production and regulate the domestic market supply and demand is an effective measure to check inflation. It is necessary to use the guiding plan and economic means to encourage the import of raw and processed materials, semi-finished products and some products, of which there is a relative shortage at home. The import plan should have greater foresight and flexibility, and avoid the phenomena that some goods are imported insufficiently or excessively. When the exchange reserve is fairly strong, we can think of removing some of the import restrictions to increase imports.

(II) Accelerate and perfect the reform of the foreign trade system, and practice a policy of orientation for export to reduce the outflow of resources

The mutual combination and supplementation between the domestic economy and the international economy means the full use of two kinds of resources (domestic and international), two markets (domestic and international), and the combination of production elements to achieve the optimum allocation of resources advantageous to the country and the relatively optimum mutual supplementation. This is the inevitable trend of large-scale socialized production and the development of the world economy. With the world economy internationalized, the international division of labor intensified among countries, and the mutual dependence for existence and mutual relations deepened, the domestic economy of one country and the international economy will be mutually combined and supplemented.

The mutual combination and supplementation of the domestic economy and the international economy is the successful experience of many countries (the four small dragons in Asia, for example) in fostering their economic growth. It is also the practical experience of China in its economic development since 1978. In a word, the mutual combination and supplementation of the domestic economy and the international economy in one country is beneficial to the participation in international competition and international economic cooperation, to the full use of the two markets and two kinds of resources for the optimum allocation of resources, and to the standardization of foreign trade according to international standards for the constant increase of total national power and international competitive power.

The pre-requisites for the mutual combination and supplementation of one country's domestic economy and the international economy are: an independent and all-inclusive industrial system, a given technological and managerial level, a market economy system, and an economic operation mechanism compatible with the international economic standards. China has already acquired the first two pre-requisites, but not yet acquired the last two pre-requisites which are precisely the foundation and targets for China's reform in its foreign trade system. To push forward the reform in the foreign trade system is the key for China to achieve the mutual combination and supplementation of its domestic economy and the international economy.

An outstanding question at present is to improve the macro-control of foreign trade. The market is not all-powerful. It has spontaneity. It needs macro-control. The three principles for macro-control over foreign trade are the compliance with the needs of the market economy, compliance with international standards and compliance with China's national conditions so as to make the full use of the two kinds of resources and the two markets and achieve the mutual combination and mutual supplementation of the domestic economy and the international economy. The macro-control over the foreign trade should be shifted from direct control to indirect control. In accordance with the existing conditions of macro-control of foreign trade in China, we should establish and improve the foreign trade coordination mechanism, complement the foreign trade statutes and policies, improve the administration over imports and exports, and improve the administration over direct foreign investments.

1. Improve the foreign trade coordination mechanism.

In accordance with the needs of the market economic system, the government department in charge should no long directly control the business activities of foreign trade enterprises, but chiefly exercise macro-control through the economic means of interest rates, tax rates, exchange rates, price signals and industrial policies. In recent years, some new problems have cropped up as a result of the extension of the independent decision-making power of foreign trade enterprises and the weakening of the administrative binding force of the government department in charge. For example, some enterprises raised prices to purchase goods at home and sell goods to other countries at reduced prices in blind competition. China suffered from anti-dumping several times in 1993; some enterprises resold their permits and quotas to get profit from rent; some enterprises transferred goods illegally; and some enterprises sold fake and inferior goods. The macro-control of foreign trade calls for the intensified role of the intermediate organization.

As the medium organization between the government department in charge and the foreign trade enterprises, the Import and

Export Chamber of Commerce can combine organically the governmental function of macro-control with the business function of the foreign trade enterprises. The measures of macro-control taken by the government shall become the rules and compulsory will through discussion by the Import and Export Chamber of Commerce and be obeyed by all foreign trade enterprises effectively.

The Import and Export Chamber of Commerce represents the interests of foreign trade enterprises. Its function and role are coordination and service. It is not a correct idea and practice to turn the Import and Export Chamber of Commerce into an administrative organ of the government and make its power administrative. Only by preserving the special feature of the Import and Export Chamber of Commerce as a trade association and regarding it as a third party between the government and the enterprises, can it play the role of fair coordination and service.

In the light of the present conditions in China, the principal mission of the Import and Export Chamber of Commerce is to maintain the economic order of the foreign trade market, supervise and guide foreign trade enterprises to do business lawfully, and check on illegal acts of business, organize or represent its member enterprises to bring up or accept suits against dumping, subsidies and monopoly, convey the requests of enterprises to the government, provide information and advice to enterprises, distribute export quotas and permits for the industry, call for bids and conduct auction as entrusted by the government, and represent the industry in making contact with and making exchanges with other countries.

Apart from giving full play to the role of the Import and Export Chamber of Commerce, we should also improve the supervisory and service functions of the foreign trade lawyer's offices and accounting and auditing offices and give play to the information and service functions of the consulting organs, research organs, societies and associations.

2. Complement the foreign trade statutes and policies.

The foreign trade statutes and policies are the system by which the government uses its administrative power in accordance with the market economic operation mechanism, international standards and the national conditions, and which the subjects of the market must observe. The purpose is to put the economic acts of the subjects of the market on a reasonable, orderly basis.

In China's practice of foreign trade, the construction of foreign trade statutes lags behind. It is manifested in the following aspects: First, insufficient standardization. It is manifested in the differences among the different regions and the differences of the different subjects of the market. The policies of regional inclination and the tactics of regional progress have revealed many problems, such as the local protectionism and administrative monopoly and separation, the difficulty in establishing a unified socialist market, and the lopsided regional flow of domestic capital. State-owned foreign trade enterprises, enterprises with overseas investments, and village-run enterprises, which are the subjects of the market, enjoy different policy treatments, thus affecting the establishment of a market environment of equal competition. Second, insufficient transparency and insufficient openness. The administrative approval for imports and the system of import permits are in the grey condition, while the mandatory planning and guiding planning are in the black condition. The protective subsidies for state-owned foreign trade enterprises with losses do not comply with international standards.

Attention should be paid to the uniformness and transparency of foreign trade statutes and policies in the construction of foreign trade statutes and policies in China. The uniformness of foreign trade statutes and policies calls for the uniformness and coordination of all aspects of foreign trade statutes and policies and the standarization of all aspects of the market, and the foreign trade statutes and policies of all localities must not contradict the foreign trade statutes and policies of the central government, but obey them. The policy of regional inclination must gradually change to the policy of industrial inclination, as it is beneficial to the improvement of China's industrial structure and to the establishment of a unified socialist market. All subjects of the market must not seek preferential treatment with the extra-market power. They can only do business according to law, compete equally and make independent choices in the face of the two markets. The transparency of the foreign trade statutes and policies calls for the openness of the foreign trade statutes and policies to all subjects of the market. This is the pre-requisite for the subjects of the market to do business lawfully, effectively and in an orderly fashion. China has already promulgated the Foreign Trade Law and the Law Against Illegal Competition. It will also promulgate the Anti-Subsidy Law, Anti-Dumping Law and Rules of Conduct for Enterprises.

3. Perfect the administration over imports and exports.

Under the conditions of the socialist market economy, the foreign trade plan can make up for the insufficiency of market regulation. The stress of the regulations by the foreign trade plan should be put on the rules of the total strategy of the foreign trade: total balance, speed guidance, structural readjustment and interest coordination. In the administration by the foreign trade plan, there is still mandatory planning. It should change to one of guided planning. Guided planning can help to solve the contradiction between state-owned foreign trade enterprises assuming sole responsibility for gain and loss and the mandatory import and export plans. Guided plans should be implemented for import and export quotas, export earnings and import payments of foreign trade enterprises. Total quota control should be exercised over the large imports and exports of major commodities that have close bearing on the national economy and the livelihood of people. The competition mechanism should be introduced into planned management. A standard bidding system for the government purchases should be established.

The overelaborate procedure of approval through examination for imports has no transparency, and it is not permitted by international trade standards. It is likely to lead to the occurrence of advantage-seeking phenomena. The administrative procedure of approval through examination must be simplified to increase transparency.

In 1993, China's import increase was 21 percentage points higher than its export increase and the trade deficit was U.S.$

12.18 billion. To a developing country, an appropriate trade deficit is normal, because domestic construction needs high technologies and new equipment. The way of eliminating the deficit can only be to increase exports, not to reduce imports. The major measures to increase exports at present are: perfect the drawbacks for exports, simplify the procedure and make drawbacks in time; develop export credit policy, provide credit and risk guaranty for exports, improve measures to organize exports, such as organizing and participating in trade fairs, strengthen the construction of the information network, strengthen the administration of goods transfer, reduce trade disputes and improve measures for special economic zones.

The measures to regulate imports must comply with international standards and meet the needs of protecting China's national industries.

As a means of regulating imports, tariffs are one of the international standards and are recognized by GATT. It is transparent. It must be understood that high tariffs must not necessarily help to protect the national industries, and that inappropriately high tariffs may encourage the subjects of the market not to seek progress nor take the initiative to take part in market competition and cause consumers to suffer losses. The problems in China's tariff policy are: the tariff structure is not reasonable, the tariff rates are too high, the preferential treatment for tariffs varies from region to region, and there are too many temporary tariff reductions and local exemptions. Make appropriate adjustments to tariffs on raw materials, semi-finished products and finished products to raise China's level of industrialization. Reduction of tariffs is an urgent matter, and it is what is demanded from China by some nations party to the GATT. They should be reduced to the general level of the developing countries. The different preferential treatments for tariffs in different regions affects the establishment of a market environment in China that has equal competition. It should be reformed in the direction of establishing national treatment.

The use of the competition mechanism to standardize the granting of the quotas and permits has proved effective in all countries in controlling quotas and permits. It helps to avoid unfair distribution, the advantage-seeking acts of enterprises and corruption of government officials. Through open bidding with compensations, the government get most of the monopoly profit for its revenues. The foreign trade enterprises can transfer them with compensations conditionally after they get the quotas and permits through competition and bidding.

To promote the development of foreign trade, it is necessary to extend the business scope of foreign trade, to grant enterprises the decision-making power in imports and exports, remove the general import and export restrictions step by step, and accelerate the institution of open bidding and auction system on import and export quotas.

It is necessary to strictly control the exports of domestic raw and processed materials and primary products, especially the export of resources of which there is a great shortage at home, and encourage the export of processed products with high added value.

Set up a mechanism, which can be adjusted in time the import and export of major commodities, strengthen the organization of imports and exports of some major commodities, and readjust the quantities of imports and exports of major commodities to ensure the domestic market supply and check market price rises. The foreign exchange and funds needed for the import of major commodities must be guaranteed with priority.

(III) Deepen the Reform of the Border Area Trade and Establish Transnational Economic Cooperation Zones

In recent years, a new model of inter-regional cooperation —transnational economic cooperation zones—has been developing swiftly in Asia. Transnational economic cooperation zones, or growing triangular zones, are a new form of economic cooperation in a small scale along the border areas of several countries. Through the special policies adopted by these countries for these zones, they give full scope to the mutual supplementation of their economies to set up transnational all-embracing economic zones which mainly absorb foreign capital to expand foreign trade.

They do business in many areas, including production, trade, transport, telecommunications, energy, tourism and the development of natural and human resources.

The transnational economic cooperation zone has the following characteristics:

1. Its scope of establishment involves only a part of a country's area. If it succeeds, the country benefits greatly. If it fails, its unfavorable influence can be restricted. Therefore, the political and economic risk is small.

2. It can make use of the resources and markets of several countries at the same time, and give full play to the mutual supplementariness of their economies.

3. It has an export-oriented economic form, and can make full use of resources, capital funds and markets of the nonmember countries.

4. It is a type of overall economic cooperation, and the cooperation in all fields supplements each other and promotes for common progress.

5. It has a good prospect for expansion. When the time is ripe, the participating countries can extend the scope of cooperation to other areas of their countries.

In 1989, Goh Chok Tong, Deputy Prime Minister of Singapore at that time, used the term "growing triangular zone" for the first time to describe the economic cooperation zone comprising Singapore, Johore of Malaysia and the Riau Archipelago of Indonesia. Supported and coordinated by the governments of the three countries, large-scale economic cooperation is being quickly formed in the zone, and 30% of Singapore's companies and firms have set up factories in Johore and on the islands.

People have also called the economic cooperation of the special economic zones in China's Guangdong and Fujian provinces with Hong Kong and Taiwan the South China Triangular Zone. As it started early, the large-scale economic cooperation has extended to the Pearl River Delta and even to the whole areas of Guangdong and Fujian.

The third cooperation zone is centered in the Tumen River Delta, comprising the border areas of northeast China, Russia and the Democratic People's Republic of Korea. Japan, the Republic of Korea and Mongolia have cooperated in the zone in different forms. The whole cooperation zone will receive an investment of 30 billion U.S. dollars. It is expected to be built into a large commodity collecting and distributing center similar to Rotterdam and Hong Kong.

The fourth cooperation zone is also called the Northern Triangular Zone of ASEAN. It includes the four northern border provinces of Malaysia, the five adjoining southern provinces of Thailand, and the two northern provinces of Sumatra, Indonesia. Organized by the Asian Development Bank, a ten-year development plan has been completed after a year of preparation. The governments of the three countries are organizing forces to implement this plan.

The last cooperation zone is the Eastern Triangular Zone of ASEAN. It includes Davao of the Philippines, Eastern Malaysia and Menado of Indonesia. The summit meetings of the three governments have included the development of this zone in the long-term plans of their countries, and preparations have already started. The Asian Development Bank recently decided to take part in the planning work of the zone.

The biggest characteristic of the economies of the big countries is diversification. Apart from taking an active part in all forms of economic cooperation in the Asian-Pacific region, China should also make full use of the model of transnational economic cooperation to promote its cooperation with neighboring countries. It has a vast territory and friendly relations with many countries. From a realistic point of view, the areas where there is a brisk border trade can possibly be grown into transnational economic cooperation zones.

The establishment of more transnational economic cooperation zones in China has important practical significance.

First, the establishment of transnational economic cooperation zones is an idea for deepening the reform of border trade. In recent years, China has made fairly good achievements in border trade. However, it should also be seen that border trade in many areas has been greatly limited. This is because without the close cooperation of the related countries, it is difficult to enlarge the scale of border trade and protract it. Without the help of the cooperation in other fields, it is also very difficult to develop the border trade effectively. The transnational economic cooperation zones precisely solve these two problems.

Second, the establishment of transnational economic cooperation zones can narrow the development gap among the regions. Most of the border areas in China are inhabited by people of minority nationalities and are economically underdeveloped. Since the reform started and China began to open to the outside world, the gap between them and the coastal areas has been further enlarged. The greatest advantage of these areas is their geographical positions. The establishment of transnational economic cooperation zones to strengthen their economic exchanges with the neighboring countries and give play to their unique advantages is shortcut to accelerate the economic growth in these areas. This is different from the general development zones. Give some financial support to and adopt special policies for these areas, and the other zones have no reason to compare with them.

Third, by establishing transnational economic cooperation zones, China can find markets in neighboring developing countries. At present, China's export markets are overconcentrated in a few developed countries. There bears a certain risk both economically and politically. Japan and the four small dragons in Asia all experienced the process of spreading their markets from developed countries to the developing countries. The success of other countries shows that it is insufficient to rely only on traditional means to find markets in developing countries. Very often, many countries rely on capital exports to pave the way for commodity exports. For example, they establish joint ventures to export their finished products, semi-finished products, machinery, equipment and technologies. It can be foreseen that China will also take this road in the near future. Most of our neighboring countries are now still in the primary stage of development. We can show our comparative advantages by making investments in these regions. Likewise, by absorbing their investments and resources, our market can also obtain what we don't have so as to help meet each other's needs.

Fourth, with transnational economic cooperation zones support and participation of other countries is easier to get. Just like China, most of the areas of other countries neighboring China are economically underdeveloped, and their governments are all eager to develop the economies in these areas. Only if we present good plans and there is the prospect of mutual benefit and common prosperity, will transnational economic cooperation zones be accepted by other countries.

Last, from the long-term point of view, the establishment of transnational economic cooperation zones is the best measure to maintain an enduring stability at the border areas.

Although the transnational economic cooperation zones have many advantages, experience has to be accumulated before more are established. It is suggested that experiments be started in one or two areas where conditions are ripe. When the experiments are successful, the lessons learned can be used to popularize cooperation zones in other areas. Concrete measures for the implementation follow:

(1) Entrust the government department in charge to make an overall study of the available experience of all countries. And then form several groups, and with the support and participation of local governments, start investigations and research, and put forward their primary cooperation proposals.

(2) The foreign affairs departments or friendship associations with foreign countries or other people's organizations should put forward cooperation proposals to the governments of other countries. After a series of talks, both parties should reach common understanding on the basic issues.

(3) The governments of both countries jointly put forward their request for help and financial aid regarding the cooperation plan to international organizations such as the Asian Development Bank and the World Bank. International experience shows that as the economic cooperation involves a great deal of interests, plans formulated by a neutral organization are easier to be accepted.

(4) Under the leadership of the international organization,

work out a concrete plan for economic cooperation in around six months, including policy and project proposals.

(5) The government departments concerned of both countries examine and finalize the plans and put forward concrete measures for the implementation of the plan.

After active preparations for a period of time, an economic cooperation zone of considerable size can be put into operation.

Chapter 5
Curbing Inflation while Perfecting Macro-Control

I. Macro-Control Under the Pressure of Inflation

(I) It is necessary to reach a common consensus of the necessity of strengthening macro-control. To seek development, enterprises should not place their hope on raising prices and borrowing money, and local governments should keep the overall situation in mind

Since the malpractice of the investment system is the root cause of China's inflation, a fundamental measure to avoid inflation is to reform the traditional investment system and set up a restriction mechanism for investment. However, the substantial stage of this reform started only in 1994, and you cannot expect immediate results from it. For the present, we can only depend on effective macro-control, including macro-control by economic means, administrative means, legal means and discipline. Therefore, it has urged us to acquire a common consensus on some questions relating to macro-control so that all of us will work with one mind to sincerely attend to the affairs of the whole nation.

1. The question of the necessity of government interference.

As people follow the question of prices with increasing interest, the central and local governments have strengthened their interference with administration over and checks on market prices. The price mechanism is indeed the most important mechanism in the operation of the market economy. However, it has never been all-powerful. Moreover, its formation and functioning call for a relatively perfect market system, fitting economic environments and a legal system. There must also be a risk restriction mechanism for enterprises, which are the subjects fixing the prices. Don't think that everything is fine once restrictions on prices are removed. The countries that have a free market like the United States, Japan, Germany and France have all tightened their control over prices. The prices of major commodities and services that have close bearings on the people's livelihood including oil, coal, air transport, public housing, real estate, rice, cigarettes and salt are all under the direct control of the government. As to fixing prices of commodities and services not under the direct control of the government, there are complete sets of statutes to be observed and government interference is frequent. The socialist market economy system in China is still being established, and after price restrictions are removed, the government cannot let things go uncontrolled. The price increase planned for 1993 was 6%, but the actual increase was 13%. Most of the seven percentage points above the plan was due to the lack of standards or even violations of the laws. Therefore, we must reduce the percentage points of unstandard and unlawful price increases to the minimum through macro-control.

2. The question of changing the way of thinking about development.

The high rate of the economic growth in China in recent years has been rarely seen in the post-war world history. The annual average growth rate in the 18 years of fast economic growth in post-war Japan (1956-1973) was 9.7%. The highest rate of 13.5% was witnessed in 1961. Counting from the early 1980s, both the average growth rate and the highest growth rate in China have surpassed those of Japan of that time. Compared with the peripheral countries of Thailand, Malaysia and Indonesia, China is also a frontrunner. However, the growth rate of our actual economic results is not as high as theirs. One of the reasons is that there has been no substantial change in the development road of the extending management mainly with enlarged reproduction, which we have taken in the past years. From 1950 to 1973, the annual average rate of investment in Japan was around 29%. From 1950 to 1960, the annual rate of investment was 23.8% in

West Germany, 21% in Italy, and under 20% in the United States, Britain and France. The highest was only 33% when South Korea jump-started its economic growth. In China, it was above 30% in six of the nine years between 1985 and 1993, and the highest was 37.7% in 1993. Data shows that the results and the growth rate were best, and the prices were stable when the rate of investment was kept within 30%. To achieve a high growth rate through a high rate of investment, the inevitable results are low results and high prices. Therefore, there must be a new way of thinking. We should really change to the track of improving the economic results instead of continuing to take the old road of blindly seeking the growth rate of output value and extending the scale of investment. From the viewpoint of checking inflation, it is quite necessary to change the way of thinking for development.

3. The question of the relationship between macroeconomy and microeconomy.

Now, there are loud voices calling for raising the prices of products and also for more bank loans. To handle these two questions correctly, it is necessary to have a correct understanding of the dialectical relationship between microeconomy and macroeconomy. It is natural that enterprises hope to have the prices of their products raised, but the indiscriminate raising of prices under the pressure of this anticipation will not only lead to a rise in the general price level, but also deprive their own products of competitive power. Therefore, the correct road to eliminating losses and increasing profits is to change their mechanism, improve the management, rely on science and technology to raise quality, reduce the cost and make their products marketable. They should not place their hopes on raising prices. It is also natural that enterprises hope to have more loans from the bank when they are short of funds, but if the banks grant whatever is requested to increase the funds for overstocked goods, it will not only lead to inflation, but will also make the debt burdens of the enterprises even heavier. Since the fourth quarter of 1993, the People's Bank of China has increased the number of loans granted, and the total sum of loans is no longer small. The question of funds shortages should be solved through different channels; the most important thing is to control the total scale of investment in fixed assets and stop its continued expansion.

Anyone who does not take the overall situation into consideration can hardly do anything good for a region. Only when he has the whole situation in mind can he move every piece well on the chessboard. As the reform develops, more and more regions are now playing their own chess games. There is no reason for criticism when every region concentrates on its own game, but any local game is inseparable from the national game. If all regions want to play their local games well, they have to work with one heart and one mind, and take care of everyone in the same boat.

(II) The Fundamental Cause for the Powerlessness of the Macro-Control Policies

Since the beginning of the reform, indirect macro-control policies have formed a relatively complete system, and the market mechanism has been playing a more and more important role in economic operations. However, the problems of the undesirable structure and especially the drawn-out undesirable economic results have shown that the macroeconomic control policies in China have not yet played their due role. The cause is usually not that these policies are to blame, but that the micro-foundation for these policies to play their role is weak, and the delayed reform of the property rights system of enterprises has restricted the results of the implementation of the macro-control policies. Now the frictions and contradictions arising from the delayed reform have developed to such a stage that if we do not really do something to reform the property rights system of the enterprises, there is no foundation for the existence of macro-control policies.

The cyclic imbalance of the operation of the macroeconomy in China is usually believed to be caused by macro-control policies, but so far as the foundation of the system is concerned, the micro-levels, especially the enterprise level, have a deeper influence. It is precisely the latter that forms the foundation for the formation of macro-control policies, which people usually ignore.

Without a strong micro-foundation, it is impossible for the macroeconomic control policies to obtain their due results. Because the macro-control policies which do not fit the micro-foundation are often twisted or obtain opposite results in the antagonistic economic acts of the micro-levels, such friction or antagonism results in tremendous economic cost and social cost.

What we call the micro-foundation for macro-control is referred to as the micro-foundation for the market economic system. It means that the inhabitants, owners of the elements, and the enterprises, owners of the products, and labor services exist, the border of property rights between them is clear, and they treat each other as equal owners of commodities. Without this prerequisite, exchange is impossible, and the market cannot be established. Only when the operation of the market loses its balance, because of its congenital defects, is the government needed to make necessary regulation from outside. The purpose of such regulation is to maintain the market order for fair competition.

We find it necessary to investigate the current conditions in China in this respect.

First, as a result of the reforms in the employment and wage systems and the stress on distribution according to work and material benefit, the consciousness of the labor power being owned by the laborer himself has been evidently intensified, and the property right of the labor power has been made clearer and clearer.

Second, after the reform, the ownership and the business operation right are separated, the operator of an enterprise is no longer the equivalent of a government official, but a staff member of the enterprise who has a business operation right and is engaged in operation and management.

In this way, the relations of the property rights of state-owned enterprises, between the right of the business operators and the right of the laborers are defined and demarcated. They act more and more according to the principle of maximum gains.

However, in state-owned enterprises, the property is owned by the state, but because there is no form of personification, they are still in a state of nobody assuming the responsibility.

Although many measures have been worked out and adopted in the hope of establishing personified representatives for state-owned properties, all individuals who represent the interests of the state-owned properties are the representatives of their individual interests. In this sense, they also tend to safeguard their individual interests.

Conditioned by the factor of this property right system, the variable input of macro-policies is often distorted.

1. The simple change in the operation mechanism without touching on property rights makes financial policy control powerless.

From an overall point of view, the controlling power of financial policies over the economy is being weakened. The rate of imbalance of the state revenues and expenditures (the percentage of the deficit to the total revenues and expenditures) dropped gradually once since the reform was started, but it has been on the rise again in recent years. It shows that so far as the system of macro-control policies is concerned, the energy of the primary reform has been mostly released, and the bottleneck of the system has become an outstanding problem.

Take tax policies as an example. Since the reform started, tax policies have effectively promoted the development of the economy through preferential treatment, tax reductions and cuts in the profit delivered to the state. However, these policies no longer play positive role any more.

In the last few years, the proportion of state expenditures to the GNP has fallen year by year: 0.31 in 1978 to 0.18 in 1992, a decrease of nearly 42%. The role of state expenditures in the economy—the output elasticity fluctuated greatly, the average output coefficient of elasticity was 1.5851 during the Sixth Five-Year Plan (1981-1985) and 1.1714 during the Seventh Five-Year Plan (1986-1990). It rose slightly in the first two years of the Eighth Five-Year Plan. However, the general trend shows that the promoting role and controlling power of state expenditure on the economy are weakening.

From the angle of the micro-level, the weakening role of financial policies is obviously the accumulated effect of the current contract financial system. A universally acknowledged defect of the contract system is the contracted responsibility for profit, but not for loss. As a result, the macro-taxation effect is that when an enterprise profits more, the government gets none, and the extra part above the contracted target becomes the consumption funds of the individuals, but when an enterprise loses, the government has to bear the loss by giving a subsidy. From the angle of dynamic equilibrium, the total tax volume of the state will be progressively lower than the expected level (namely, the actual losses will offset the increases).

The contract system also leads to the expansion of investment. This is because the interests of the enterprise contractors and the laborers are directly related with the rise of the investment. The rise of investment means a rise in state-owned resources under their control, and this enables them to get more material benefit through the contracted quotas. Moreover, the extension of the enterprise helps to increase their weight in the state management system. As these factors act, the expansion of investment is unavoidable.

2. The absence of market subjects makes monetary policy control powerless.

So far as the macro-monetary control functions are concerned, the past few years has shown that monetary policies are relatively loose, the response is slow, and the sway is too quick. The stimulating effect of the increase in the money supply to the total output is relatively weak.

Since the reform, the growth rate of the money supply in the broad sense M2 has been represented in two-digit figures in all years; the highest was 29.7% in 1984, and the lowest 17.5%. As a result of the oversupply of money, the marginal result of the money has been on the down side. Compared with the early years of the 1980s, the marginal supply result in the early years of the 1990s dropped nearly by half.

It is true that the situation is attributed to the imperfect monetary policies and means, but more important, the policies have been distorted by an incompatible micro-foundation. The state-owned banks in China have never become enterprises, they are nothing more than administrative organizations. The state-owned enterprises are called "enterprises," but they are all directly controlled by the government, and are fairly far from being the subjects of the market economic interests. As a result, the implementation of monetary policies are to a great extent distorted by the administrative interference.

Since the government fund allocations were changed to loans to the enterprises through the state-owned banks, they are actually financial investments in the form of credit. The reason is that such loans are influenced greatly by the interests of finance, not by the changes in interest rates. In order to implement the financial policy, loans, always inclining toward the state-owned enterprise, can be granted without asking whether they will be returned, nor is any property needed as a mortgage. The state-owned enterprises which have suffered losses for many years borrow loans from the banks to pay employees or subsidize the production of unmarketable and overstocked goods. As far as the enterprises are concerned, there is not much difference between the bank loans and the government allocations. Since it is the money of the state and the government assumes the responsibility, the enterprises tend to keep the money for a long period of time, turning the loans into bad or dead debts. The bank loans become the foundation-laying funds for the enterprises' production. At present, about 10-15% of the loans from the specialized banks are at risk to become idle loans, and it is very difficult to get them paid back.

It is also true for interest rates. Interest rates must be changeable, and only when the changes reflect the changes in the supply and demand of the capital market, do the interest rates have the function of regulation. More important, regulation through the interest rates urges the enterprises and inhabitants to respond quickly to the rate changes. To achieve this, the enterprises and the inhabitants must become the interest subjects in the market economy. In the past few years, readjustments in interest rates have exerted an increasing influence on the population, because the Chinese people at present are the subjects of clearly stated economic interests of property rights in the field of monetary property. But the state-owned enterprises in China are not yet the subjects of the market, and they are not sensitive to interest rates. This is why interest rate changes usually have little effect on the enterprises, and lack the flexibility of regulation.

3. The absence of property right restriction and the benefit stimulus mechanism lead to a distortion of the income distribution policy.

Since the reform, giving more decision-making power and profit to state-owned enterprises has always been the goal. However, because the reform has not touched upon the relationship of property rights, and an effective restriction mechanism has not yet been set up, the macro-removal of some restrictions has given the enterprises under the restrictions of the interests of the operators and laborers a chance and means to strive with the state for more benefits.

When the state decided on profit quota contracts how much money is handed over to the state with an enterprise they resorted to bargaining one to one between them; they lacked an objective means of appraisal. The contract system, in the form of negotiation, pushed up the cost of transactions, forcing many local governments to give it up. On the other hand, no matter how perfect the quota is, it can only be decided on the basis of the historical production level and the existing technical level of the enterprise. This gives rise to a great elasticity. The contractor can strive for low quotas for various reasons and at the same time turn great profits into the income of individuals. Even if there is a loss, he is responsible only for the profit, but not for the loss. The result must be that the state revenues decrease year by year while the income of the individuals rises greatly year by year.

From the angle of the macro-regulation by the state, the control over the growth of individual income met with the demands of workers for higher wages. In order to maintain social stability, the government has no choice but to ensure that workers' wages grow at least equal to the rise in prices. As a result, staff and workers receive both pay and bonuses even when an enterprise suspends its production and the work is halted. Even when the government calls for the reduction of expenditures, the enterprises still hope to get more investment funds, more allocations or more loans from the fixed distribution plates. The local governments also yield to the interests of the enterprises in this respect and join the enterprises in exerting pressure on the central government to strive for more benefits for their localities, forcing the central government to use its money-issuing power to meet the social demand, which is above the effective supply. This results in oversupply.

It is worth noting that if only from the angle of the workers' wages, the above-described inclination is not clear. The total wages of staff and workers increased by an average of 12.4% during the Sixth Five-Year Plan and 16.4% during the Seventh Five-Year Plan. The wage increases were high as compared with the average annual increases of 10% and 7.5% in national income in the same periods. However, the actual average wage growth rate was 4.2% and 2.4% respectively in these periods, while social labor productivity was 6.7% and 4.91% respectively in the same periods. Therefore, the distribution inclined towards individuals was reflected mainly in non-wage income. The main part of the non-wage income is insurance and welfare funds. For example, the insurance and welfare spending for all staff members and workers of state-owned enterprises in 1991 totaled 90.487 billion yuan RMB, accounting for 83.2% of the total insurance and welfare expenditure or 54.47% of the total volume of taxes and profit turned over to the state from the state-owned enterprises. Most of the expenditures were medical expenditures and retirement pay. The absolute sums of the two expenditures were 26.753 billion yuan and 22.456 billion yuan respectively, the combined total of which accounted for 53.35% of the total insurance and welfare expenditures. As the non-wage income is distributed on a per head basis, there is the tendency towards equalitarianism in the distribution. The tendency is especially evident in state-owned enterprises where the welfare treatment is stable, the economic results is not good and the pay barely rises.

4. Industrial policies were distorted in the course of implementation.

In the present system, it has become a very difficult matter to reach the goals set by industrial policies. The causes are: One, the solidification of inventory composition and the lack of channels for the outflow of production elements; and two, the identity of the investment structure. Both causes are related with the enterprise system at the micro-level.

The identity of the investment structure is not caused by the competition mechanism as many people have said, but by the state monopoly. Because the state has controlled the prices of basic industries and hindered the entry of the enterprises not owned by the state, it is impossible for market mechanism to operate in these industries. Without competition, there is no lasting results and it is impossible to absorb capital inflow. On the other hand, in the area not controlled by the state, large numbers of enterprises not owned by the state compete equally and the market mechanism operates normally. Through competition, resources are allocated optimumly and fairly high economic results are achieved. And this in turn absorbs the entry of large quantities of resources. Both factors act jointly, leading to an identical flow of investments to the processing industries.

In order to protect the interests of local enterprises and local financial interests, local governments also rely on their administrative power and adopt irrational preferential policies to protect local enterprises from the "menace" of competition, such as forbidding good-quality products made in other regions to enter the local markets and forcing the local enterprises to use local raw and processed materials and parts. Such measures have created an anti-market regulation tendency of helping inferior-quality products to drive the good-quality products out of the market.

The rigid structure is also a serious problem which has remained unsolved for a long time in the Chinese national economy. The direct cause is the lack of a market mechanism, leading to the solidification of the economic structure in China. Once capital funds are invested, they are deposited and the deposition almost never flows.

As the rights of state-owned property in state-owned enterprises are not clear, the enterprises always request the state to make more investments in order to increase the safety coefficient of increased production. On the other hand, the large quantity of production elements lying idle can be counted as an "irresistible factor" arising from market changes, and the enterprises will not, or cannot find it possible to sell or lease the idle production elements through the market channels, but let them be stockpiled year after year, leading to the ossification of the inventory structure.

State-owned enterprises in China now embrace production, life services for the employees, social insurance and administrative management in one entity and form a typical small society. Every employee not only is entitled to free medical service, retirement pay and all sorts of social welfare, but also accepts the leadership of the state and the organizations at all levels. The employment vigidity thus formed has gravely hindered the flow of labor power. Without the flow of labor power, the readjustment of the industrial setup loses its most basic prerequisite.

Besides, China's production element market is far from being perfect, and there is no effective channel for the readjustment of the industrial setup.

(III) The key to controlling price rise is to adopt an appropriate macroeconomic policy

Nineteen ninety-four marked a big step in the reform of China's economic system. Five major reforms were introduced in the taxation, banking, investment, foreign trade and exchange, and state-owned property management systems. Most of the past reforms were to destroy the old, adjust policies and give part of the power and profit to local governments and enterprises. The new reforms are mainly to set up a new mechanisms, harmonize the basic relations among the different economic sectors and readjust the vested interests of all sides involved. It was more likely to cause a social shock. The greatest threat to the maintenance of stability is the excessive rise of prices. Because whether prices rise excessively is an important symbol of whether the economy is stable or not. Economic stability is the foundation for social stability. If inflation continues to develop, and price increases continue to enlarge, it will keep people in a constant state of fear and will inevitably affect smooth progress in reform and make it difficult for the fast economic growth to continue.

In order to control the rise of high prices, the government must adopt a safer macroeconomic policy. Both domestic and foreign experience shows that the direction of the state macroeconomic policy has a decisive influence on the price tendency. If the government adopts a safer macroeconomic policy, tightens both financial and monetary policies, strengthens and improves the macroeconomic control, appropriately checks the local enthusiasm in striving for investments, building new projects and accelerating construction, stops the tendency of accelerated development of inflation, controls the quick rise in the general price level and keeps the price rise within a scope acceptable to all sides, it will be able to create a better and relatively loose and comfortable environment for reform, maintain economic stability in the reforms and vigorously promote economic growth.

It is worth noting that the macroeconomic policies of the state were often under the pressure from local governments, departments and enterprises. Proceeding from their own interests, they wanted the credit and money supply to be increased just to ensure increased production but relaxed their vigilance against inflation and price hikes. They tried every way to oppose or boycott tighter macro-control by the state. For example, in order to seek the results of the growth rate, and alleviate the local financial difficulties and employment pressure so that they could make more accomplishments in their administration, some regions kept on requesting more investments and seeking still higher growth rate. This created more difficulties for the central government in adopting a safer macroeconomic policy and keeping it under control. Once the investment was out of control, it would force the bank to increase the money supply and inevitably aggravate inflation, and the prices would rise more quickly, thus affecting and even undermining economic stability. In that case, it became difficult for the economy to achieve a soft landing through minor readjustments, and a major readjustment was needed for a hard landing, just as in the fourth quarter of 1988. The loss it inflicted on the development of the reform was also very big.

It is only a few years since 1988, but China has once again suffered from the attack of inflation. It seems to show that China has not yet adopted a consistent and definite macroeconomic policy or the macroeconomic policy has not yet found the best way to ensure both growth and price stability, there is still a big difference between theoretical understanding and the policy choice. It needs further discussion.

The experience and data in some countries and regions shows that economic growth and price increases have a relationship of substitution between them. High economic growth often leads to high price increases, because high economic growth is caused by high investment growth which is accompanied by the shortage of materials supply and pre-schedule growth of the money supply, thus pushing prices up. On the contrary, keeping price increases smaller depends on the slowing down of economic growth, thus cutting down the economic growth rate. An important task of the economists in all countries and regions is to find a better combination point of economic growth and price increases, a point that is suited to the conditions in their own countries and regions and is a basis for governments to adopt macroeconomic policies. Although the economic growth rate differs from year to year because of the influence of the economic growth cycles, a relatively suitable solution can be found.

In the light of Chinese conditions, an economic growth rate of 9% and a price growth rate of around 6% or not higher than 10% may be a relatively good combination point in China at present. Based on this estimation, it can be assumed that the excess price growth in 1993 and 1994 were closely related to the high growth of investments since the beginning of 1992, and to the fact that the investment system was not well reformed and the macroeconomic policy of the government was somewhat relaxed.

What should draw our attention at present is that inflation has self-accelerating mechanism, just as when people eat opium. Once they are addicted, they smoke more, find it very difficult to abandon it and destroy their health in the end. A country (a developing country in particular) once haunted by inflation, finds it very difficult to free itself from it. After inflation grows to a two-digit figure, it often tends to speed up, and its harm is more and more exposed, thus undermining the stable and coordinated development of the economy, and a high price has to be paid to eliminate inflation. We must realize the harm done by the high inflation rate and high price growth, readjust the macroeconomic policy, strive for a soft landing of the economy through minor readjustment and avoid great losses.

(IV) It is necessary to strengthen the government's macro-control over economic operation, and control prices according to law

Establishing the market economic system and giving play to the foundation role of market mechanism in the allocation of resources does not mean that everything becomes fine once the control over the prices is removed. On the one hand, the formation of a price mechanism is a relatively long process in which some government interference is still needed so as to ensure the healthy operation of the economy and to help establish the new system and perfect it step by step. On the other hand, a perfect market system and compatible economic environment and legal system are also needed for the price mechanism to play its due and positive role after it is formed. There must also be a restrictive mechanism for the enterprises which are the subjects in fixing the prices.

The market economy does not reject government interference, but urges the government to make interference in accordance with the laws and demand of the market economy. The reason why countries in Europe and North America which practice the market economy have only a slight inflation rate is that government interference in these countries plays an important role. They not only control the money, but also exercise direct governmental control over the prices of most major commodities, resources and services that have close bearings on the national economy and people's livelihoods, such as oil, coal, air transport, public housing, land, rice, cigarettes and salt. Frequent interference is also made in accordance with the complete statutes over how prices are fixed for commodities and services not under the direct control of the government.

Even developed countries with market economies have governmental interference; it is natural that developing countries which are changing their economic pattern should need to strengthen their macro-control over their economies. In this respect, it should be said that we also have learned some lessons. In the opinions of some people, the planned economy is not good because the control it exercises is too much and too tight, and the market economy should exercise less control, the less, the better. Some people even advocate that the government should "govern by doing nothing." They have committed a metaphysical mistake in their way of thinking. It was precisely under the influence of such thinking that inflation rate rose quickly in 1993. The total price index of national retail sales had been planned for 6% that year, but the actual figure was 13%. This was chiefly because we lost our vigilance against big price increases towards the end of 1992 and failed to confirm the high total social demand. Moreover, because of insufficient understanding of the further growth of the total social demand and the inflation of dragging-type demand, we did not introduce any supplementary measures to check the price rise while continuing to make big price reforms in the same year. As a result, prices rose too drastically. Secondly, the government relaxed its macro-control and administration over the prices after the price restrictions were removed, and circulation was in disorder. In 1993, after the prices of most of commodities and services were not restricted, the proportion of commodity prices regulated by market accounted for around 90%, higher than some of the countries with seasoned market economies. However, as the self-restricting mechanism for market prices has not yet been set up, the laws and statutes for standardizing the subjects of the prices are not yet complete, the system of indirect macro-control over the market is not yet perfect. At one time, the problem of raising prices and charges willfully became very serious. Some law-breakers even monopolized the market to raise prices by big margins at their own will, upsetting the price order and giving high rise to price.

To strengthen macro-control over the economy to effectively check inflation, the government must constantly raise its ability to exercise macro-control. The problems cropping up in developing countries which are changing their economic pattern are all new problems, and their inflation is not inflation in the general sense. Therefore, they can find no ready solutions to these problems to effect a smooth change in economic patterns, nor can they copy the experience of other countries. This urges the policy makers to take precautions, keep a close watch on the operation of the economy, correctly use economic means and legal means, with the assistance of necessary administrative interference, to control inflation within a scope acceptable to the state, the enterprises and the individuals.

First of all, the government should exercise control over the change of the general price level. The change of the general price level is the overall manifestation of the operation of the national economy, and is a mirror of whether the macroeconomy operates in a healthy way. Therefore, the control over the general price level depends on the macroeconomic policies of the government, chiefly the financial policy and the monetary policy. At the same time, it is also necessary to establish and improve the reserve system and price regulation funds system for major commodities. With a sound reserve system for major commodities and a fairly sufficient reserve of major commodities, it is possible to regulate the market by purchasing goods when the supply is greater than the demand and selling the goods when the supply is shorter than the demand so that the prices of major commodities do not fluctuate too much and the price changes are regulated by the long-term relations between supply and demand, not by the short-term relations between supply and demand or sometimes even by artificial manipulation. It is obvious that the relative stability of the prices of major commodities has tremendous influence on the stability of the general price level. For example, the price trends of food grains, cotton, coal and steel products play an important restrictive role in the change of the general price level.

It is also very important to establish a system of price regulation funds. Practice shows that it is absolutely necessary to establish and use price regulation funds at present in the light of the Chinese conditions to mainly maintain the basic stability of the basic daily necessities of the people (chiefly a small number of the most essential food items). It accords with the need of developing the socialist market economy, and is beneficial to economic growth and to the improvement of the people's livelihood.

Secondly, it is necessary to make laws to restrict the pricing acts of enterprises and other subjects of the market, such as opposing monopoly prices, opposing the pursuit of huge profits, marking price tags and supervising and examining the prices of the basic daily necessities and services of the people. The marking of price tags for commodities and services helps to maintain the normal order of market prices, promote legitimate competition and protect the legitimate rights and interests of consumers. It also helps consumers to compare the goods in different shops and expose the unlawful acts of pursuing huge profits. The Regulations on Marked Prices for Commodities and Services took effect on March 1, 1994. It showed that the control on prices had been legalized. The State Council had decided to strengthen the supervision and examination of the prices of daily necessities and services of the people. The following twenty items are under supervision and examination: wheat flour, long-grain nonglutinous rice, round-grain nonglutinous rice, edible oils, pork, beef or mutton, hen eggs, cow milk, table salt, sugar, soy sauce, detergent, kitchen coal, liquid petroleum gas, kitchen gas, housing rent, drinking water, tuition fees, child-care fees, medical charges and transit fares. It has been stipulated that when the prices of some items under examination are to be readjusted by local governments, the higher level must be reported to the price control department for the record. When the price control department of a provincial government decides to readjust prices, it must be reported to the State Planning Committee for the record within ten days before the readjustments are made. When production and commercial enterprises readjust the prices of commodities items under market regulation, they must report it to the local price control department for the record five days in advance. This is also a major measure to standardize the pricing acts.

Furthermore, it is necessary to conduct price checks in accordance with laws and stop all acts of raising prices unlawfully to infringe on the interests of consumers so as to ensure the normal operation of the socialist market economy. Although price check organs have been set up in all parts of the country and many law-breaking acts have been found and penalized every year, violations have never been completely halted. Therefore, the efforts to check price rises should not be relaxed. The work must be done from time to time. General price checks should be conducted on a nationwide scale regularly so as to create a fairly good environment for reform and development.

Lastly, it is also necessary to strengthen the supervision through the media and the masses. The question of prices is a matter of importance to the vital interests of all families. All sides of the society should seriously listen to and deal with complaints about unlawful pricing acts infringing on the interests of consumers. This not only helps to establish a good market order, but also helps to introduce a good social custom.

Establish a system of responsibility for the risk of macro-control to ensure the scientific nature of macro-control and prevent subjective decisions. After the new macro-control system is established, the government's macro-control should be changed from strong regulation following inflation to regular micro-adjustment to reduce the cost of control and cut down the big waste of resources arising from the big rises and big falls. In other words, macro-control cannot place hope on readjustment following the economic expansion and inflation. Stress should be laid on the prevention of big rises and big falls in economic development through micro-control measures.

Don't think that market economy is to let the "invisible hand" to play the role. The modern market economy also needs the "visible hand," and this hand is to control prices. It is necessary to determine a reasonable limit. In a country with a population of 1.2 billion and an imbalance of economic development, restrictions on the prices of some commodities can be removed step by step, and the restrictions should not be removed on the prices of some other commodities, and they should be controlled by the government for a fairly long period of time. The basic basis is: the supply and demand of commodities, the degree of shortage of resources, the elasticity of consumption, and the relationship with the national economy and the people's livelihoods.

—Restrictions should not be removed on the commodities of which the demand is bigger than the supply. If the restrictions are removed, it is beneficial to fraudulent traders, not beneficial to producers and consumers. If the restrictions are removed, new links for the circulation of commodities will be added so that production and consumption will be seriously separated and the rise and fall of prices cannot correctly reflect the actual situation of production and consumption and therefore cannot correctly guide the acts of the producers and consumers. In that case, market regulation loses its original sense.

—Restrictions should not be removed on the commodities for which resources are scarce. Because the resources are scarce, they cannot be replaced by other resources. If the restrictions are removed, the situation will be like this: the producers will make up the quantity by producing inferior goods, the circulators will monopolize the market and the consumers will be entrapped. Some people believe in the creed that "the prices are raised once the restrictions are removed, the goods are plentiful when the prices are raised, and the prices fall when the goods are plentiful." This is conditional, in fact. When the resources are scarce, even if the prices are raised without limit, it is still difficult to stimulate production.

—Restrictions should not be removed on the commodities with little elasticity for consumption. This is because such commodities are mostly the daily necessities of the people, from which the people have not much room to choose. If the prices tend to rise after the restrictions are removed, it will affect the actual income of the people in large numbers and in the same quantity.

—Restrictions should not be removed on major products

vital to the national economy and to peoples' livelihoods, of which the supply falls short of the demand. If the restriction are removed, the shock will be tremendous and is detrimental to social stability and development of the national economy.

—When China's resources are relatively scarce, generally speaking, the restrictions can be removed gradually on the prices of the industrial goods for daily use, because the use value of such goods is easily replaceable. After restrictions are removed, the people have a greater choice. The restrictions can be removed gradually on the prices of the commodities of which the supply is slightly short of the demand. It will help to stimulate supply with the aid of other conditions. Restrictions can be removed gradually on the prices of commodities with a good elasticity of consumption, because consumers also have a great choice among these commodities. It is necessary to set up a reserve for major commodities. When the prices are high, sell them in great quantities to check further price rises. When the prices are low, purchase and store them to stop the downward tumble. At the same time, it is necessary to give price subsidies. The hidden subsidies should not be canceled. A protective price policy should be adopted for farm products.

Eliminate price monopoly. Western countries that have had a market economy for a long time regard anti-monopoly as an important measure to check inflation. Its main content includes: stopping enterprises from becoming monopoly enterprises, disorganizing or disintegrating the monopoly enterprises which have come into being, restricting conspiracies to monopolize the market, opposing regional blockades and banning price discrimination. Namely, the customers must be treated equally without discrimination, otherwise the enterprises will be charged with the crime of price discrimination. As to public utilities, such as gas, electric power, telephone service, telecommunications and railway service, because these industries, when properly concentrated, can easily produce good results on scale production, they are often allowed to do business exclusively, but exclusive business operation is likely to lead to price monopoly. Under these circumstances, the government should fix the ceiling and floor prices for these industries, to protect the interests of both the consumers and the producers.

Reduce the intermediate links to avoid the raising of the prices level by level. For this purpose, it is necessary to reform the system of commodity circulation. In 1994, the State Council combined the production and marketing of oils in a complete network and the prices of oils fell immediately. This was a successful example. The subsequent change in the circulation system for cotton will probably produce the same results.

Give play to the self-discipline role of trade societies. Trade societies in other countries play a very strong role in self-discipline, including prices. Trade societies should be set up as soon as possible in China to play the same role in this respect.

Establish an effective market competition order through legislation. The experience of the developed countries have shown that this is an important measure to prevent inflation and protect the interests of consumers. For example, Germany has set up a complete system of market statutes gradually in the development of its social economy, including laws against restrictions on competition and laws against unlawful competition, to create conditions for the establishment of a normal market order. After removing restrictions on the prices in 1986, France replaced its state price bureau with a general administration of prices, competition, consumption and punishment of fruitless practices, whose principal function is to strengthen price supervision and protect the interests of consumers. China should make price laws, anti-monopoly laws and anti-huge profit laws to supervise and control the prices of basic living necessities of urban and rural inhabitants. The acts of asking exorbitant prices and cheating customers must be severely punished according to law.

Push price reform forward cautiously and safely. In the world today, all countries which are switching to the market economy system or developing market economy have all witnessed inflation. Judging by the results, economists in most countries, including the developed countries, have adopted a positive attitude toward China's progressive reform program, but a negative attitude towards the radical "pains" or even the "shock" therapy used in some countries with acute inflation. Although China has removed restrictions on the prices of the overwhelming majority of the consumer goods and means of production, restrictions have not yet been removed on the prices of a small number of basic industrial products, which exhibit a big difference from international market prices. This is especially true of land, housing rent and charges for public utilities. This is detrimental to the optimum allocation of resources and is also apt to give rise to speculation and corruption. Therefore, it is necessary to continue to push forward price reforms safely and cautiously in accordance with the development of the economic situation and the supply and demand of the market. We should not waver in our determination to reach the goal of price reform because of current inflation. However, in a big country with a low per-capita income and an imbalance in economic development, any major question involving price reform must take into full account the actual ability of people to bear the consequences. We must grasp the timing and the dynamics well, solve the real problems arising from reform and truly strike a balance among reform, development and stability. If inflation grows too powerful, and affects development and stability, we must slow down price reforms for the time being. The delaying of the readjustment of the railway transport price is an example.

It is necessary to resort to economic, legal and administrative means to keep down the current excessive price increases.

Economically, it is necessary to grasp the farm production and the "food baskets" projects well on the one hand, and establish risk funds for food grains and non-staple foodstuffs on the other to increase reserves at the national and local levels to benefit the international and domestic markets and effectively handle the market supply and demand and check the rise of the market prices in good time.

Legally, all local governments and ministries should, in accordance with current laws and statutes, improve price order, strengthen price supervision, punish those who seek huge profits by raising prices without authorization in the name of reform, and resolutely ban all unreasonable charges. At the same time, it is essential to seize time to formulate the price law, sell goods at marked prices, and strictly supervise and examine the prices of basic daily necessities and services of the people.

Administratively, it is necessary to continue to practice the system of responsibility for control target of the general price level for governments at all levels, and use price controls as a principal criterion for the assessment of the achievements in their administrative work. Price figures will be made available to the public month by month and are subject to mass supervision.

(V) Readjust the internal proportions of the national economy during the reform

It is necessary to correctly handle the internal proportions of the national economy to strike a balance between total demand and total supply. One, full attention must be paid to the foundation position of agriculture. The output value of light industrial products made of farm products as raw materials in China accounts for 70% of the national output value of light industry, and whether the prices of farm products in market are reasonable and stable is a matter of vital importance to the stabilization of money value and the gratification of the popular feelings. To check inflation, agriculture and the rural economy must be greatly developed. To increase the production of food and vegetable crops is a key move to control inflation. To maintain social stability, first of all, it is essential to ensure the stability of rural areas, which hold 80% of the population. If something goes wrong with agriculture, the consequences will be beyond imagination. Two, a major surgical operation must be performed on the reform of government organization. It is necessary to choose better troops and simplify the administration and reduce the heavy load that the huge government organization has brought to the state revenues and expenditures. For example, if the 10 million government employees depending on the government for pay and supply are reduced to six million, state expenditures will be cut down by 20 billion yuan. This will help to put an end to the financial deficit and to corrupt practices of dilatory work and unprincipled disputes in office work. Three, the five major reforms call for attention to the readjustment of the proportion between the development of the state-owned economy and the development of the economy not owned by the state, to balance of the burdens between the state-owned economy and the economy owned by foreigners, overseas Chinese and individual businessmen in accordance with the market laws, equal the tax burdens, and reduce the pressure of state-owned enterprises on state expenditures and credit. Four, make and carry out industrial policies in earnest and gradually change the underdevelopment of the infrastructure and basic industries.

(VI) Constantly improve macro-control

How to exercise effective macro-control under market economic conditions is a question to be answered in the course of practice.

First of all, it is necessary to mark a clear line of macro-control. Macro-control is not equal to administrative interference, and it is essentially different from administrative interference under the planned economy. Macro-control means total control of the economy. It does not interfere with the decision-making power of the enterprises and microeconomic activities, but administrative interference in the past was interference in all affairs of an enterprise, including its manpower, financial power and material power, and also its production, supply and marketing.

Macro-control is chiefly to use economic means and certain administrative and legal means, while administrative interference was basically the use of administrative means.

Macro-control is to guide the enterprises to conduct its activities in accordance with market economic laws, to establish an orderly market operation system, invigorate the market and discard the rigid model under the old system.

The scope of macro-control must be improved. Macro-control is not only to control the total, but also the structure. For example, in investment, it is to control not only the total amount, but also its structure. Moreover, it is to control not only the input, but also the distribution, including the distribution of consumer goods and the income of individuals. It is to control not only economic growth, but also to coordinate the relationship between reform and development and opening to the outside world.

The method and dynamics of macro-control must be considered from the practical point of view. For example, in the use of the monetary policy and financial policy in macro-control, stress on taxation or credit differs from time to time, depending on the situation of the time. Macro-control can tighten or relax the money supply, the use of these also depends on the situation.

It is necessary both to strengthen macro-control and to give full play to the independent decision-making power and initiative of the local governments and the enterprises. Only in this way, is it possible to invigorate the market and the economy.

It is necessary to prevent and overcome the overheating of the economy through the system. It is true that the impulse of the economic leaders of governments at all levels, departments and enterprises for expansion has a bearing on the overheating of the economy, but it should be said that the acts of these leaders are reasonable, because it is beyond criticism that everyone of them wants to expand what they are in charge of. What has caused the overheating of the economy is not the expansion impulse itself, but the current mechanism for expansion impulse. It has two characteristics: First, it is the expansion impulse under the restriction of a soft budget. That is to say, in the system of soft finance and soft credit, the expansion impulse of every individual economic leader is not restricted by the resources in his hands, because he can meet the needs of his expansion impulse by absorbing what is needed from the government and the bank. Second, it is an expansion impulse to seek economic growth through high input and extension. Talking of expansion, it is to build a new project. If this expansion impulse mechanism is not changed, the expansion impulse inevitably gives rise to big rises and big falls in the economy. Therefore, to prevent big rises and big falls in the economy fundamentally depends on, first, the reform of the economic system to harden the budget restrictions on the economic leaders with expansion impulses, and second, on a change in economic development strategy. In view of the cause for the economic overheating arising from the current system, a major reform measure to bring inflation under permanent control is to solve the problem of soft budget restrictions in the system and cut off the father-son relations between the central government and the local governments, and between the state and the enterprises, thus eliminating the macro-foundation for economic fluctuations. The enterprises and local governments can no longer, as they did in the past, depend on bargaining, a soft budget distribution, soft taxation and soft credit to absorb capital funds to meet the needs of their expansion impulses. Once hard budget restrictions is in force, the expansion impulses of local governments and of enterprises have no choice but to obey the market. Their acts of expansion are self-restricted, so that their micro-acts do not give rise to economic overheating.

The aggravated instability of the Chinese economy in recent years has exposed the limitations of the reforms in the previous years. However, further reforms, including property rights reform, and reforms in the financial and banking systems cannot produce good results in a short time. In a fairly long period of time, the Chinese economy will remain in a state of "double-track system," and the problem of the state-owned economy cannot be solved very soon. The system of the state-owned economy with the power divided will remain in force for a fairly long period of time, and give rise to a number of micro- and macro-problems. How to exercise macro-control to maintain stability and at the same time keep the economic growth and deepen the marketization reform in the period of "double track transition" is a very thorny question.

A basic difficult question is: there is no macro-control means which can maintain macro-stability on the one hand, and does not cause the economy to lose the vitality of its reform and growth on the other. On the one hand, because the national economy is still holding sway in the whole national economy, the policy means of macro-control under the market economy cannot get the desired results. For example, through the adjustment of interest rates and the indirect control of the money supply, it is still impossible to effectively check the acts of investment expansion of local governments and enterprises in the state of soft restriction. On the other hand, because of the existence of a great deal of economy not owned by the state, the market mechanism is already acting in a certain scope. If direct control only is used, for example, the direct control of the credit, to exercise control over the economy, it will lead to the inefficiency of the allocation of resources and check the development of the market mechanism.

A basic conclusion can be drawn from this that in the period of transition, different means should be used to exercise overall control over the economy in the different sectors of the economy in the light of the different situation of the different micro-economic subjects.

Be sure not to exercise administrative control over the whole economy, even less to exercise administrative control over the economy not owned by the state. So far as the economy not owned by the state is concerned, it is essential to use all effective indirect control policies, such as monetary and tax policies, especially to strengthen the use of interest rates, even if the current state-owned sectors of the economy are not sensitive to it. However, we have, after all, a fairly large economy not owned by the state, which is more sensitive to interest rates. To them, all indirect control policies have proved fairly effective.

A current question in dispute is how to look at interest rates, especially the interest rates for loans. On this question, the following points should, first of all, be made clear: (1) Due to obstruction by certain interest groups, the loan interest rate has been kept down to a very low level, not only far lower than market interest rate, but also lower than the inflation rate. This constitutes a most grave distortion of the Chinese economy. To ignore this and the grave fact that a large number of low-interest loans have become the source of "rent-seeking" acts of individual bank officials or state-owned enterprises and continue to artificially control all interest rates for the loans at a fixed low level is a serious policy mistake. (2) The question of the influence of interest rate changes on the macroeconomy. There is no doubt that rising interest rates help to check the demand for capital funds to a certain degree, especially when the economy not owned by the state accounts for more than 60% of the national output value at present, and its investement more than 30% of the total. The elasticity of the interest rates of total demand has been raised somewhat; however, because 80% of bank loans are granted to state-owned (at least in the primary distribution), overestimation should not be made of the effectiveness of interest rates in macro-control.

In light of the current economic structure and interest pattern, it is perhaps unrealistic to exercise market regulation through interest rates. In this basic situation, as to the interest rate--the price of using capital funds, we can also adopt "double-track transition," the feasible experience gained from price reforms in other fields. First, preserve part of the low-interest loans for state-owned enterprises, but at the same time leave a part from the total amount of loans as the newly-increased loans, which will be lent openly and legally at marked "prices" decided in accordance with the market supply and demand (the central bank "adjusts" the interest rates for the re-loans while the loan interest rates of the special banks are decided by the market). Then gradually reform the interest rates and use the market means to exercise control over the total demand.

(VII) Macro-control has helped the Chinese economy to achieve a soft landing

1. The situation of the macroeconomy has tended to be better after the macro-control, and the economy has achieved a soft landing.

The economic situation in 1994 as a whole was good. It was manifested chiefly in two aspects:

First, a number of major reform measures had been introduced in finance and taxation, banking, foreign exchange and trade, investment and price since the beginning of 1994, and rewarded with satisfactory results. These measures had already exerted and continue to exert deeper and deeper impact on the establishment and perfection of the socialist market economic system.

One of the important reasons why these major measures were possible to adopt was that the macro-control symbolized by

16-point measures issued in the middle of 1993 had initially checked the abnormal phenomena of four highs and two disorders emerging in economic operations with high economic growth (high investment, high money supply, high price and high imports, financial disorder and means of production market disorder). The preliminary results achieved in the implementation of the 16-point measures have created necessary social and economic environmental conditions for the introduction of the major reforms.

The negative influences that emerged for a short time after the major reforms were introduced in foreign exchange and trade, finance, taxation, and banking were smaller than expected, but the actual results were better than expected. After the exchange rates were combined into one, the rates of exchange between RMB and foreign currencies remained stable, and the value of RMB did not drop sharply, but rose or remained stable. The unfavorable balance of international trade was narrowed and the national exchange reserve increased. The reforms in the financial and taxation systems was stable and smooth, and domestic revenues and industrial and commercial taxes increased notably as compared with the previous year. Banking continued to operate smoothly. It not only effectively controlled the increase of money in circulation and effectively controlled the total credit of society, but also guaranteed the needs of structural readjustment and fast economic growth. It can be said that the introduction of the major reforms in 1994 has increased the momentum in establishing and perfecting the socialist market economic system, and laid the foundation for the sustained, fast and healthy development of the national economy.

Second, fairly conspicuous results were achieved in macro-control for most of the quotas. This is manifested in the fact that in the course of exercising macro-control, there was no big rise and big fall in economic operations, the overheated economy was cooled down to a certain degree, not only did economic growth remain fast (although it slowed down steadily), but the macro-economic environments were obviously improved, and the balances of finance, foreign exchange, revenues and expenditures, and materials all turned for the better. In the first half of 1994, the GDP rose by 11.55% as compared with the same period of 1993. Although it was still fast growth, it dropped by 2.5 percentage points as compared with the same period of the previous year. The investment in the fixed assets of the whole society rose by 25.2% as compared with the same period of the previous year, but the increase margin was nearly 36 percentage points lower than in the previous year. The excess growth of investment was checked to a certain extent.

These macro-control measures were more successful than before, chiefly because the moment for exercising macro-control this time was more appropriate than in 1988. While using administrative means, great stress was laid on the use of economic and legal means in exercising macro-control, and special attention was paid to the use of financial means. An even more important reason was that we withstood the pressure both from the urge to relax controls due to the difficulties of state-owned enterprises and from the urge to adopt more severe control measures in order to check the overheating of the economy in a short time. Because the dynamics of macro-control were properly handled, we successfully controlled the overheating and ensured the major development needs. Besides, the fact that we have been able to positively draw lessons from previous macro-control measures, and the improved environment provided by the macro-system after the reform was deepened, were also quite important factors. The macro-control started in 1993 created the conditions for the introduction of major reforms in 1994, and the two supplemented each other. The positive results scored in macro-control not only made it more and more possible for an economic soft landing to succeed, but also helped us accumulate more experience and lay the foundation for further raising macro-control standards.

Because satisfactory results were scored in the major reforms, macro-control continued to report new successes. At the same time, some problems existing in the general economic life were also outstanding. Therefore, macroeconomic operations in 1994 had the following characteristics:

(1) The economic growth rate dropped steadily, but the

economy still continued to grow quickly. The growth rate of the GDP in 1994 was around 11.5% and China continued to be one of the most eye-catching and quickly growing countries in the world. The growth rates of the increased value of the first, second and third industries were 3.0%, 16.0% and around 10.2% respectively.

(2) The expansion of investment was somewhat checked, but the investment growth was still strong. The total investment in fixed assets of the whole society was more than 1,500 billion yuan in 1994, or more than 18% above the actual growth in 1993. It was still faster than the actual growth rate of the GDP. Therefore, the investment growth was still the chief motive force pushing the economic growth forward. The growth rate of investment was obviously smaller than in the previous year, the proportion of investment in the third industry rose, but the small proportion of investment in the first industry was nothing to be optimistic about.

(3) The income of people continued to grow, but the increase in the volume of the retail sales was small. The gap in the growth of income between the urban residents and the rural residents was narrowed, but the growth of the income of the rural residents was still under that of urban ones. The total volume of retail sales of social commodities increased by 25% nominally, but the actual growth was far lower from the economic growth.

(4) The monetary situation was stable, but the financial situation brooked no optimism. The bank savings of the residents increased by a big margin. There was not much gap between new deposits and new loans. State revenues rose, but the deficit was a bit too big.

(5) The foreign trade situation turned for the better, and the balance of imports and exports was reduced. The total volume of imports and exports was around 235 billion U.S. dollars.

(6) The increase in prices of the means of production was obviously smaller. Consumer prices kept increasing. The margin of increase in the prices of the means of production in 1994 was smaller than in the previous year, but retail prices of commodities and consumer prices of residents rose too much. Inflation was an

outstanding problem.

Through micro-control over some time, the overheating of the Chinese economy has been mainly eliminated. This is manifested in the fact that the economic growth rate was not only lower than in the two previous years, but also in the following aspects: (1) Except for food, all categories of commodities are now on the buyer's market, the prices of the means of production are on the downside because of overproduction, the supply of domestic appliances, clothing and some other consumer goods is also bigger than the demand, and there are grand sales that were rare in the 1980s. (2) The money supply and demand are in the main balanced. After withdrawing all the money supplied from circulation in the first half of 1994, a thing that rarely happened in the past, the money supply was controlled within the green light limits in the second half of the year. (3) There was a favorable balance of trade, exchange reserve increased, and the value of RMB to the U.S. dollars was stable and on the upside after the double exchange rates were integrated. This shows that the growth of the Chinese economy enjoys a high integral prestige. (4) In spite of the high price level, the actual income of the urban and rural inhabitants rose quite quickly. The growth rate of saving deposits was higher than in the two previous years. In short, judging by the growth rate or by the relationship between total supply and total demand, the operation of the national economy is basically normal and balanced, and a soft landing has been achieved.

2. Combine slight upward adjustment with relaxation of structural demand.

Economic growth is now slowing down. The stress of the relaxation this time should be laid on slight upward adjustments to some anticipations instead of the numerical expansion in all fields as in the past. The essential points of the policy relaxation should include the following two: One, make a slight upward adjustment, the relaxation of demand should not be too fast and hasty. Two, the relaxation of demand should be structural, not comprehensive. The policy requirements of combining slight upward adjustment with the relaxation of the structural demand are: (1) Strictly control the money supply to prevent the hidden danger of high inflation in the future as a result of the oversupply of the money; (2) prevent the redundant construction of similar new projects in different parts of the country, and guide local governments and enterprises to use their extension funds for technological transformation; and (3) make use of the power of the central government in concentrating capital funds so that most of the extension funds made available by the policy relaxation will be used for infrastructure facilities, and put the dynamics of the relaxation on transport, telecommunications, electric power, urban water supply, medical facilities and rural water conservancy facilities so that infrastructure facilities will develop at an accelerated speed simultaneously with the steady growth of the other industries.

Accelerate the change of savings into investment funds and readjust the expenditure structure of the government, enterprises and families so that a part of the consumption funds will be turned into investment funds. At present, the value of bank deposits in all banking institutions and ready money of residents almost equals the domestic gross product, but the scope of their investments is very narrow. Their basic choices are either to seek luxurious consumption or turn a great part of their funds into non-productive speculative capital like stocks, resulting in excess demand on the speculative capital market. Enterprises, and some investment companies and state banking institutions also put large funds into real estate and the stock market.

II. The Financial Policy to Check Inflation

(I) The serious imbalance of revenues and expenditures and the soft restriction on the budget are important factors for inflation

In the course of switching from the traditional planned economy to the market economic system, rapid economic growth in China is once again threatened by inflation. How to effectively check inflation so as to keep down the loss, which inflation causes to the high growth of the national economy, to a minimum is one of the basic targets of the macroeconomic policy adopted in China at present. Financial policy is an important part of the government's macroeconomic policy, and whether the financial policy is good or not will exert a direct influence on inflation rates.

The current inflation has a great deal to do with the growing financial deficit, which is made up for through overdrafts from the bank, leading to a money expansion by the central bank. As a result of the shortage of financial power, the financial subsidies to state-owned enterprises, and the investments in the public utilities and infrastructure facilities which should be made from state expenditures, are all made available through bank loans, forcing the central bank to increase the money supply.

Since the beginning of the 1990s, the financial deficit has grown bigger and bigger. In addition, the policy of tax and profit reduction was adopted over and over again in the course of the reform in previous years, the financial policy of the government has shown the color of expansibility.

The degree of influence of the financial deficit on inflation depends on how the deficit is made up for, namely, by debts or by the money supply. A deficit made up for by debts, generally speaking, has little influence on the expansion of the money supply, mostly indirect if any (except for government bonds directly subscribed for by the People's Bank of China). The deficit made up for by the money supply (namely the hard financial deficit overdrawn from the central bank) has direct influence on inflation. A quantitative analysis can be made of this. In the ten years between 1984 and 1993, the combined hard financial deficits came to 112.826 billion yuan, and the central bank increased the money supply by 315.02 billion yuan, although financial deficits accounted for only 35.8% of the increased money in the same period, the influence of the financial deficit on inflation did exist.

If the influence of the financial deficit on inflation is visible, the influence of contradictions in the allocation of resources related to the revenues and expenditures does not draw the attention of people. But these influences cannot be underestimated. For example, when a modern enterprise system compatible with the needs of the development of the market economy has not yet been established, all funds that the enterprises should have obtained from state revenues were advanced through bank loans. The investments in some basic industries and infrastructure facilities which should be made by the government, as limited by the shortage of the financial power, have to be made through bank loans. All these can force the central bank to increase the money supply, thus putting more money in circulation.

(II) Control the financial deficit and properly adjust the fiscal demand and supply

China is a developing country in the stage of economic upstart. The contradiction between the need and possibility of financial power will exist for a long period of time. As a policy instrument for regulating supply and demand, the budget deficit is a form of implementation of the expansible financial policy. Therefore, when supply is short of demand, deficit financing is also a policy choice for consideration. However, when there is already inflation, it is very dangerous to continue to adopt the expansible policy. In the light of the actual situation in China at present, the current size of the deficit should be strictly controlled. The amount of debts arranged in the 1994 budget adopted by the Chinese government accounted for around 4% of the gross domestic product, obviously a big proportion. Measures should soon be taken to keep it under 3%. For this reason, on the one hand, efforts should be made to increase revenues, strictly control tax exemptions and reductions, and strengthen the administration over the collection of enterprise and personal income taxes so that all taxes that should be collected are collected. On the other hand, control expenditures as tightly as possible: reduce financial subsidies, appropriately control the administrative expenditures, and gradually remove all the items from the budget that the government should not bear.

(III) Intensify the dynamics in the structural readjustment and increase the effective supply

In the application of the macroeconomic policy, the structure policy and the stability policy are equally important. This is the basic condition for improving supply. Because the mere increase of total supply is restricted by the structure of demand, it is necessary to adjust the production structure to increase the effective supply. Agriculture is the foundation of the Chinese economy. To increase the agricultural input and improve the conditions for the agricultural production form an important aspect of the structural adjustment. China's experience has shown that only when agriculture is stable, there is no big fluctuation in the whole macroeconomy. Construction of infrastructure facilities is also a key point in the structural adjustment. The investment portion of the state budget should be concentrated on solving the bottleneck contradictions in economic operations. Give more support to the high and new technology industries to strengthen the future power of economic development. Moreover, efforts should be made to adopt measures to invigorate the deposition of current properties, support the production of marketable and profitable products, and make every effort to increase the effective supply.

(IV) Further deepen financial and tax reform and give play to the role of the "internal stabilizer" of finance

In the final analysis, inflation is a phenomenon of money. Because the tax system in China before the reform had no natural elasticity or progression, the growth of state revenues always lagged behind the rate of the economic growth while the tough expenditure mechanism forced budgetary expenditures to increase from time to time under the conditions of inflation, resulting in an inevitable increase in the financial deficit. To a certain degree, therefore, finance is also a victim of inflation and has difficulty in playing its regulation function of "internal stabilizer." The tax reform introduced in 1994 has helped to establish the elasticity function basically so far as the tax system is concerned. The question is that the Chinese tax laws are not tough enough, and moreover, the progression mechanism has not yet been set up for enterprise income tax. Therefore, it is necessary to accelerate the making and perfection of the enterprise income progressive tax law and further increase the elasticity of taxation and give effective play to the role of finance as a "internal stabilizer." It is necessary to strengthen the legislation of taxation, collecting taxes strictly in accordance with the tax laws and establishing a system of severe punishment for the tax evasions; and to set up effective taxation organs at the central and local levels to meet the needs of the reform of the financial system aimed at the separation of taxes to ensure the tax collection process and the timely delivery of full sums to the state.

(V) Coordinate financial and monetary policies

Strengthen the cooperation between the financial departments and the banks in the issuance and circulation of government bonds, and gradually increase the proportion of negotiable securities, mainly government bonds, in the properties of the People's Bank of China to create the necessary conditions for the central bank to do open-market business. With a view to checking inflation and maintaining a fairly fast economic growth, it is necessary to adopt a measure of mutual cooperation between a tight-and-loose financial policy and appropriately tight monetary policy. By using these tactics, we can both avoid big fluctuations in economic development and help to check the tendency of further rise of the actual interest rate and the further increase of the financial deficit.

(VI) Accelerate the establishment of the social security system to suit the development of the socialist market economy

In some developed market economic countries, the raising and use of the social security funds is regarded by the governments as an important financial policy tool to regulate economic cycles, and it has played a positive role. As China's reform in the social security system has just started, it has not yet played the role of social security as a "safety network," nor the role of regulating the cycles of economic operation. Therefore, whether to improve the financial policy tool or to check inflation, it is an urgent task to accelerate the reform of the social security system. It is essential to establish, step by step, an old-age retirement insurance system in enterprises in a few years to come, combining the basic state old-age insurance, the enterprise supplementary insurance and individual savings insurance, and make an overall plan and arrangement at the provincial level. Further improve the measures to raise and use insurance funds and include workers' old-age insurance funds and unemployment funds in the budgets at all levels. Insurance for the staff and workers of administrative units and institutions shall be taken into overall consideration in conjunction with the reform of the public servants' system. Continue the reform in the system of free medical service and labor insurance medical service and gradually establish a socialized medical insurance service system. Social insurance will be gradually put under a unified state law and administration.

(VII) Strictly control revenues and expenditures

It is necessary to strengthen the administration over the tax collection and collect taxes strictly in accordance with laws to increase state revenues. It is necessary to perfect central and local tax organizations, reform the tax collection system, change the tax collector system to the tax declaration system, and establish a system of severe punishment for tax evasion. It is necessary to introduce the consumption tax and control the consumption demand. Establish the personal property declaration system and strictly collect personal income taxes.

Excess direct investment by finance will aggravate the imbalance of revenues and expenditures. It is necessary to strictly control the proportion of direct financial investment. Financial investment should be controlled within the scope of the public utilities, infrastructure facilities and primary industries. Increase the dynamics of the structure adjustment, and concentrate efforts on solving the contradiction of the bottleneck restriction to increase the effective supply.

It is essential to increase revenues, central revenues in particular, and gradually include extra-budgetary funds in the budget and strengthen the macro-control ability of state revenues and expenditure so as to give play to the function of optimizing the allocation of resources, make the distribution of income fair and maintain economic stability.

Properly control expenditures, readjust and optimize the structure of the expenditures, and increase the transparency of the expenditures. Expenditures for construction projects should mainly be used for basic industries and building infrastructure facilities. Strengthen the supervision over expenditures and ensure the fairness of expenditures.

In the administration over financial investments, establish a system of registered capital funds for appropriations, while the question of other funds needed by projects can be solved through the direct and indirect short-term loans among the banks.

In financial policy, efforts should be made to increase revenues and cut down expenditures. The government should make a public statement to restrict the size of the financial deficit. The total sum of government bonds should also be controlled. Don't think that since bonds can be used to make up for the financial deficit, the government can increase the deficit and the sum of the bonds at will. International experience shows that in a developing country, the financial situation of revenues and expenditures has a tremendous influence on the macroeconomy. Since the tax system reform has been introduced, the government should strictly practice its administration over the tax collections, fill up the leaks, gradually improve the financial situation and get out of its difficult position.

III. The Monetary Policy for Checking Inflation

(I) The Background of the Role of Monetary Policy

Before the economic reform, under the highly centralized system of economic administration, all economic activities including investment, consumption, imports and exports were organized by the central planning department, and money was nothing more than a planning symbol. Therefore, under the system of central planning, it can be said that there was no monetary policy. The reform in the past dozen and more years has brought a profound change in the economic system. The subjects of the economic operations and the operation mechanism have both changed. On the one hand, these changes have greatly strengthened the role of monetary policy, and on the other, the role of monetary policy is restricted as the economic system is still changing its track and some of the mechanisms of the old system are still functioning. Therefore, the Chinese economy has certain special features.

At the beginning of the reform, the goal of the reform was to change the highly centralized system of economic administration, and therefore, the government adopted a number of reform measures to give part of the decision-making power to local governments and enterprises and reduce the amount of profit turned in to the state. These measures gave local governments more power and enterprises the power to make their own decisions in organizing their economic activities, thus turning them into the subjects of economic operations.

First, the measures motivated local governments to show a strong demand for investment.

Following the reforms in the financial and planning systems, local governments had more power in handling local affairs. For example, the power of examining and approving investment items and the power of using a guiding plan for locally raised investment funds gave local governments the power to make decisions on local investments, while the system of responsibility for local finance gave local governments more financial power and increased the funds at the disposal of local governments. It should be especially pointed out that as most of the revenues in China come from an indirect tax, which is linked with the sales income, the system of responsibility for local finance not only aroused the enthusiasm of local governments in organizing revenues, but also motivated them to make the extensional economic expansion and stimulated their demand for investment. On the other hand, they were governments, so they did not take the responsibility as owners for the loss and waste of resources. Therefore, their acts of investment are of soft restriction. The combination of the interest stimulus and the soft restriction have made their investment impulse very strong.

Second, with more decision-making power, enterprises have acquired the mechanism for expanding both investment and consumption.

After these measures were adopted, state-owned enterprises have acquired more decision-making power in their business operations and more interest stimulus. This is true especially with the reforms similar to the contract system and that of "the wages linked with results." Because the "results" refer to the profit and tax turned in to the state (including the indirect tax linked with sales income), this system has strongly stimulated enterprises to seek output value, and enlarge their production and investment. For a long time, enterprise reform almost remained in the primary stage of acquiring decision-making power and keeping a portion of profit, and nothing was done to make a deeper reform in the property right system. Therefore, when enterprises have the interest stimulus, they are not restricted by the property right, nor by the risk. This is why the state-owned enterprises still have the soft restriction mechanism.

The reform of the system of distribution of personal income which accompanies enterprise reform includes setting no ceilings on the bonus, and linking income with work efficiency. These measures all have helped enterprises to distribute their income inclining towards individuals. Very often, the growth of the individuals' income surpassed the growth of their labor productivity. At present, enterprises have a strong investment impulse and also the mechanism to increase individuals' income and stimulate their demand for consumption.

The mechanism for the quantitative development of enterprises instinctively demands expansion. However, when a tight policy was adopted, the results of the enterprises dropped drastically and individual income also dropped. This state of affairs has influence on state revenues and also on the livelihood of staff and workers and social stability. This mechanism of the state-owned enterprises put the monetary policy in a state of neither being loose nor being tight.

Third, price reform will give rise to price increase prompted by increasing costs. A major reform in the track-changing period is to change planned prices to market prices. Theoretically speaking, the price reform is to adjust relative prices and not to push the general price level up. But this needs the market environment with full competition, something not present in China yet. Moreover, the market supply and market demand are relatively balanced. If the demand is too high, the combination of the cost push and the demand pull will bring the price level up by a big margin.

(II) Monetary Policy and Inflation

In the period of changing the track of the economy, for reasons arising from its system and mechanisms, China's monetary policy has its peculiar influences on the formation and control of inflation:

1. During periods of economic expansion, the central bank often finds it difficult to control the money supply, and the money supply expansion leads to inflation.

During periods of economic growth, the central bank wanted to adopt a relatively tight monetary policy to prevent overheating of the economy, but often found it difficult to implement the policy because the strong investment impulse of local governments and enterprises prompted them to use their power to intervene in the economy, and use loopholes in the management of the bank system to force the central bank to increase the money supply. The channels for inducing the central bank to increase the money supply are:

(1) Exerting influence to the local office of the central bank to increase the money supply through the local government. For example, in early 1988, the head office of the central bank made a relatively tight monetary policy demanding that its branch offices in different parts of the country withdrew all loans issued in the first half of the year, which amounted to 25 billion yuan. However, due to intervention by local governments, some of the

branch offices failed to withdraw the loans and others reissued loans after they withdrew them. As a result, almost none of the 25 billion yuan loans of the central bank were paid back. At that time, the central bank had not exercised the quota control on the loans of the special banks, but controlled the total sum of the loans of the whole society by controlling the loans of the central bank. Therefore, controlling the loans of the central bank was the most important means to carry out the monetary policy at that time.

(2) Use the "pressing" mechanism to force the central bank to increase the money supply. In accordance with China's credit policy, the Chinese banking organizations must ensure the supply of funds needed by the major state-owned enterprises and the funds needed for purchasing farm and sideline products. However, local governments, enterprises and local banks joined hands in using the funds they had raised for investment in fixed assets and supplying funds within the local loan quotas to local enterprises, leaving the demand of the major enterprises directly under the central government and the demand for funds to purchase farm products unsatisfied, forcing the central bank to make additional loans.

(3) With the diversification of banking institutions and the development of the financial market, the state-owned banks made use of the short-term loan market and bypassed the loan quota control to increase the money supply to gain profit. This channel played an important part in the money expansion and the flow of large capital funds to the real estate market and stock market in 1992 and 1993.

As these mechanisms functioned, the credit scale of the central bank was often exceeded. Under the managerial system of "more deposits more loans" instituted before September 1988, the central bank could hardly put into effect the control plan for basic money, and the banking system became the supplier of capital funds for economic development. With the increase of the money supply resulting from economic development, the money expansion became the motive force for the overheating of the economy and the growth of demand.

2. When galloping inflation emerged, the monetary policy could not but tighten money supply forcefully, and as a result, caused a violent shock.

In the period of changing the track for the economic system, the subjects of the economic operations, the governments and the enterprises, have strong expansion impulse, but lack the inherent risk restriction mechanism. Their expansion mechanism can be checked only when there is outside intervention. If the intervention is not strong enough, they will do everything to resist. Only when the contradiction between supply and demand is very acute and the outside intervention is very strong, can the excess demand and overheated economy be checked. However, a very high price has to be paid for this powerful tightening measure. The situation in September 1988 was exactly like this, when the economic operation reached its peak, the demand expansion and the removal of the restrictions on the prices of some industrial consumer goods gave rise to soaring prices, and panic purchasing on two occasions was immediately followed by another panic purchasing, this time a nationwide one. Therefore, the State Council decided to adopt an overall tightening policy. In the monetary policy: One, the interest rate was raised, with a preserved value interest rate added for the deposits of three years or longer; two, the loans were strictly controlled. The three months between September and November 1988 were the peak period of issuing loans when large sums of funds were needed by the enterprises to purchase raw or processed materials and by commercial departments to purchase farm and sideline products. However, in the three months, not only the loans were not increased, but reduced by more than 600 million yuan. This resulted in an acute shortage of funds for the purchase of farm and sideline products, and the purchasing departments in various parts of the country had to give signed paper slips instead of money to the peasants in a crisis of payment. In short, this was a drastic reduction.

The drastic reduction of loans, assisted by other tightening measures, helped to check the acute inflation and prices dropped. But a very high price was paid. Industrial production fell drastically. The industrial growth rate was negative in October in 1989, many enterprises suspended production, workers were laid off, and the financial situation was worse.

Not only such reduction is drastic, but it is done mainly through direct control, depending on the administrative means. Because both the government and the enterprises have no risk restriction mechanism, the market means and economic variables are not sufficient enough to change their acts and check their demand. Only direct control and administrative means can do. In the monetary policy, it mainly relies on the loan quota control. Direct control helps to achieve the goal of quick reduction, but it also does greater harm to the economy, and its negative role is also big, especially in China. For example, when drastic reductions occur, the banks withdraw loans. They can not force the enterprises with poor performances and inability to pay the loans to sell their property or announce bankruptcy to pay the loans, and to the enterprises with good performances and sales income, the banks can withhold their sales income to pay the loans. As a result, the tightening policy has no effect on the enterprises with poor economic performances, but has effect on those with good economic performances, thus leading to the drastic drop in production.

In short, drastic reduction causes big harm to the economy.

3. When the economy was at a low ebb, monetary policy was often used to aid state-owned enterprises, but delayed economic recovery and structural adjustment.

After the drastic reduction, the economy was at a low ebb, and state-owned enterprises were in a very difficult position—no production, jobless workers and losses. In order to protect these enterprises and stimulate an economic comeback, the government poured in large amounts of funds. In September 1989, the central bank adopted the monetary policy of expansion, and the focal point of the credit policy of that time was to protect the state-owned enterprises, major enterprises in particular. Therefore, the measure of "designated loans" was adopted, namely, the government departments concerned designated a number of state-owned enterprises to which the banks were obliged to grant loans. However, since the market was weak or the products were unmarketable, and large quantities of commodities were kept in stock, the funds that poured in were held in the form of overstocked products. Since the products were kept in stock, the enterprises had difficulties making payments, thus giving rise to the "triangular debts" among the enterprises. As a result, there was still no power for the economic recovery despite the pouring in of large quantities of funds.

Up to the fourth quarter of 1990 the central government did not decide to enlarge investments in fixed assets, and since then banking institutions had granted loans to the investment projects. Subsequently, with the increasing demand for investment, production was pushed up.

In the period from September 1988 when the reduction began, to September 1989, it was above criticism for the central bank to make the money market easy. As any monetary policy needed time to bring out its result, the central bank should perhaps have made the credit easy earlier. The question was that large amounts of funds had been supplied to state-owned enterprises with poor or little economic performances and their products were overstocked. If the funds had been used for investments in basic industries at the very beginning to stimulate investment demand and pull up production, and at the same time readjusted the prices of the primary products while the market was weak, it would have been able to promote economic recovery earlier and support the development of basic industries to lay down the foundation for alleviating the bottleneck in the next round of economic development.

(III) A stable monetary policy is an important requirement for the stable development of the economy

The inflation in 1988 and the subsequent tightened money market have showed that to avoid big rises and big falls in the economy and to keep the economic cycle from rising and falling too much, a stable monetary policy is quite essential. However, it is extremely difficult to maintain the stability of the monetary policy when the basic track of the economic system is being changed. To do this, it is very important to improve the control system of the central bank, but it is also an important aspect to change the environment for the function of the monetary policy through reform.

First, to maintain a stable monetary policy, the money authorities must have a very high authority. Therefore, it is very essential to promulgate and implement the Bank Law.

As the track of China's economic system changes, the pressure of the demand for money from all sides is very strong. The pressure comes not only from the enterprises, but also from the various levels of government. If the money authorities do not have a very high authority, it is very difficult to resist the pressure. For example, the central bank made two decisions in order to implement the monetary policy of proper reduction in 1988: to withdraw all its loans amounting to 25 billion yuan and to raise the interest rate. The former was boycotted under pressure of the local governments, and the latter was also boycotted by the ministries and commissions of the central government concerned. Some feared that these measures would increase the cost of investment and expenditures on capital construction investments because of the higher interest rate; some were afraid that the higher interest rate would increase the losses of enterprises and affect their revenues; and some feared that the higher export cost would affect exports. As a result, the measure to raise the interest rate was delayed until September when high inflation occurred. If the two decisions had been put into effect at the beginning of the year, there would have been no acute inflation in the third quarter. If the policy measures adopted in June 1993 to strictly control the loans and improve the financial order had not been decided and backed by the State Council, it would also have been very difficult to implement them.

Second, improve the control system of the central bank.

1. Bring the loans of the central bank under control. The experience in losing control of the loans of the central banks in the first half of 1988 and in bringing the loans of the central bank under control in June 1993 show that the link is very important. With the diversification of the monetary institutions and the development of the money market, it is very difficult to control

money effectively through the use of loan quotas. Therefore, to exercise strict control over the loans of the central bank, the main sluice-gate has become a very outstanding problem.

2. Pay attention to the control over extra-quota reserves of the special banks. The excess extra-quota reserves of the special banks in 1988 were important sources of credit expansion then. The present extra-quota reserves of the special banks are fairly high. Because of the strengthened control over loan quotas of the special banks and the intensified control over short-term loans made in violation of the rules, the excess extra-quota reserves have not yet become sources of credit expansion. But we should draw attention to it or withdraw the loans of the central bank or operate the common market to bring the excess extra-quota reserves under the control of the central bank.

3. Start using the interest rate instrument. The role of using the interest rate policy to stabilize savings deposits and check consumption demand was confirmed in 1988 and 1993. The use of the interest rate policy to check the demand for investment should also be taken into consideration. With the increased proportion of the economy not owned by the state and the entry of the state-owned enterprises in the market, the interest rate will also have an effect on control of the investment demand. The current negative interest rate should be regarded as a stimulus to investment demand. Of course, a big and overall increase in interest rates is beyond the reach of the enterprises, and it can be a good solution that the old interest rates apply to old loans and the new interest rates apply to new loans. Moreover, use open subsidies to replace the hidden subsidies of low interest rates for the enterprises and industries that have to be subsidized.

4. Supervise and control the money supply quota. Strengthen the supervision and control over the money supply, and at the same time study issue of reasonable growth quotas for the money supply and study the influence of deepening financial reform and price increases resulting from price reforms on the money supply so as to find out a reasonable growth quota for control.

Third, deepen economic reform, especially the reform of the

enterprise system, and carry out reform of the property right system of the enterprises to change the soft restriction mechanism. At the same time, change the function of the government and remove the direct control of the government over the enterprises so that the enterprises can really enter the market.

As monetary enterprises, state-owned banks should also make the same reform. As a first step, they should separate the policy factors from business, then make reforms of the property right system and set up the risk restriction mechanism. Only with this micro-foundation can the central bank switch from direct control to indirect control.

(VI) The central bank should carry out monetary policy relatively independently

Monetary policy holds a very important place in the macroeconomic control of China. However, to give full play to this role, it is essential to give the central bank the power to carry out monetary policy relatively independently.

Monetary policy is the most principal part of the macroeconomic policy. Chinese monetary policy is made by the State Council. The People's Bank of China should, under the leadership of the State Council, carry out monetary policy independently, take a positive part in the macroeconomic control, support the increase of the total social supply, control the money supply and regulate the total social demand in order to stabilize the value of money and prices.

China's money market is unified, and RMB is in smooth circulation throughout the country. If more money is put in circulation in any place, it will affect money circulation in the whole country. The starting of a new project in one place without approval aggravates inflation, and the loss from the devaluation of the increased money supply is shared by the people of the whole country. A small number of local government leaders, regardless of the reality of the possible imbalance between the total supply and the total demand, sometimes ask the central government to approve and support the construction of their new projects. This is why local governments should not share the power to exercise macroeconomic control. Therefore, the power to exercise macroeconomic control, including the issuing of currency, the fixing of the standard interest rate, the regulation of the exchange rates, and the readjustment of the major tax categories and tax rates, must be concentrated in the central government. The provinces, autonomous regions and municipalities can only formulate local statutes, policies and plans in accordance with the unified laws and macro-policies, make full use of local resources and promote the economic and social development of their localities. They should not be treated as a level of macroeconomic control, nor should they interfere with the central bank in carrying out monetary policy.

Some people suggest that the central government should give part of the macroeconomic control power to the local governments, thus making clear the definite division of labor between the central and local governments and exercising macro-control at two levels. This view is open to question. Holders of this view may have understood macroeconomic control as administration over the major economic and construction affairs. They think that the power should not be overconcentrated, but be decentralized properly so as to mobilize the enthusiasm of all localities. In reality, macroeconomic control is an economic concept with a given implication—total control. Its goal is to balance total social demand and total social supply. The macro-control policy and measure can only be formulated and implemented directly by the central government. If the different localities and ministries are permitted to exercise separate control and decide their own quantities of money supply, it is impossible to balance the total demand and the total supply of the whole society and it is difficult to avoid inflation.

Will the concentration of macroeconomic control affect the development of the local economy? Absolutely not. After the socialist market economic system is established and the market plays a foundation role in the allocation of resources, the economies in the different localities can release their vigor, accept market guidance, compete for the survival of the fittest and fast growth. This serves not to increase, but reduce the restrictions on the development of the local economies.

Mix up macro-control with planned management of the past intentionally or unintentionally. As soon as they hear of strengthening macro-control with the power concentrated in the central government, they fear that it would restrict the invigoration of the microeconomy. In fact, macro-control is quite different from the planned management of the past. The planned management of the past directly restricts the microeconomy. The more it is planned, the greater the binding force on enterprises, and the more difficult it is to invigorate the economy. Macroeconomic control is mainly to regulate and control the total demand and the total supply of the whole society, leaving the economic activities of the individual enterprises entirely open and subject to regulation by the market. To strengthen macro-control and ensure the stability of the value of the currency are to give full play to the vigor of the enterprises, accelerate development, clear the way and set the stage. If macroeconomic control is not exercised, the balance between the total demand and the total supply of the whole society is lost, inflation occurs. Thus, the environment and order for economic development are undermined, and enterprises cannot organize production normally. There is no talk of invigorating the economy. The concentration of macro-control power in the central government is precisely intended to promote the invigoration of the microeconomy. If all localities and ministries are permitted to share macroeconomic control power and to exercise control at two or even more levels, turning macro-control into micro-control, certain defects of the planned management of the past might reappear in the macro-control of the micro type.

To ensure that the central bank carries out monetary policy independently, governments at all levels must change their functions. The function of the government in administering the economy is mainly to make and execute macro-control policy, build infrastructure facilities and create a good environment for economic development instead of intervening in the microeconomy and instructing the banks to grant loans to help enterprises out of their financial difficulties. It should be up to the commercial banks and other monetary institutions to make their own decisions on whether and how much they should loan to an enterprise on the basis of their own financial power and the request of the enterprise.

Some experts say that to fundamentally solve the question of independence of the central bank in macroeconomic regulation, it is essential to change which governmental organ has jurisdiction over it, that is, from under the State Council to under the Standing Committee of the National People's Congress. But others argue that in light of the real life in China, if the government does not change its function, but continues to directly control the microeconomy, it will make arrangements for funds for national capital construction projects and funds needed by state-owned enterprises for production and business operations. Even if the central bank is placed under the Standing Committee of the National People's Congress, when local governments transfer state funds for purchasing food grains, cotton and edible oils to other ends, the shortage of funds makes it impossible to continue purchasing food grains, cotton and edible oils, and major state-owned enterprises have no money to pay out workers' wages. The Standing Committee of the National People's Congress cannot run the risk of having urban inhabitants being starved and the workers expressing grievances against the government by refusing to instruct the banks to increase loans and money supply.

When the socialist market economy system is established, and the government changes its function and no longer intervenes directly in production and business activities of enterprises, they have to get loans directly from banks or to raise the funds they need from the market. Except for the construction of infrastructure facilities, the government no longer makes arrangements for capital construction investments. The government will have less and less pressure from a shortage of funds, and gradually concentrate its energy on macroeconomic control. In this way, when the bank is under the government, it will not bring any unfavorable influence on stability of money.

The separate management of banks and stocks is also a measure to ensure the independence of the central bank in executing monetary policy. The stock market is apt to fluctuate, and stocks are more risky. Only when the stock market is separated from the banking system, will it be possible to avoid the fluctuation of the stock market and stock risk, avoid affecting bank credit and the money supply of the central bank.

(V) Adopt a tighter monetary policy and control the money supply

The monetary policy must ensure the steady growth of the money supply. The current market interest rate has climbed to around 20%, and the raising of the interest rate of loans helps to reduce the demand of fixed assets investment for loans, reduce the money supply and check inflation. In the immediate future, the loan interest rate of the special banks may float appropriately.

A tighter monetary policy can check inflation effectively. If the economic growth rate is around 8%-9%, and the inflation rate is around 6%-8%, the annual growth rate of the money supply M2 should be around 20%-23%.

The central bank should control the sluice gate for the circulation of basic money. One, withdraw loans from non-bank monetary institutions, which amount to 30 billion yuan; two, gradually reduce direct policy loans, which now total more than 60 billion yuan; three, control reloans of the special banks; and four, pay attention to the control of the exchange transactions on basic money. In times of inflation, part of the exchanges should be sold out to help increase the domestic supply and reduce basic money.

It is urgent for the central bank to reform its management pattern of "limited funds scale and fixed interest rate" for the special banks. The main reasons are:

—Many social funds are not within the scope of the loan scale control and the loan scale only controls state-owned banks.

—Adopt fixed interest rates for state banks. When inflation climbs up, there will be negative interest rate and the banks will use every means to leak funds. As a result, state-owned enterprises get less and less proportion of loans from the state-owned banks and become short of funds although they enjoy a low interest rate.

On the other hand, the enterprises not owned by the state can get more loans at the market interest rate. Therefore, in the course of controlling inflation, state-owned enterprises and banks will, on the contrary, have to pay an even higher price.

Adopt floating interest rates for state-owned banks. For example, float the interest rate 60% for rural credit cooperatives, and at the same time reduce the limits for the scale of loans and supervise and control loan sizes. This will not only help to increase the competitive power of state-owned banks, but also control the total quantity and support the growth of state-owned enterprises with good economic performances and help them change the business operation mechanism. If this cannot be done at once, it is advisable to first raise short-term interest rates for bank deposits and loans.

Restructure the policy investment and bank-to-bank loan setup and complete the organization and formation of the policy banks. Cut off the direct connection between policy loans and basic money and ensure the initiative of the central bank in regulating and controlling basic money.

IV. Check Inflation, and Control and Guide Consumption Funds

(I) The excess growth of consumption funds is an important factor for inflation. It is necessary to control and guide use of consumption funds to check inflation

1. The over-distribution of national income leads to the expansion of consumption funds.

The expansion of consumption funds is the direct root cause of inflation and leads to a sharp rise in social purchasing power, causing an imbalance between demand and supply. The universal rise of commodity prices has been so serious that it has to be checked. Counting on the basis of the comparable prices between 1989 and 1993, the labor productivity in China rose by 30%, but the per-head income of urban people went up by 45%. The gap between the labor productivity and the per-head income inevitably led to an imbalance between demand and supply and increased inflation pressure. As a macro-phenomenon, it was manifested chiefly in the microeconomy: (1) The readjustment and reform of wages for the government functionaries towards the end of 1993 and at the beginning of 1994. It has given an impetus and is giving impetus to the upward climb of the wage level of enterprises and non-governmental institutions, resulting in a big increase in the income of the residents, and the urban residents in particular. (2) The increase in numbers of people in the high income strata. According to the estimation of a department concerned, 80% of the 1,500 billion yuan savings deposits of the inhabitants are owned by a small minority. (3) The extra-wage incomes are increasing tremendously. (4) Group consumption is side-tracked and deformed.

2. Attention should be paid to the fact that the overgrowth of consumption funds has given rise to an overheated demand and an accompanying price rise.

The expansion of consumption funds resulting from the overgrowth of social group consumption and wages has tremendous influence on inflation. According to estimates, when the investment demand expands, about 40% of the investment was turned into wages and social group consumption funds. Such huge figures emerging in the sphere of consumption inevitably leads to the overheating of demand.

It is essential to strictly control group consumption. Group consumption, which accounts for a very big proportion of the growing consumption funds in China, not only leads to growing demand and price increases, but also to increases in the expenditures of the Party and government organizations and the expansion of investment demand. It is particularly necessary to control group consumption of the Party and government offices and the part of the investments turned into group consumption. Specific measures should be taken to solve the problem.

3. It is necessary to control the big growth of wages, and the growth of wages should be synchronous with the growth of productivity.

The planned growth rate of total national wages in 1994 was

18.4% over the previous year, but the actual growth rate was more than 30%, the fastest in many years. The extra-wage income of the state-owned departments grew even faster, equivalent to one third of the wages or even more than the wages in some departments. However, the per-head labor productivity of the state-owned enterprises grew only by an average of 8%. The wage growth led to the rise of the cost and consumption level, and inevitably pulled up the rise of consumption prices. Therefore, the overgrowth of the wages should be controlled in order to avoid the increases of wages and prices in turn. In state-owned enterprises, the measures to control wage growth can be combined with the acquisition of property right of the labor power. The staff and workers in enterprises are entitled to the property right of their labor power through shareholding plans and it is in line with their long-term interests. It provides a reliable foundation for controlling wage growth, helps to eliminate the contradiction in interest between the enterprises and their employees, and arouses the enthusiasm of the workers.

4. Take care to direct society from short-term consumption to long-term consumption.

Accelerate the reform of the housing system by selling houses to the buyers at the cost price. This not only can divert part of the consumption funds to long-term consumption, but also can help to hold less bank credit in housing construction and achieve the self-circulation of housing funds. The staff and workers of the enterprises should be encouraged to buy shares of their own enterprises. It can be considered that the internal shares of the staff and workers be turned into workers' shareholding funds on a voluntary basis.

5. Hold the surplus purchasing power of the urban residents stable and turn consumption into investment.

After World War Two, the United States, West European countries and Japan all experienced the "consumption revolution" characterized by the purchase of durable consumer goods in large quantities. Japan witnessed its first consumption revolution in the fast economic growth period from the late 1950s to early 1960s. During the 1956-1963 period, the annual growth rate of the per-capita national income was 12% and the universal ownership of black-and-white TV sets, washers and refrigerators climbed up sharply. The years between 1964 and 1970 were the period of the end of the first consumption revolution and conservation and preparation for the rise of the second consumption revolution. It was about seven years. This period was a long period of prosperity and stable growth in Japan. Beginning with the early 1970s, luxurious consumer goods represented by the three C's (car, color TV sets and coolers) began to enter the ordinary families.

As a late developing country, color TV sets entered Chinese families ahead of time during the first consumption revolution. The current urban consumption demand is in a period of preparation for the second consumption revolution. A new generation of home appliances of the 10,000 yuan class, represented by house equipment and decorations, cars, motorcycles, telephones and other telecommunication equipment, coolers and personal computers will constitute the second consumption revolution. Since 1989, the savings of urban inhabitants have clearly increased at an accelerated speed. Between 1989 and 1992, the remainder of the per-capita savings of urban inhabitants increased by an average of 30.38%. In 1992, every family (3.37 persons) had a surplus purchasing power (cash and savings deposits) of 9,543.03 yuan or a saving of 10,000 yuan, including the banking property. Growing at an annual rate of 30%, every urban family will have a saving of 60,000 yuan by the year of 2000. It means that a considerable number of Chinese families will participate in the second consumption revolution.

However, in order to make the second consumption revolution successful, China must upgrade the industrial structure successfully under the inducement of a change in the structure of the consumption demand while inhabitants accumulate their consumption payment capacity. If the income of urban inhabitants surpasses economic growth for a long time, the readjustment of the industrial structure will inevitably lag behind the rise of consumption income, giving rise to another "time difference." When the first consumption revolution occurred in the 1980s, the demand for home appliances of the 1,000 yuan class grew so fast that it greatly surpassed the technological level and supplying capacity of the home appliance industry in China. China had to import complete sets, parts for assembly at home, and complete installations for production lines or key parts to alleviate the acute shortage. It depended on imports or semi-imports to complete the first consumption revolution in the urban areas. When the producing capacity of the domestic home appliance industry reached a certain scale, the proportion of homemade parts rose to a certain level and the technologies became gradually mature. But the heat wave of consumption of urban inhabitants was already over. If a situation in which the income rise of urban inhabitants is faster than economic growth is not appropriately controlled, the change in the industrial structure will lag behind the upgrading of the structure of the consumption demand, the old drama of the 1980s will be repeated around the year 2000 and the inhabitants' payment capacity will exceed the supplying capacity of the new generation of consumer goods. The inevitable result will be sustained inflation and rapid growth of imported consumer goods. It is now the period of accumulation and preparation for the second consumption revolution, and the surplus purchasing power of the inhabitants is relatively stable, thus providing a favorable condition for the readjustment of the industrial structure in the economic upsurge beginning in 1992. Induced by the demand of the second consumption revolution, the structure of investment is clearly inclined toward the transport, telecommunications, motor vehicle and real estate industries. Take 1993 as an example: the investment of the whole society in fixed assets increased by 50.6%, but the investments in real estate rose by 88.1% (commodity houses by 124.9%), investment in the basic industries of transport, post and telecommunications by 106.7%, and motor vehicles by 117.6%, all above the average investment growth rate. In order to speed up the readjustment of the industrial structure, it is essential to hold stable the current surplus purchasing power and turn consumption funds into investment funds while appropriately controlling the growth of income of urban inhabitants. By the middle of the period of accumulation and preparation, the surplus purchasing power of the inhabitants will reach a fairly high level and the pressure for the expansion of consumption demand will further increase. It is even more necessary to induce the consumption demand to climb step by step and prevent its rise like a platform synchronous with the purchasing power.

It is necessary to direct the shift of social consumption funds to investments. For the present, there are some concrete measures for consideration: One, appropriately develop domestic investment funds and direct the shift of part of the socialist consumption funds and personal savings to investment funds; and two, gradually enlarge the proportion of personal accounts in the reform of the social security system and create conditions for a gradual transition to public accumulation funds. For the present, it is advisable to institute the housing accumulation funds system.

6. Make a rational policy of income and distribution.

A rational policy of income and distribution itself cannot produce the effect of checking inflation, but it can greatly buffer the social instability arising from inflation. Because when income increases and the distribution is reasonable, the people can bear it even if prices rise. There are three important points in correctly handling the relations among price, income and efficiency: First, change the way in which personal income (mainly wages) is decided by the state, and give play to wages in market regulation. If wages are controlled by the state, it is certain to lag behind price increases. Therefore, the power to make decisions on wages should be given back to the enterprises as soon as possible so that wages will reflect the real price of the labor and wage increases will not be lower than price increases. Second, the government should strengthen the regulation of the differences in the distribution of the income, including the personal income and the imbalances among the localities. Third, perfect the social security system to eliminate fears of trouble coming from unemployment and retirement.

(II) Turn the tables in the situation whereby consumption income of inhabitants exceeds economic growth as soon as possible, and alleviate the pressure on the potential expan-

sion of consumption demand

Total demand is made up of consumption demand and investment demand. Likewise, total supply is made up of consumption supply and investment supply. The balance between total demand and total supply depends on the balance between investment demand and investment supply, and it also depends on the balance between consumption demand and consumption supply. In studying the balance between consumption demand and consumption supply, China has always used the method of comparison between the social commodity purchasing power and the total quantity of social retail commodities that can be supplied. An outstanding defect in this method was the disagreement of the approaches. One, the source of commodities as the supplier only reflects the total supply of material consumption while the purchasing power as the demanded includes the demand for commodities and services. Two, the sources of retail commodities include both the sold consumer goods and agricultural means of production and the consumer goods in stock while the purchasing power includes the money to be used to buy the agricultural means of production and consumer goods and the surplus money of the urban and rural inhabitants. The consumer goods in stock will be sold to the urban and rural inhabitants, social groups and foreign visitors, but the owners of the surplus money are limited only to the urban and rural inhabitants. Because of the defect described above, people have been looking for new methods. One of them is the growth rate comparison method for the consumptive income of the inhabitants and the GNP, namely, studying the relationship between the rate of economic growth and the rate of consumption growth. When economic growth is faster than or as fast as the growth of the consumption income, it will not lead to the expansion of consumption demand. Otherwise, if the growth of the consumption income is faster than economic growth for years on end, it is bound to give rise to the expansion of demand.

In order to find out the consumption income of urban and rural inhabitants more accurately, specialists concerned used the money spending method to calculate the disposable income of urban and rural inhabitants which can be used for consumption expenditures and financial assets investment (referred to the net money income of the inhabitants plus the self-sufficient consumption of the peasants). Between 1979 and 1993, the disposable income (DPI) of the inhabitants in China increased annually by an average of 16.8%, and the gross national product (GNP) increased annually by an average of 15.3%. The annual average growth rate of the disposable income was 1.5% higher than that of the GNP. Of the 15 years (1979-1993) with comparable data, only the three years of 1989, 1990 and 1991 witnessed the growth of the consumption income of the inhabitants lower than the economic growth, but it was higher than the economic growth rate in all other years. Precisely because the growth of the DPI has been faster than the growth of the GNP, the distribution of the GNP is evidently inclined to the personal income of the inhabitants. (See the following table for the details).

Comparisons for the Growth Rate between the Income of Inhabitants and the National Economy

Year	DPI Annual Growth Rate (%)	GNP Annual Growth Rate (%)	Ratio	Proportion of DPI to GNP (%)
1978	--	--	--	49.1
1979	18.0	11.43	1.57	52.0
1980	18.1	11.80	1.53	54.8
1981	10.7	6.78	1.58	57.0
1882	9.0	8.79	1.02	57.1
1983	13.2	11.86	1.11	57.8
1984	21.0	19.84	1.06	58.4
1985	23.5	22.91	1.03	58.6
1986	16.3	13.31	1.24	60.2

1987	17.7	16.54	1.07	60.8
1988	25.8	24.48	1.05	61.4
1989	10.3	13.68	0.75	59.6
1990	9.6	10.64	0.90	59.0
1991	13.5	14.36	0.94	58.6
1992	20.6	18.78	1.10	59.5
1993	26.0	25.66	1.01	59.6
1979-1993 Average	16.8	15.3	1.10	

The fact that the growth of the consumption income of the inhabitants is faster than the economic growth has led to the possibility of expanding the consumption demand. Of course, it is not that if the growth of the DPI is faster than the growth of the GNP in a given year, it will turn the possibility of the expansion of the consumption demand into reality immediately. It is true that the overheating of the consumer goods market in 1985 and 1988 was related to the overgrowth of the DPI that year, but they were foreshadowed by the nonstop overgrowth of the DPI over the economic growth in the two or three preceding years. With the advent of a new round of economic upsurge beginning in 1992, the proportion of the DPI to the GNP in 1993 has risen again and reached the 1989 level of 59.6%. If the DPI continues to rise faster than economic growth, the potential pressure on the expansion of the consumption demand will be accumulated to a fairly high degree.

To figure out to what degree the potential pressure on the expansion of the consumption demand has accumulated, it is essential to make an overall analysis of the payment capacity of the inhabitants for consumption. In the real life, the whole payment capacity of the inhabitants for consumption is equal to the net monetary income of the year plus the surplus purchasing power of the preceding year (cash in hand and savings deposits).

The Whole Payment Capacity of the Inhabitants for Consumption

Unit: billion yuan

Year	Net Monetary Income	Previous Year-end Surplus Purchasing Power	Whole Payment Capacity	Proportion of SPP to WPC (%)
1978	124.58	43.64	168.22	25.9
1979	150.91	48.07	198.98	24.2
1980	188.47	58.52	246.99	23.7
1981	203.39	79.05	287.44	27.5
1982	227.29	98.05	325.34	30.1
1983	260.31	117.90	378.21	31.2
1984	326.08	145.07	471.15	30.8
1985	416.09	187.43	613.52	32.2
1986	492.40	252.43	744.83	33.9
1987	587.47	320.96	908.43	33.9
1988	751.23	423.46	1,174.69	36.0
1989	836.91	549.46	1,386.37	39.6
1990	923.97	698.52	1,622.49	43.1
1991	1,054.98	912.32	1,967.30	46.4
1992	1,291.26	1,162.09	2,453.35	47.4
1993	1,651.23	1,495.26	3,146.49	47.5
1978-1993 Annual Average Growth	18.8%	26.6%	21.6%	

The figures show that the net monetary income of the inhabitants increased at an average rate of 18.8% annually between 1978 and 1993, 3.5 percentage points higher than the annual growth rate of the GNP. The year-end surplus purchasing power of the inhabitants during the 1978-1993 period rose more than 34 times with an annual average increase of 26.6%. Its proportion to the whole payment capacity of the inhabitants for consumption rose from one fourth in 1978 to nearly one half in 1993. According to the 1993 year-end estimates of the State Statistic Bureau, the year-end surplus purchasing power of urban and rural inhabitants in 1993 would come to 1,966 billion yuan, surpassing the net monetary income of the inhabitants of the same year for the first time. It would come to around 2,500 billion yuan in 1994. This shows that the degree of difficulty in the macro-control over consumption by the state has increased. Even if the income distribution policy and the monetary policy are adjusted and the situation of the consumption income surpassing the economic growth is controlled, if there is a slight oversight in the price policy and the interest rate policy or the anticipation of inflation of the inhabitants increases, part of the surplus purchasing power that has withdrawn from the sphere of consumption will be concentrated and put into the consumer market again, and the potential pressure on the expansion of the consumption demand will burst out.

Properly control and guide the growth of consumption demand. One, to set up and perfect the check and balance mechanism for the gains of state-owned assets and the personal income of the enterprise operators and workers to ensure that the growth rate of total wages of the enterprises is lower than that of the economic results and that the growth rate of the average wage of the workers is lower than the rise of the labor productivity of the enterprises, and to prevent the increase of individual income through the corrosion of state-owned assets. Two, to set the reference standards for the enterprise wages in the different industries and the ceilings for wages of the enterprise operators and standardize the measures for the distribution of the individual income for the contracted business operations of the enterprises. Three, to use economic means to regulate personal income, strengthen taxation, especially the collection of a personal income tax. Four, to continue to control the consumption of social groups.

(III) The effect and limit for taxation to check consumption

When the elements income is fixed, taxation on commodities reduces the purchasing power of consumers by raising prices. Although the prices of taxable commodities are raised directly, they reduce the total demand for commodities and services in the economy, thus exerting a deflationary influence on the general price level. Therefore, indirect taxes reduce the relative purchasing power of the element income and lighten the pressure of inflation by raising prices while income taxes reduce the consumption capacity to lighten the pressure of inflation by reducing the disposable income.

In a developing country like China, the biggest contribution of indirect taxes lie in the fact that it can reduce the incremental consumption of low-income families or raise the marginal consumption. This is beyond the reach of the direct tax. Because the low income strata constitute the overwhelming majority in China, and at the same time their tendency for marginal consumption is very high, the indirect tax reduces the actual consumption by raising the prices of taxable commodities. Therefore, when there are equal tax revenues, the retrogressive indirect tax, in a certain degree, perhaps has a greater anti-inflation effect than the progressive income tax. Under general conditions, the expenditure-savings ratio of many low-income families is quite high, and it is impossible for low-income families to use their savings or borrow money to avoid an actual decline in their consumption like high-income families. When indirect taxes increase, low-income families can only reduce their consumption spending.

Besides, indirect taxes also affect the consumption spending of high-income families. Generally speaking, in order to give the tax system certain progression and raise ample income, indirect taxes levy heavily on luxuries. Because the spending of the high-income families on luxuries constitutes a great proportion, these taxes will reduce their consumption. Moreover, the absolute expenditure of rich families is very high, so an indirect tax can, in a large degree, reduce the incremental consumption, producing an anti-inflationary effect on the price level.

When some commodity prices tend to rise, foreign trade taxes can also be usually used as a tool to stabilize prices. When commodity prices rise in the same international market, tariffs can be used to control the same tendency in the domestic market. Import duties are levied on the input elements like raw and processed materials, machinery and equipment, and intermediate products as well as finished goods. So far as the input elements are concerned, when their international market prices rise, they will increase the production cost of the domestic departments, thus leading to a rise in the price level. Reduction of import duties levied on these commodities can be used to check (block) the rise of the prices of these input elements so as to maintain domestic production. Likewise, when an abnormal situation emerges in the international market, it is necessary to levy export duties to prevent the influence of foreign inflation on the domestic market and stabilize the domestic price level. When the prices rise due to the short supply of commodities, the government can use import duties to stabilize prices. The government can cut down the import duty rate and encourage imports to make up for the short-term short supply. With large quantities of goods are imported, prices in the domestic market will tend to drop.

The backward personal income tax in China has tied up the anti-inflationary ability of taxation. The prescription of Keynesian economics is to raise personal income taxes, cut down the disposable income of the people and lower the total demand to check inflation. This is undoubtedly a powerful tool to check inflation in the United States where the revenues from the personal income taxes account for around 45% of the total tax revenues. However, the current tax structure in China attaches equal importance to circulating taxes and income taxes, but the income tax system is backward. The chief manifestation of this is that enterprise income taxes constitute the overwhelming majority, and the personal income tax revenues accounts for less than 1% of the total tax revenues. This tiny figure, which can be possibly neglected in the statistics, cannot influence the economic situation. In other words, a change in the personal income tax rate will not affect the disposable income of individuals. It can be seen that it is impossible for China to follow the example of the United States and place the heavy task of stabilizing the prices on the readjustment of personal income taxes.

V. Macro-Control and Regional Economic Development

(I) The imbalance of inter-regional development and inflation

The imbalance of inter-regional development can possibly lead to an inconsistency in regional development policies and central macro-policy. The regions with fast development want to develop even faster, and the regions with slow development want to catch up with the fast-developing regions. Therefore, when the rate of growth contradicts with price rises, none of the regions are willing to maintain the national stability of the prices and sacrifice their own growth rates. A certain difference in the regional development is beneficial to the total economic development of the whole country, but the spread of the high prices of the more quickly developed coastal regions to the other parts of the country is far quicker than the spread of their funds, technologies and talents to relatively slowly developed regions. Take the four neighboring provinces and autonomous region of Guangdong, Guangxi, Guizhou and Yunnan in the south for example. Their GNP growth rates in 1992 were 22%, 18.3%, 9.2% and 10.9% respectively, but there were no distinct differences of their price increases in 1993, 18.2%, 18.9%, 14.8% and 18.9% respectively. According to statistical figures, more than 60% of the growth of the national production, investment and consumption in the last two years was brought about by the coastal regions, but the disparities of the price increases in the different regions were much smaller. The increased imbalance of the inter-regional development was unable to transmit the high growth to every relatively underdeveloped region, but transmitted the pressure of inflation to the whole country.

In reality, the problem of investment scale, the problem of

state-owned enterprises and the problem of the imbalanced development of the regions are often entangled to exert influence on inflation. The influence is typically manifested in the form of the contradiction between macro-administration represented by the central government and nonmacro-administration represented by local governments and enterprises. The goal of the former is to achieve the most effective allocation of total resources while the goal of the latter is to maximize local interests. When our system has not yet completely harmonized the relations, because the division of the administrative power and the change of the government functions have lagged behind, and because of the incomplete information obtained by the central government in the organizational structure of multi-level administration, the contradiction between macro-administration and nonmacro administration is often a deep-level cause of inflation. This contradiction is manifested in various forms. For example, the readjustment of the structure of the different sectors of the economy has progressed slowly, local governments and enterprises often forced banks to increase the money supply, and the problem of negative interest rates has existed for a long time.

(II) Proceeding from the reality of the imbalanced regional development in China, deal with different regions in different ways and make regional inflation-controlling policy

Since the 1950s, an important breakthrough has been made in the study and application of the theory of poles of economic growth in the regional economic development. The theory has gained obvious results in regional development and planning of many developed countries and developing countries. The essence of the theory is the stress on the imbalanced development of the regional economy, and the concentration of the limited rare and scarce resources in a small number of departments or regions with big potential of development and with obvious returns from scale economy and investment to strengthen the economic power at a point of growth to form a difference of momentum with the economy in the surrounding areas, and guide it to economic development in all regions through the forces of conduction and medium in the market economic mechanism. France once used the pole theory to solve the problem of overexpansion in the Paris region. The theory is of great importance to the development of the Chinese economy. China is a vast country, and the imbalance of the regional development will remain a problem for a long time. It is essential to deal with different regions in different ways and make regional inflation-controlling policies in the light of the specific conditions in China.

1. The imbalance of regional development is an objective existence, and inflation varies from region to region. Therefore, different policies should be adopted for different regions in light of the different conditions.

The opening of China to the outside world began with the opening of regions. Priority was given to the development in a few areas and then it was radiated to the surrounding areas to pull up the development of the whole economy. The development differs from area to area, so does inflation, and the inhabitants in different places have different psychological abilities to stand the pressure of inflation. Some specialists have cited the example of Hainan to illustrate the point. Between 1990 and 1993, the retail price index in Hainan rose by less than 30 percent while the per-capita income of the urban inhabitants rose from 1,574 yuan in 1990 to 2,774 yuan in 1993, up by 76%, thus raising the ability of the inhabitants to resist inflation. In a region with many outstanding historical problems and underdeveloped infrastructure facilities and basic industries like Hainan, it is extremely difficult to rely entirely on its own accumulation for development. To a large extent, it has relied on high input to achieve its high growth. Controlled within the unified investment credit scale, Hainan faces a great obstacle to its development. Therefore, how to solve the contradiction between the single monetary and credit policy and the difference of real economic growth in different regions is a question that warrants serious study.

2. Pay attention to the study of the regional inflation and its solution, and permit all regions to make different inflation controlling policies suited to their own conditions.

A realistic problem is that the inflation problem has different influences on the economy in different regions. Therefore, it is essential to proceed from the reality and deal with different regions in different ways. The macroeconomic policy should be beneficial to the national control of inflation, and also to the sustained development of the regional economies throughout the country. In controlling inflation, the problems should be solved in the course of the economic development. Development is the hard theory.

Since the whole province of Hainan became a special economic zone and real estate has become the hottest industry for investment, the high growth of the real estate industry in Hainan has not only led to the development of commerce, services, building, transport and other related industries, but also promoted the construction of infrastructure facilities in Hainan cities, thus greatly improving the environment for investment in this special zone. Of the investments in real estate in Hainan, 40% come from other provinces and one third from overseas. Real estate has become an important channel to absorb capital funds from both inside and outside the country. The pre-development of the real estate industry in Hainan has provided the primitive accumulation of capital for its basic industries, thus playing a leading role. Hainan has uniquely used tourism as its leading industry. Its special industrial policy is determined by Hainan's unique geographical and historical surroundings and social-economic conditions. The real estate industry is closely related to tourism. Real estate and tourism have conditioned each other, supported each other, and thus have started integrated development. The leading industry of tourism should be greatly developed, and the real estate industry must not lag behind. The pre-development of the real estate industry has become the prerequisite for the fast growth of the whole economy in Hainan. At present, Hainan faces the contradiction between the development of advantageous and pillar industries and the credit and industrial policies of state macro-control. The unified credit policy has put many corporations that center on real estate development into a difficult position. This shows that while strengthening macro-control over the banking work in real estate, we should take into consideration not only the whole situation of the macroeconomic development of the country, but also the realities in the different regions, not only stick to the principles, but also show flexibility, and not only ensure the smooth implementation of the government decrees, but also protect the good development momentum of the local economy.

(III) Alleviate and overcome the negative effect of controlling inflation

Any economic policy has both positive and negative effects. We know the negative effect in order to overcome the negative effect and increase the positive effect. To control inflation itself does not have a very big negative effect. The question is what method we choose to control inflation. So we have to consider the price and cost, namely the degree of force and method with which we control inflation.

First, pay full attention to the negative effect produced by the method of reducing demand.

Inflation in China was indeed propelled by demand, and we have already used this method for more than a year. The question we face now is whether the next move to control inflation will remain to be the relatively rigid method of reducing demand, after keeping demand tight for one year. Reducing demand inevitably gives rise to problems. In the light of the current situation, China still maintains a fairly high rate of growth. However, we must notice that the current high rate of growth is achieved mainly through the extra-systematic part of the economy, namely, the enterprises run by the townships and villages and the enterprises with overseas investments, while the rate of growth of state-owned enterprises is greatly restricted. Moreover, although we have kept a growth rate of more than ten percent, the enterprises run by the townships and villages have registered a growth rate of around 20%, especially in Jiangsu Province, while state-owned enterprises have reported only 5% growth. Since demand has been reduced, the problems of stopping production and poor economic results have been quite outstanding. These problems will give rise to new problems like inflation, problems produced by the negative effect.

Second, the question of structure.

The chaos of the economy is also manifested in the chaos of the economic structure. The structural contradictions that have led to inflation have now become the factors for growing inflation. The overheating of the economy is mostly the overheating of the structure. Economic expansion is first of all the expansion of the processing industries. Although the expansion of the processing industries will promote the expansion of the basic industries, the cycle of investment for the basic industries is long. When the macro-control of the government puts a brake on the overheated economy to reduce demand, the expansion of the processing industries with a short cycle of investment may have already completed several production cycles, but the expansion of the basic industries may have been just started. Therefore, it is, in fact, the basic industries which receive the severest blow from the tightening policy. This practice has produced the negative effect of further worsening the structure. So inflation-controlling measures must be coupled with readjustments in the structure. The tightening policy should not affect all. We should adopt a structural tightening policy. Processing industries should be tightened, but the basic industries should not be tightened. In other words, to control inflation, it is essential to adopt a policy of structural growth, while continuing to control the investments in the fixed assets of the processing industries, properly loosen the control over the investments in the fixed assets of the basic industries. It is true that inflation in 1993 was pulled up by demand. It was the demand that caused the economic overgrowth, but it did not push up the development of the underdeveloped transport and basic industries. Therefore, if we persist in adopting a rigid tightening policy, it might affect our long-term stable development. If the demand is tightened too much, it produces a negative effect on the economic structure. As to how tight the demand should be, we should also consider the relation between the current money demand and the current money supply. Many specialists think that the current money supply is quite great, and in the face of the great money supply, we should not mainly control the inflow of overseas capital, because the foreign capital inflow can support our high growth rate and increase our supply, and thus provide the material foundation for controlling inflation. Of course, we should avoid short-term and speculative inflow of foreign capital. Therefore, we have raised the question of the limit for the tight money market. Because in deciding how much money should be put into circulation, we must take into consideration the great part of it held by the foreign exchanges. If the money market is controlled too tightly, the negative effect of tightening the demand might increase. Therefore, after the demand was tightened for one year, the control over the demand should be appropriately loosened. It is necessary to properly increase the investments in basic industries, because in some provinces, many investment projects are in the infrastructure.

At the same time, we should support loans for the circulating funds with better results. The reason why our economy is not stable is that our growth rate is mainly based on high input. We must adjust our development strategy so that our growth rate will be based on results. However, because of the progress in the reform at present, it is impossible for us to effect the change very soon, but we can adopt transitional methods, that is, the loans should be granted to the enterprises, departments and regions with better results. In that case, our growth rate will be based on the results.

Third, on the method of price adjustment.

The current method of adjusting prices has given rise to cycles of price adjustment. Adjust the prices of the farm products, coal, electricity and oils, and then adjust the prices of transportation. Every price adjustment results in the rise of the prices. As a result, a round of price adjustment is accompanied by a round of price rises. Because the price adjustment has led to a general price rise, the prices remain irrational. A dozen years ago we said that the prices of food grains were not rational and transport fares were not rational, but today the prices of the food grains are still irrational, and transport fares are still irrational. In fact, we have already done a lot of work on the prices. Therefore, in adjusting the prices, we are now trying our best to find a non-price channel.

Because many market problems are solved not through the market itself. In readjusting the prices, can the problem of the structural readjustment be solved through tax reduction, subsidies or the use of industrial profit to benefit agriculture? In Jiangsu and other areas, for example, the ability to stand inflation is slightly stronger, because the enterprises run by townships and villages there are obliged to provide different subsidies to agriculture.

Fourth, on the method of distribution.

To solve inflation problems, we usually use the compensational method. At present, the compensations depend on subsidies within the enterprises. Because the social security system is not yet perfect, the dependence on the internal security measures of enterprises has given rise to unfair subsidies under the pressure of inflation, the differences of subsidies and the multitude of channels. It is essential to change the security of the enterprises to social security and turn the method of distribution into an automatic stabilizer for economic fluctuations instead of an accelerator for inflation.

Fifth, local governments should be able to do something.

In order to prevent and overcome the negative effect in controlling inflation, it is essential to make some necessary readjustments to the acts of the central government and the acts of the local governments. The central government should strictly control demand, and under this premise, should permit the local governments to be able to do something, and make up for negative effects of inflation through the local governments. For example, Jiangsu Province has much to do this time to tighten demand, but as a whole, the province, especially the areas south of the Yangtze River, has a stronger ability to withstand the tightening, because the areas south of the river are stronger economically, especially the enterprises run by the townships and villages and the enterprises with overseas investments, which can use their flexible mechanism and continue to develop considerably, when the central government tightens the demand. This shows that some of the negative effects can be overcome through the actions of the local governments. When we control inflation, we should not ask the central government and the local governments to take only one action. If they all take the same action, the negative effect will increase.

图书在版编目(CIP)数据

中国经济快速发展与抑制通货膨胀:英文/高尚全,迟福林主编.—北京:外文出版社,1997

(中国市场经济研讨丛书)

ISBN 7-119-00025-X

Ⅰ.中… Ⅱ.①高… ②迟… Ⅲ.①经济发展-高速度(经济)-关系-通货膨胀-中国-研究 ②通货膨胀-对策-中国-研究 Ⅳ.F822.5

中国版本图书馆 CIP 数据核字 (96) 第 12870 号

责任编辑 程钦华 胡开敏

封面设计 唐 宇

中国经济快速发展与抑制通货膨胀

高尚全 迟福林主编

*

外文出版社出版

(中国北京百万庄大街 24 号)

邮政编码 100037

北京外文印刷厂印刷

中国国际图书贸易总公司发行

(中国北京车公庄西路 35 号)

北京邮政信箱第 399 号 邮政编码 100044

1997 年(大 32 开)第 1 版

(英)

ISBN 7-119-00025-X /F·2(外)

02800

4-E-3093P